BET 18.50

Chekhov

Chekhov

A Study of the Four Major Plays

Richard Peace

Yale University Press
New Haven and London
1983

To my Parents

Designed by Stephanie Hallin.
Set in Linotype Baskerville by Alan Sutton Publishing Ltd., Gloucester.
Printed in Great Britain by Butler & Tanner Ltd, Frome, Somerset.

Library of Congress Cataloging in Publication Data

Peace, Richard Arthur.
   Chekhov, a study of the four major plays.

   Includes bibliographical references and index.
   1. Chekhov, Anton Pavlovich, 1860–1904 — Dramatic
works. I. Title.
   PG3458.Z9D755 1983 891.72′3 83–40001
   ISBN 0-300-02961-6

CONTENTS

ACKNOWLEDGEMENTS

QUOTATIONS from the plays are taken from Elisaveta Fen's *Chekhov's Plays* (Penguin Classics) but reference has also been made in the notes to Ronald Hingley's *Chekhov: Five Plays* (O.U.P. World's Classics). The art of translation is notoriously difficult and both these translators aim, quite rightly, at rendering Chekhov's Russian into good colloquial English, yet inevitably there are occasions when it proves virtually impossible to convey the ambiguities and eccentricities of the original in a way which does not appear forced or unnatural in English. In such instances I have provided my own, less stylistically elegant, but more literal, translations, which are marked by an asterisk and may be checked against Miss Fen's versions in the notes.

Miss Fen has adopted spellings of Russian names designed to guide English-speakers in their pronunciation, but, as in many instances these spellings are at variance with received systems of transliteration, I have felt obliged to substitute more standard spellings of such names.

My analysis of the texts is based on the Soviet Academy of Sciences complete edition of Chekhov's works (*Polnoye sobraniye sochineniy i pisem v tridsati tomakh*, Moscow, 1974 -) I owe the editors of this fine edition a scholarly debt, in particular A.I. Revyakin and the editorial team responsible for *Sochineniya* vols. 12 and 13 (Moscow 1978).

I warmly thank Elisaveta Fen (and her publishers) for allowing me to use her very readable translations. I also acknowledge the work of my wife as proof-reader, and the help with the typescript given, at various times, by Jean, Sheena and Tanya of the Department of Russian Studies, University of Hull.

INTRODUCTION

CHEKHOV, as a playwright, is the inheritor of a Russian tradition which, deeply indebted to Western models, nevertheless has its own recognisable idiom; in the words of one critic it exhibits 'a magnificent picture gallery, but no great narrative ingenuity'.[1] Although this characterisation specifically refers to the 'comedic tradition that leads from Griboyedov to Chekhov', the observation is broadly true for Russian literature as a whole, with its emphasis on character (i.e. psychology) at the expense of the neatly tailored plot.

Chekhov is also the inheritor of another Russian tradition, according to which seminal plays were written by authors excelling in other genres (Pushkin, Gogol, Lermontov, Turgenev, Tolstoy). Chekhov only achieved success in the theatre towards the end of his life, when he already enjoyed an established reputation as a writer of short stories. This fact undoubtedly conditioned his approach to dramatic art; his stage settings at times contain evidence of a striving for total authorial control more appropriate to description in the short story than to the business-like deployment of properties and scenery for a producer and actors. Thus in Act IV of *Uncle Vanya* the stage directions describe the map of Africa as: [*obviously useless to anyone here**]; the setting for the first act of *The Three Sisters* has the direction: [*outside it is sunny, gay**]; and Chekhov's prescriptions for the set of Act II of *The Cherry Orchard* (with its town *'which can be seen only in very good, clear weather'* *) push the technology of scenic illusion to its limits.[2] Such directions are at once specific and yet intangible. They recall the descriptive devices of Chekhov's short stories; for they are in essence indicators of mood.

'Mood' may seem a term over-used in Chekhovian criticism, but it is an indispensable concept. The very essence of mood is its lack of precision: it is a complex, emotional, only just sub-rational reaction to meaning and significance not clearly apprehended: a response to elusive suggestion rather than precise statement. Unfortunately its very vagueness has often led to its being used in criticism as a woolly dampener to further analysis and discussion.

Chekhov's preoccupation with the elusive, less dynamic emotions of 'mood' appears to cut across the traditional concept of drama as action. Thus Harvey Pitcher comments on the development implied in the reworking of the earlier *Wood Demon* into *Uncle Vanya*: 'What Chekhov has done is to replace a play of action by a play of emotional content.'[3] The observation is good as far as it goes, but Pitcher (who wishes 'to bury alike both Chekhov the social partisan, and Chekhov the ironist') reduces everything to 'emotion' and is against 'vast coded documents which can only be deciphered with the utmost patience'.[4] The truth lies somewhere in between: literature is not an abstract art — it cannot abrogate meaning. Chekhov's world is poised between emotion and reason, and his drama combines mood with action, much as his comedy mixes laughter with pathos.

The emotional atmosphere (mood) of a Chekhov play is achieved through numerous devices. His titles may call obvious attention to symbol (*The Seagull, The Cherry Orchard*) but for the creation of mood such symbolism must retain a degree of ambiguity throughout. The sets, in their evocation of significant place, are also redolent of symbolism (the nursery in *The Cherry Orchard*; the study-cum-estate office in *Uncle Vanya*; the garden and the trees in the final act of *The Three Sisters*). A natural setting may be conducive to a lyrical mood, and atmosphere can be evoked through sounds — some musical: piano, guitar, concertina, snatches of song; some ominous: a distant shot, a breaking string, the thud of axes. Omen itself has a distinct role to play in the building up of vague feelings of presentiment. Akin to this is the extensive use of literary quotation, which surrounds each play with a penumbra of partially stated meaning. This shadowy periphery is also the abode of non-appearing characters, whose influence upon those on stage may often be considerable, and from this realm beyond the wings there stray from time to time odd episodic characters, vatic vagrants whose presence is inexplicably disturbing. Conversations, which seem disconnected and are interrupted by random remarks, contrive, nevertheless, to suggest some interrelated significance.[5] The device is most obvious at the beginning of *The Three Sisters*, where two apparently unrelated conversations form a dramatically meaningful whole. Nonsense words (*tram, tam, tam* or *ta-ra-ra bumbiya**) can also be imbued with significance, and gestures and small actions communicate meaning symbolically and visually (Gayev's imaginary billiard game, and the constant looking at watches). Above all there is the adroit use of pauses, where silence takes on an eloquence denied to mere words.[6]

All these devices have a common factor: they are referential and allusive — they suggest rather than state. As such they invite interpretation, and must have seemed to Nemirovich-Danchenko and Stanislavsky ready-made material for the new director-dominated productions of the Moscow Arts Theatre. The interpretation of mood was one of the chief sources of disagreement between author and producer, but although Chekhov on occasion seemed to be in despair at the way his plays were being staged, the only advice he seemed capable of giving was to hint in the enigmatic, elusive spirit of the plays themselves. To Stanislavsky's appeals for elucidation Chekhov replied: 'But I have written it all. I am not a producer. I am a doctor.' Such observations as he did vouchsafe were felt by Stanislavsky to be 'puzzles' (rebuses).[7] In this respect Chekhov's attitude to his later plays appears to differ markedly from his earlier urge to analyse and interpret *Ivanov*.[8]

Chekhov did not invent 'mood' in the theatre, but he brought its techniques to perfection. A. N. Ostrovsky's play *The Thunderstorm* (1859) has many of the lyrical, poetic qualities often associated with Chekhovian theatre. The symbolism of the title and the motif of birds are developed in the play itself. Ostrovsky's outdoor sets breathe an almost Chekhovian magic, and atmosphere is created through omens (the mural depicting

Gehenna) as well as by episodic vatic characters (the mad noblewoman). Particularly Chekhovian are the sounds of the guitar, the snatches of song and the literary quotations: Ostrovsky's autodidact Kuligin seems to find at least a nominal echo in Chekhov's representative of provincial intelligentsia in *The Three Sisters* — Kulygin. Moreover, like Chekhov, Ostrovsky is interested in the psychology of his characters (particularly his heroine) rather than in dramatic action as such.

Turgenev's play *A Month in the Country* has also been seen as a forerunner of Chekhovian theatre. Here too action is subordinated to psychological portraiture. Valency, in comparing Chekhov's methods with those of Turgenev, has made a strong case for the innovatory nature of Turgenev's characterisation, which he claims is the technique of impressionism: the characters 'discover themselves little by little, and are constantly surprised at the things they feel and do'.[9] Nevertheless for the purposes of his plot Turgenev relies on the well-worn device of eavesdropping — a stock situation also found in his novels. It is significant that Chekhov uses this theatrical cliché in his early plays *Platonov* and *Ivanov*, but in his later plays it is used only once (*Uncle Vanya*) and there its psychological role transcends any suggestion of a mere hackneyed mechanism of plot.[10] Indeed the recurrent situation of the true Chekhovian play is not overhearing but 'underhearing' — the inability, even refusal, of one character to listen to another. Such psychological 'deafness' had already been developed as a social theme in Griboyedov's *Woe from Wit* (1825), indeed Chekhov's comic characters Ferapont (*The Three Sisters*) and Firs (*The Cherry Orchard*) may owe something to Griboyedov's Tugoukhovsky, but, more importantly in *The Cherry Orchard*, as in *Woe from Wit*, the younger generation is the bearer of truths which an older generation does not wish to know; Lyubov Andreyevna, like Famusov before her, covers up her ears in a symbolic act of non-hearing.[11]

Nevertheless, *A Month in the Country* is obviously far closer than *Woe from Wit* to the later plays of Chekhov. It is closer in its naturalism as well as in its poetic symbolism. Turgenev, as he does elsewhere, uses trees symbolically. Thus Rakitin, whose very name is derived from a tree (*rakita* = 'willow') attempts to evoke a romantic mood in his wayward mistress by poetic words on nature, but his contrast of the strong oak to the radiant birch is obviously to be taken as a symbolic statement about himself and Islayeva. Like Gayev in *The Cherry Orchard* he is rebuked for such elevated thoughts on nature. The motif of trees recurs frequently in Chekhov's plays, but his symbolic use of the theme is at once more subtle and more generalised. This scene between Rakitin and Islayeva strikes yet another Chekhovian note in the 'silences' which Turgenev calls for in his stage directions.[12]

The allusive quality of Turgenev's writing is important. In Act IV of *A Month in the Country* Shpigel'sky seeks to explain himself through a song, but more significant is the use of literary quotation. Rakitin is the friend of Islayeva's husband, and when in Act I Islayeva tells Rakitin: 'You see, I, like Tatyana, can also say: "What's the point of dissembling?"' her fragment of quotation alludes to far more than it actually states: it indicates her love for Rakitin, whilst at the same time asserting her faithfulness to her husband. Every Russian audience would catch the reference to Chapter Eight, stanza XLVIII of Pushkin's *Eugene Onegin*, would know what precedes these brief words and what comes after:

> I love you (what's the point of dissembling)
> But I have been given to another.
> I shall be eternally faithful to him.[13]

The impact of any play depends as much on its audience as it does upon its performers, and the special susceptibilities of a Russian audience are often overlooked by Western critics. Education in Russia has traditionally been based on oral skills to a greater extent than in most English-speaking countries. Every educated Russian has a rich fund of poetry which he knows by heart, and public recitations of poetry, both classical and contemporary, are a prominent feature of Russian cultural life. Anyone who has attended such a recital, given perhaps by a well-known actor, will know that the performer has only to falter a moment for there to be innumerable voices from the audience prompting him with the correct lines, so that the impression may be gained that the audience knows the poem better than the reciter himself.

Far more, perhaps, than in any other culture, a writer in Russia can play upon the literary memory of his audience or of his readers. It is important to bear in mind this ability of a Russian audience to participate in the creative act through its literary memory, when we come to look at the use Chekhov makes of literary quotation in his own plays (such as the repeated quotation in *The Three Sisters* of lines from Pushkin's *Ruslan and Lyudmila*).

The tradition of censorship in Russia has been such that readers and audiences alike have long been attuned to the finer points of oblique statement and innuendo. Theatre in Russia can be particularly vibrant; producers and actors have a way of bringing pointed meaning to words which look innocuous on the printed page. Thus classics of the nineteenth-century repertoire, such as *Woe from Wit*, or the stage adapation of Dostoyevsky's story *The Village of Stepanchikovo and its Inhabitants* can be played in such a way that without any deviation from the text a Soviet audience is aware of its relevance for contemporary life.[14]

Having said this, it must also be conceded that Chekhov could not always count on his audiences. The dispiriting failure of the opening night of *The Seagull* was as much due to the audience's expectations (see p. 17), as was its spectacular success when it was later produced by the Moscow Arts Theatre. Chekhov's plays were unfamiliarly new; but for all that, they built on the work of previous dramatists. When Styan lists among Chekhov's new techniques: 'experiments with the empty stage, his use of sounds to enlarge the area of our perception or to illuminate the condition of a character', we must not forget that, almost seventy years before, Gogol had shown him the way.[15] At the end of Act IV of *The Government Inspector* the stage is left empty for the departure of Khlestakov, which is impressionistically conveyed through off-stage conversations, cries and the sound of troyka bells. Chekhov, like Gogol, shuns the subplot, but suggests intrigue beyond the confines of the stage through his use of non-appearing characters — a device which goes back, in fact, to Griboyedov.[16]

Elements of the Chekhovian play may even be seen in eighteenth-century comedy. Thus in *Uncle Vanya* Marina's 'comic' prop of the knitted sock, has its precursor in D. I Fonvizin's *Brigadier* (1769) which opens, like the Chekhov play, with one of its characters (the brigadier's wife) knitting a sock on stage.[17] V. V. Kapnist had also experimented with the ironical effects of the interdependence of apparently unrelated conversations in his comedy *Malicious Litigation* (*Yabeda*) of 1798. In Act I scene viii of Kapnist's play an attorney conducts one conversation with the chairman of a civil court about his employer's litigation, whilst at the same time he carries on another with the chairman's wife concerning goods which he has brought with him as bribes.[18]

One can sense Chekhov himself experimenting with his techniques in the earlier playlets. Thus *Swan Song* (1887) which is the dramatic reworking of the short story *Kalkhas*, can be seen as an exercise in the extended use of literary quotations, and *Tatiana Repina* (1889), which is Chekhov's theatrical reply to Suvorin the dramatist, has been seen by at least one scholar as: 'the first glimmerings of the drama of mood'.[19] The playlet is remarkable in that it is constructed entirely of parallel and apparently unrelated areas of speech, through which Chekhov suggests ironical commentary (scandalous gossip conducted against the background of the wedding service). A second Chekhovian feature is the centring of *Tatiana Repina* not on dramatic action but on a ritualised event, capable of charging the playlet with its own 'ready made' atmosphere and drama.

Success in the theatre for Chekhov was by no means immediate, yet he wished to write plays almost from the start of his literary career. His first attempt dates from 1878 — a play without an authenticated title, which is usually referred to as *Platonov* in English (after its chief protagonist) but should perhaps be called *Fatherlessness* (*Bezotsovshchina*). It has a long rambling plot, but it is full of glimpses of the mature Chekhov, and Donald Rayfield is probably right to see it as the source of all his later plays.[20] *Ivanov*, Chekhov's next full-length play, certainly appears to be a reworking of *Platonov*. It exists in two versions (1887 and 1889) both of which, unlike the earlier play, were staged. In its revised version *Ivanov* enjoyed a measure of success, nevertheless it cannot be regarded as a truly Chekhovian play. Its hero, Ivanov, is married to a young Jewish heiress, who has not brought him a dowry because she has been disowned by her staunchly religious parents. Heavily in debt, Ivanov becomes involved in a liaison with another heiress, Sasha, the daughter of a friend and neighbour. Ivanov's behaviour drives his consumptive wife to an early death, but when he is free to marry Sasha he is denounced by his wife's doctor, and because of this, and the malicious gossip which surrounds him, he commits suicide (in the first version he succumbs to the pressure and dies a rather improbable natural death). Ivanov is hardly an edifying character, yet it is obvious that Chekhov is presenting him as a candidate for his audience's sympathy.

John Tulloch has persuasively argued that Chekhov based his portrait of Ivanov on the scientific theories of the time, and that the play has to be seen more as a socio-medical case study of neurasthenia. He stresses that Chekhov had the professional outlook of a doctor, which in the Russian tradition implied medicine with a sociological bias.[21] Yet one might also quote the words of Ivanov himself: 'It is possible to be an excellent physician and at the same time not know anything about people.'[22] If *Ivanov* shows evidence of Chekhov's professional outlook as a Russian doctor, it also bears the trademarks of his other, and more important, profession — the calling of a Russian writer. His hero fits into that tradition of Russian writing (Griboyedov, Lermontov, Turgenev, Goncharov, Dostoyevsky among others) which sought to create typical 'heroes' of their time. Chekhov's very insistence on the name Ivanov seems designed to assert the typicality of his 'Russianness'.[23]

The decade of the 1880s, after the assassination of Tsar Alexander II in 1881, was a period of political repression and stagnation in Russian intellectual life. It was a time when heroism seemed impossible; a period of so-called 'little deeds' (*malyye dela*). It is in these terms that Sasha angrily taunts local society, in her defence of Ivanov:

> Or if you could all *do* something, something quite small, hardly noticeable, but something a bit original and daring, so that we young ladies could look at you and say 'Oh', admiringly, for once in our lives! [24]

Ivanov, himself, is a typical intellectual figure of his period, but as such he is aware of literary echoes from a previous age:

> I'm dying of shame at the thought that I, a healthy, strong man, have somehow got transformed into a sort of Hamlet, or Manfred, or one of those 'superfluous' people, the devil knows which! There are some pitiable people who are flattered when you call them Hamlets or 'superfluous', but to me it's a disgrace! It stirs up my pride, a feeling of shame oppresses me, and I suffer. [25]

The term 'Hamlet' was almost synonymous with 'superfluous man' (cf. Turgenev's story *The Hamlet of the Shchigrovskiy Region*). References to Hamlet are particularly pronounced in *Platonov* (as well, of course, as in the later play *The Seagull*). Nevertheless the true era of the so-called 'superfluous man' had been the three decades between 1825 and 1855 which corresponded to the reign of Tsar Nicholas I. Like the period of the 1880s this was a time of repression, which had also been occasioned by a political event — the suppression of the Decembrist uprising in 1825. Ivanov exhibits the characteristics of key figures in the literature of this earlier period. Like Griboyedov's Chatsky he is at odds with local society. [26] Like Turgenev's Rudin he is a man full of great potential, which he seems incapable of realising; and again like Rudin, he demurs when his 'heroine' suggests that they should abscond. Nevertheless the terms of his reply suggest yet another of these 'superfluous' heroes: 'I feel too lazy to walk to that door, and you talk of America . . . ' [27]

The laziest man in Russian literature is the hero of I. A. Goncharov's novel *Oblomov* (1859). Like the other figures discussed above, Oblomov is incapable of forming a serious relationship with a strong heroine, yet she, Olga Ilinskaya, wishes to 'resurrect' him. In a similar way Sasha is accused by Ivanov of having set herself the goal of resurrecting the human

being in him and he characterises their love affair as a literary
stereotype:[28]

> And this love affair of ours is all just something commonplace and trite:
> 'He lost heart and lost his grip on things. She appeared, cheerful and
> strong in spirit, and held out a helping hand.' It's beautiful, but it's only
> like what happens in novels. In real life you don't . . .[29]

In Goncharov's novel the psychological motivation of Olga
Ilinskaya is equally as fascinating as that of Oblomov himself.
Sasha provides us with an insight which could be just as valid
for Olga:

> There are a lot of things men don't understand. Every girl is more
> attracted by a man who's a failure than by one who's a success, because
> what she wants is active love. . . . Do you understand that? Active love.
> Men are taken up with their work and so love has to take a back seat with
> them. To have a talk with his wife, to take a stroll with her in the garden,
> to pass time pleasantly with her, to weep a little on her grave — that's all.
> But for us — love is life.[30]

In a variant of this scene Sasha actually calls Ivanov
'Oblomov', but Chekhov discarded such open identification.[31]
In reinterpreting Goncharov he undoubtedly wished to avoid
the ready-made stereotype, and a polemical point is the
disowning of positive features which certain critics had
attributed to Oblomovism itself:

> IVANOV. I can't enjoy spiritual idleness and see it as something noble and
> lofty. Idleness is idleness, weakness is weakness — I don't know any
> other names for them.[32]

Central to the play is the assertion that man is psychologically
far more complex than the gossip-mongers of local society and
the self-appointed moralist, Dr Lvov, can ever imagine. In an
important speech in Act III, scene vi, Ivanov not only rebukes
Lvov for his simplistic view of human motivation, but at the
same time appears to take up Lebedev's observation in the
preceding scene, that man is a mere samovar.[33] This polemical
point about the complexity of human psychology will be illustrated more impressively in the later plays: in *Ivanov* itself it has
more the role of a programmatic statement.

Nevertheless it is national psychology and sociological inter-

pretation which are uppermost in the detailed explanation of his
play communicated to Suvorin in a letter of 30 December 1888.
It appears from this that *Ivanov* is about the Russian temperament itself, which Chekhov sees as conditioned by periods of
excitability followed by troughs of depression. He even draws a
graph to illustrate his argument showing that with each successive phase the troughs of depression get lower:

> Disillusionment, apathy, nervous instability, being easily tired are the
> invariable results of excessive excitability and such excitability is character-
> istic of our young people in the highest degree. Take literature. Take the
> present . . .*34

Although Chekhov here seems to be offering a national and
social account of the medical condition known as manic depression, his view of the polarisation of the Russian temperament
between excitability and depression, bouts of activity and
periods of lethargy, is not new. The critic N. A. Dobrolyubov,
pointing to a similar pattern in Russian history, had likened the
intelligentsia of his day to the legendary folk hero Ilya
Muromets who slept for thirty years then awoke to perform
doughty deeds.35

Chekhov's argument in his letter to Suvorin, as we have seen,
is partly based on literature, and here he may have had *Oblomov*
in mind; for there had also been 'high-points' of activity in
Oblomov's life (initially, as a young man, under the influence of
Shtolts and later in response to Olga). Indeed, in giving his
hero both the name and the patronymic of Ilya (Ilya Ilyich)
Goncharov may have been seeking to link him with the
symbolic figure of Ilya Muromets.

In *Ivanov*, the aristocratic Shabelsky says of Ivanov's self-
appointed critic Dr Lvov, that he thinks of himself as a second
Dobrolyubov, and regards him (Shabelsky) as a rogue and a
serf-owner, because he wears a velvet jacket and is dressed by a
manservant.36 There are clear references in this to Dobrolyubov
as the critic of 'Oblomovism'. In 1859 Dobrolyubov had written
an extremely influential article on Goncharov's novel (*What is
Oblomovism?*) in which he had argued that Oblomov was the
summation of all the gentleman heroes in literature up to that
point: that he was the quintessential 'superfluous man'. A

similar objective seems to have been in Chekhov's mind when writing *Ivanov*:

> I cherished the daring dream of summing up all that has been written up to now about whining and melancholy people, and to put an end to these writings with my *Ivanov*. It seemed to me that all Russian men of letters and playwrights had felt the need to depict the depressed man, and that they had all written instinctively without having definite images and a view on the matter. In conception I more or less got it right, but the execution is worthless, I should have waited.*[37]

It is interesting that this same letter contains the often quoted statement about himself as a writer of lowly origin who had to squeeze the slave out of himself drop by drop and who one day woke up to find real human blood in his veins. His injunction to write a story about such a figure was never fulfilled. The nearest he came to depicting such a social parvenu in positive terms was in his play *The Cherry Orchard*. Lopakhin has certain auto-biographical features and is a more credible version of Goncharov's Shtolts — the practical man of affairs of mixed social origin.

In 1886 Chekhov published a 'Literary Table of Ranks' in the humorous publication *Splinters (Oskolki)* (No. 19, 10 May).[38] This parody of the hierarchy of ranks in the civil service left the top grade as yet unoccupied, but placed Tolstoy and Goncharov together in the second grade. Nevertheless in 1889, after the production of the second version of *Ivanov*, Chekhov reread *Oblomov* and, in a letter to Suvorin at the beginning of May, wrote of his disillusionment with the novel and its author: he had completely revised his views of its artistic merits. In his next letter to Suvorin (4 May 1889) Chekhov defends himself against the charge of laziness, but fears that he is like Goncharov: 'whom I do not like and who is ten times head and shoulders above me in talent'.[39]

In *The Wood Demon* (1889) Hélène is seen as the embodiment of laziness, and she is characterised by Voynitsky as an 'Oblomov'.[40] This reference was removed when the play was rewritten as *Uncle Vanya*, and Chekhov strongly objected to critics who attempted to interpret the play in terms of Goncharov's novel:

I have read reviews of *Uncle Vanya* only in the *Courier* and *News of the Day*. I saw an article about 'Oblomov' in the *Russian Record*, but I didn't read it. I can't stand this making something out of nothing, this forced linking with *Oblomov*, with *Fathers and Sons* etc. You can forcibly compare any play with what you want, and if Sanin and Ignatov had taken Nozdrev and King Lear instead of Oblomov, it would have turned out equally profound and readable. I do not read such articles, so as not to foul up my temper.*[41]

Given such a categorical authorial pronouncement, it might seem that any critic would be foolish to draw further parallels between Oblomov and Chekhov's heroes, yet the echoes are there in the later plays; indeed in the recurrent theme of ineffectuality confronted by the exhortation to work we have something of the dilemma which lies at the heart of Goncharov's novel.

Chekhov felt the parallel with Oblomov even in his own life. We have already seen that in reply to Suvorin's charge of laziness, he conceded that he felt like Goncharov, and he made a similar excuse to Stanislavsky towards the end of his life as he was working on *The Cherry Orchard:*

I was ill, but am recovered now, my health has improved, and if I do not work as I ought, it is because of the cold (it is only eleven degrees in my study), lack of company and, probably, laziness, which was born in 1859, that is one year before me.*[42]

The reference to the publication date of *Oblomov* is unmistakable, yet Chekhov was anything but a lazy man; he did, however, suffer from a debilitating disease, and did not wish to face up to it. A jocular condemnation of the 'Oblomov' within himself was one way of minimising his symptoms and coping with a problem he knew to be incurable. The charge of 'Oblomovism' from others was another matter — it touched on a sensitive area of his own life, even though the term was applied solely to his heroes. It is undeniable, nevertheless, that the protagonists of his plays lack drive: 'The usual Chekhovian character is a half-hearted participant in an action that barely excites his interest.'[43] Through such heroes Chekhov was not merely purging an element which he most dreaded in himself, he was also portraying a state of mind endemic in Russian society at the end of the nineteenth century. In the political reaction which

followed the assassination of Tsar Alexander II even the most
energetic leaders of the intelligentsia suddenly felt themselves
superfluous. M. Ye. Saltykov-Shchedrin (of whose great output
Chekhov felt envious)[44] expressed this mood most strikingly in
his Gogolian 'Fairy Tale' *The Adventures of Kramolnikov* (1886) —
Kramolnikov wakes up one morning and suddenly realises that
he doesn't exist.[45] Such new 'non-people' could obviously be
related to the former 'superfluous men', of whom Oblomov had
been seen as the epitome. But *Oblomov* is also a novel about
social change (it purports to have been written in answer to the
question: 'where do beggars come from?').[46] The reforms of the
1860s, anticipated in Goncharov's novel, had resulted by the
turn of the century in a rapidly changing society. The old
landowning gentry were a waning social force, losing ground to
the new and energetic entrepreneur, whom Goncharov had not
so much depicted, as prophesied, in the figure of Shtolts. The
social theme is important for all Chekhov's plays and it is
significant that its dominant motif is dispossession.

It has often been observed that Chekhov's theatrical technique combines a subtle blend of naturalism and symbolism.[47]
He wrote at a time when the Russian theatre had found, in
Stanislavsky, its great exponent of showing life as it is. The
Moscow Arts Theatre productions stressed the naturalism of
the plays to the point where, Chekhov felt, it became absurd.
The naturalism of sets, acting and effects was boldly emphasised, and Stanislavsky was particularly fond of multiplying
incidental, off-stage sounds far in excess of those called for by
the author. Stanislavsky tells the following story against himself:

> 'Listen!' Chekhov told someone, but so that I could hear, 'I shall write a
> new play and it will begin like this: 'How marvellous, how silent! No birds
> can be heard, no dogs, no cuckoos, no owls, no nightingales, no clocks, no
> bells and not a single cricket.' Of course he was getting at me.*[48]

Stanislavsky's philosophy of production, his famous 'method',
was constantly developing. Later he would take a different view
of his earlier Chekhov productions.[49]

Nevertheless, naturalism as such was not the order of the
day. Throughout Europe the 1890s marked an almost universal

flight from the humdrum and everyday; symbolism, decadence, impressionism dominated the *fin de siècle* mood. Chekhov was aware of these currents, and in his new theatre of the 1890s he contrived, whilst retaining the naturalistic surface, to incorporate an element of intangibility and mystery proclaimed in the new art forms — a dimension characterised by Valency as the 'Chekhovian "Beyond" ': 'The strangely unreal atmosphere in which the realities of his later plays are suspended. It is an atmosphere less mysterious and less explicit than the Maeterlinckian *au-delà*, and certainly more intelligible.'[50]

Chekhov's earlier heroes, Platonov, Ivanov and Voynitsky (in the *Wood Demon*) are romantic figures alienated from the prosaic world in which they live. Not only do they convey a sense of looking back to an earlier period of Russian literature, but such self-indulgent, self-destructive romanticism is artistically at odds with the naturalistic vehicle of the plays themselves. It is significant that *The Seagull*, the play which gave Chekhov his first major success, and marked the onset of the theatre of mood, should project the romantic, alienated hero at odds not merely with the society around him, but more importantly with that society's concept of theatre. Treplev, in calling for new forms, is Chekhov struggling to find a way out of his own artistic impasse. The rivalry between Trigorin and Treplev reflects a debate within the author himself. The first 'Chekhovian' play is a play of re-evaluation and self-examination.[51]

1

THE SEAGULL

CHEKHOV began work on *The Seagull* in the autumn of 1895, and the play was first performed on 17 October 1896 at the Alexandrinsky Theatre in St Petersburg. Unfortunately the occasion chosen was the benefit night of a well-known comedy actress, Ye. I. Levkeyeva, who was to star, not in Chekhov's play, but in a vaudeville on the same programme. The audience attracted to such an event was in no mood to take Chekhov's play seriously. Almost from the opening it reacted with inappropriate laughter, and by Act IV was howling for the curtain to fall. The following day press notices were almost unanimous in their condemnation of the play. Although subsequent performances went better, Chekhov was bitterly disillusioned and vowed never to stage another play. It was, therefore, with great reluctance that he allowed Nemirovich-Danchenko to undertake a fresh production of *The Seagull* for the newly opened Moscow Arts Theatre. Yet this opening night, 17 December 1898, made theatrical history: it was the turning point in Chekhov's career as a dramatist, and it established the fortunes of The Moscow Arts Theatre itself. The success of that night was as overwhelming as had been the failure two years before.

A contributing factor in the initial failure may well have been the acting and the production itself, but the play's very novelty also militated against a ready-made success. The opening directions for the stage-set of *The Seagull* are striking: within the frame of the theatre stage another but rudimentary stage is encompassed as a piece of scenery. Shortly this improvised theatre will have its own 'stage audience', but the theatre as a whole is also drawn in as its audience by the design of the set itself. It presents a wide avenue leading directly from the auditorium to the crude framework stage and the attention of the audience is focussed visually along this line, which normally would end in a view of the lake, were it not blocked out by the little curtained stage and its 'natural' surround of bushes.

This is the visual impact of Treplev's 'new' theatre, and its designer soon puts it into words:

> TREPLEV [*looking over the stage*]. There's a theatre for you! Just the curtain and the two wings and beyond it — open space. No scenery. You have an unimpeded view of the lake and the horizon. We'll raise the curtain at half past [eight precisely, when the moon rises*].[1]

Here, then, is a concept of theatre proclaiming a simple frame for a natural setting: a lake, the horizon and the rising moon. It contrasts with 'the room with three walls' of the conventional stage, decried by Treplev himself as mere humdrum prejudice. Thus the audience of *The Seagull* has before it two stages, each reflecting a contrasting concept of theatre: the conventional opposed to the experimental, and the dichotomy is carried on through two couples who are in apparent artistic opposition: the author Treplev and his actress Zarechnaya championing the new art against the actress of the conventional theatre, Arkadina, and her author — Trigorin. Thus from its very opening we are aware that this first truly Chekhovian play is about the nature of dramatic art itself.

The laughter which greeted its first performance came not merely from an audience frustrated in its expectations, but also from one perplexed by the play's inherent ambiguities. Those sitting in the body of the theatre were invited to become a double audience through the construction of the set, and in similar manner the scenery of a conventional stage was also called upon to assume a double function. Treplev's contempt for the trappings of the routine theatre and his insistence on presenting his play against a natural backdrop, seek in real theatrical terms to elevate the painted moon and lake into true originals, as if the second theatrical frame were a prism capable of transmuting image into reality. but the nature of Treplev's prism is deceptive; what naturalness there is derives from the conventions of illusion on the main stage itself, and it is the action of the main play which is naturalistic. By contrast Treplev's stage transforms the 'real' phenomena, on which it so insists, into poetic symbols; from the would-be concrete reality of lake, horizon, moon, it projects abstract, eternal images. In essence his playlet is non-naturalistic.

Chekhov in challenging the conventional theatre of his day is involved in an elaborately serious joke. The 'new forms' of Treplev's symbolist play, which rely on natural means, are not Chekhov's own innovatory theatre as such; nor yet, of course, is the main play the conventional humdrum 'three-walled stage' attacked by Treplev. Yet, just as the playlet has a real dramatic function within the wider action of *The Seagull* itself, it also has a nucleic, but self-parodying, position in respect of the new artistic manifesto which Chekhov's play proclaims; for although Chekhov's new theatre is acted on the old conventional stage, implicit within it is that very symbolic naturalism, which Treplev has reduced to such starkly bare essentials. Treplev's language may be elevated in an un-Chekhovian way, but his incantatory roll-call of nature's fauna finds a more sober counterpart in Chekhov's own symbolic use of the phenomena of the natural world throughout his plays (beginning, of course, with the 'seagull' itself) and Treplev's desire to propel his audience from the present into the future, is merely the extreme expression of a tendency observable in all Chekhov's later plays.

If Treplev's playlet can be seen as having only token and emblematic significance for Chekhov's own 'new theatre', it also exhibits a certain ambiguity as the artistic manifesto of Treplev himself. It is obvious that it also serves as a vehicle of psychological confrontation with his mother and her lover Trigorin. Before the playlet begins, his uncle tells Treplev that he has already imagined that it will not please his mother, but, that nevertheless, she really adores him. Treplev's reaction is to pull the petals one by one from a flower, as he chants: 'She loves me . . . she loves me not . . . she loves me — loves me not . . . loves me — loves me not. [*Laughs.*] You see, my mother doesn't love me.' This is more the guessing game of a lovesick swain than of a son. Although it is played half in jest, it is an early indication of the depth of Treplev's feelings for his mother.

He seems to sense that his mother is already hostile to his play, without having seen it, and that she is jealous of the fact that Nina will play the leading role. From this jealousy, and from the play's aesthetic challenge to the older writer, Trigorin, Treplev subconsciously hopes to wring some avowal from his mother (even though secretly he knows that this will not happen). The 'game with the flower' will be played out more elaborately as a direct emotional and professional challenge both to his mother (as actress) and to her lover (as writer): it will prove that Treplev is not the nonentity which he feels himself to be in his mother's eyes.

The added psychological function of the playlet introduces a new dimension of literary allusion. The 'play within the play' suggests a theatrical analogy with *Hamlet*: 'The play's the thing/ Wherein I'll catch the conscience of the king', and in this sense Treplev's play is also *The Mousetrap* (a second literary allusion in Act II will identify 'writer' with 'rat').

References to *Hamlet* are explicit before the playlet begins. They reveal the sexual guilt of the mother in the eyes of her son:

> ARKADINA (*recites from 'Hamlet'*). 'My son! You have turned my eyes into the depths of my soul, and I have seen it in such bloody, such mortal ulcers — there is no salvation!'
> TREPLEV (*from 'Hamlet'*). 'And why then have you succumbed to vice, have sought love in an abyss of crime?'*[2]

By such quotations Chekhov reveals more about the emotional relationships of the central characters than he does through direct statement or self-analysis. He is able to play on the literary memory of his audience, drawing, not only on the psychological issues of the Shakespearian play itself, but also on the Russian identification of the Hamlet theme with that of the 'superfluous man'.[3] Treplev is an introspective, ineffectual, student 'drop-out' (*nedouchivshiysya student*). When his uncle defends him to Arkadina in Act III he points both to his pride and to his sense of feeling superfluous:

> SORIN. but all the same, when all is said, he feels that he is superfluous in the house, that he is a sponger and a hanger-on here. It's an understandable thing, self-respect . . .*[4]

Self-respect (*samolyubiye*) is a concept at the centre of a key argument in *Rudin*, Turgenev's first novel about a 'superfluous man', and it is not without significance that Nina, during her final meeting with Treplev in Act IV, should quote directly from this work:[5]

> NINA. Let us sit and talk, talk. . . . It's nice here, warm and comfortable. . . .
> Do you hear the wind? There's a passage in Turgenev: 'Fortunate is he
> who on such a night has a roof over him, who has a warm corner of his
> own.' I am a seagull. . . . No, that's not it. [*Rubs her forehead.*] What was I
> saying? Yes. . . . Turgenev. . . . 'And Heaven help the homeless
> wayfarers'. . . . Never mind. . . . [*Sobs.*]

Nina is obviously referring to herself, but if she is contrasting her position with that of Treplev, her words must have a bitterly ironic ring for one who feels himself to be 'superfluous in the house'. After this meeting, Treplev like Chekhov's earlier 'superfluous hero', Ivanov, ends the ambiguity of his life by suicide.

Chekhov's use of the *Hamlet* theme goes beyond its significance for Treplev alone. It casts other characters in certain emotional roles *a priori*; thus Arkadina, through quotation, identifies herself with Gertrude, whereas Trigorin, inevitably, is projected as the wicked uncle, the usurper in the realm (of art) and in the affections of a mother. Nina, through her vulnerability, her betrayal, her giving of flowers and finally through her poetic 'madness' can be seen as another Ophelia. Treplev's father, like Hamlet's own, is present only as a disquieting 'ghost':

> TREPLEV. but according to my passport I'm a petty bourgeois from Kiev.
> My father, you see, was a petty bourgeois from Kiev, although he was
> also a well-known actor.*[6]

The internal passport places Treplev firmly in the lower social class of petty townsman or tradesman (*meshchanin*), but like the word 'bourgeois', which it also means, it carries the culturally pejorative connotation of 'Philistine'.[7] It is this inheritance from his father that Arkadina can use to wound her son: ARKADINA. 'You're not even capable of writing a pathetic little vaudeville. Kievan petty bourgeois! Hanger on!'*[8] It is his mother's sneering reference to a diabolical father which acts as the emotional trigger bringing Treplev's 'pathetic little vaudeville' to an abrupt end:

ARKADINA. The Doctor's taken his hat off to the Devil, the father of Eternal
   Matter.
TREPLEV [*flaring up, loudly*]. The play's over! Enough of it! Curtain!

Shakespeare's play, however, is not a constricting grid imposed on *The Seagull*; its role is rather to liberate by providing an added dimension of allusion and atmosphere. It is obvious that Chekhov's plot is entirely different, and whereas *Hamlet* is a tragedy, Chekhov calls his play a 'comedy', even though it ends in a suicide. This ambivalent note of 'tragic comedy' is struck at the very opening by Masha (the character who has an introductory role in each act):

MEDVEDENKO. Why do you always wear black?
MASHA. I'm in mourning for my life. I'm unhappy.

Similarly, but in more serious vein, the tragic hints surrounding Chekhov's 'Ophelia' are not fully realised, even though death by drowning is suggested from the start (like some loaded pistol which must inevitably be fired). Thus Nina on her first appearance confesses that she is drawn to the lake like a seagull, and when in Act II Treplev kills a seagull and lays it at her feet, we seem to have a portent of her death. It is Trigorin who suggests this interpretation at the end of the act through his 'plot for a fairly short story',*[9] and in Act III, Nina echoes the suggestion by inviting him to take her life, in an oblique reference to his own published work. The seagull motif is associated with a more substantial literary allusion, and the theme of drowning, at the beginning of Act IV, when Treplev likens Nina's constant reference to herself as a 'seagull' to a comparable self-identification in *Rusalka*, Pushkin's poem about a drowned maiden,[10] and when Nina makes her appearance at the end of the act, it is a stormy night, the lake has huge waves, and her own imagination, like that of Ophelia, seems correspondingly disturbed. She constantly refers to herself as a 'seagull' and reveals that: 'Ever since I came I've been walking round here . . . beside the lake.' Before she goes out into the stormy night, she says 'someone ought to kill me', but no violence is offered her, nor does she drown herself; she merely asks Treplev for a glass

)f water, as though Chekhov is underlining a point with bathos.

Direct quotation from *Hamlet*, which in Act I reveals the relationship of mother and son, is used in Act II to reveal Treplev's attitude to Trigorin, and it is now not Arkadina who is the cause of rivalry, but Nina. The older writer's growing influence over Nina is yet a further stage of usurpation, and Treplev's expression of artistic jealousy combines both fear and contempt; it mockingly casts Trigorin as the usurper of the Hamlet role, while at the same time suggesting him as Polonius — the foolish old man:

> TREPLEV . . . [*Seeing* TRIGORIN, *who comes in reading a book.*] But here comes the real genius, stepping out like Hamlet himself, and with a book, too. [*Mimicks.*] 'Words, words, words.'

Nevertheless, the most significant literary quotation in Act II comes, not from the English genius of the theatre, but from the French master of the short story. In Act I Treplev had referred to Guy de Maupassant's autobiographical work *La Vie Errante*, and in Act II Arkadina reads out a passage from his novel *Sur l'Eau*:

> The rats. . . . Here it is. [*Reads.*] 'And it goes without saying that it is as dangerous for society people to pamper and encourage writers of novels, as it is for corn merchants to breed rats in their granaries. And yet novelists are very much sought after. Thus, when a woman has chosen a writer whom she wishes to capture, she lays siege to him with the aid of compliments, flattery and favours.'

Arkadina is quick to see the relevance of this for her relationship with Trigorin, but equally prompt to point out the difference: she is following no programme; she is head over heels in love with her writer. Nevertheless, the quotation in suggesting that Arkadina is making all the running in the relationship (and this is borne out later in the act) touches on a raw nerve, and when Nina enters, Arkadina overcomes her own promptings to read further, claiming that the continuation is uninteresting and untrue. If the Maupassant quotation performs the same revelatory role for her relationship with Trigorin, that the *Hamlet* exchange in Act I had performed for her relationship with her son, its implications are nevertheless wider: it goes to the very core of the debate on art which Chekhov is conducting throughout this play.

The equation of novelists with rats is hardly flattering to Trigorin — it suggests him as the destroyer of hospitality, the ruin ,of those who harbour him. There is truth in this, but it is also clear from Arkadina's remarks that she is merely resuming the reading, and the passage, on which Dorn must have stopped before the act opens, puts the quotation read on stage in its true context. It draws a distinction between the 'poet' and the 'novelist':

> The woman who feels urged by that peculiar taste of having a man of letters in the house, as one might have a parrot, whose chattering attracts the neighbouring concierges, has a choice between poets and novelists. There is more of the ideal in the poet, and more of the unpredictable in the novelist, poets are more sentimental, novelists more positive.[11]

In terms of the play itself Arkadina has a similar choice between her son — the writer of a poetic, idealistic play — and Trigorin — more positive, but unpredictable in his affections. But the passage goes on to suggest further dangers to be associated with Trigorin:

> But a novelist presents more dangers than one encounters with a poet, he gnaws, loots and exploits everything he sees. One can never be at peace with him around, never certain that one day he will not lay you out completely naked between the pages of a book. His eye is like a pump which sucks everything in, like the hand of a robber always active. Nothing escapes him, he gathers movements, gestures, intentions, everything that passes and takes place before him. He collects the least of words, the least of acts, the least of things. From morning to night he stores up every kind of observation, from which he makes stories to sell, stories which travel to the ends of the earth, which will be read, discussed and commented upon by thousands and millions of people. And what is terrible is that he will make it true to life, the rogue, in spite of himself, unconsciously, because he sees accurately and because he relates what he has seen. In spite of his efforts and his subterfuges to disguise the characters, people will say: 'Did you recognise M. X . . . and Mme. Y . . . ? The likeness is striking.'[12]

It would be difficult to conceive a more accurate description of Trigorin's activities throughout the play, and more particularly in this act. Thus he observes Masha: TRIGORIN [*making notes in his book*]. 'Takes snuff and drinks vodka. Always dresses in black. A schoolmaster in love with her.' Almost immediately afterwards he says to Nina:

Girls don't often come my way, I mean girls who are young and interesting to meet. I've forgotten what it feels like to be eighteen or nineteen, indeed I can't imagine it at all clearly. That's why the girls in my novels and stories are usually so artificial. I wish I could exchange places with you, even if only for an hour, just to find out what your thoughts are, and what kind of a pretty little thing you are in a general sort of way.

This admission points to the real nature of Trigorin's interest in Nina, and he goes on to tell her that writing is an obsession which dominates the whole of his life:

Here I am with you, I'm quite worked up, and yet not for a single moment do I forget that there's an unfinished novel waiting for me. I look over there and I see a cloud shaped like a grand piano. . . . At once I think I must put it into some story or other — the fact that a cloud looking like a grand piano has floated by. There's the scent of heliotrope in the air. I make a mental note: 'sickly scent . . . flower — the colour of a widow's dress . . . mention when describing a summer evening.' . . . I snatch at every word and sentence I utter, and every word you utter, too, and hurriedly lock them up in my literary pantry — in case they might come in useful!

At the end of this scene with Nina, Trigorin is again writing in his notebook:

NINA. What are you writing?
TRIGORIN. Just making a few notes. . . . An idea suddenly came into my head. [*Putting his notebook away.*] [A plot for a fairly short story*]: a young girl, like you, has lived beside a lake from childhood. She loves the lake as a seagull does, and she's happy and free as a seagull. But a man chances to come along, sees her, and having nothing better to do, destroys her, just like this seagull here.[13]

This bare plot for a 'fairly short story' is almost the plan of Trigorin's own actions. By Act IV Nina is left by the lake, ruined and abandoned by her writer, and he has once more returned to Arkadina, as though nothing had happened. Yet Nina's attitude to Trigorin is more serious: she still loves him, as she confesses to Treplev. Moreover, she refers to herself in his terms as a 'seagull', and to her plight as 'the plot of a fairly short story'.

What Trigorin steals from life is a gain for his art. Arkadina's desperately lavish praise of her idol in Act III stresses this point: 'people in your books are so alive'. By contrast the more 'poetic' Treplev does not consume real life and real people for his art, and this is his weakness. Nina comments: 'It's difficult to act in your play. There are no real living characters in it.' and in Act IV Trigorin says that even Treplev's latest work contains 'not a single living character!'

Nina is not Trigorin's only victim. Treplev, who seems to have lost out to the older writer on every account, is driven to take his own life. Even his failures are in danger of becoming the artistic property of his rival. Thus at the beginning of Act III we find Masha (another of Trigorin's 'subjects'), offering Trigorin the details of Treplev's earlier suicide attempt for him 'to make use of', and in Act IV, the older writer, with a predatory lack of tact, appears to consider Treplev's abortive play a fit subject for his art:

> TRIGORIN. Besides, I want to have a look around the garden and see the place where your play was acted — you remember? I've a subject for a story, I only want to revive my memories of the scene where the action is supposed to take place.

But the stigma of Maupassant's literary 'rat' penetrates deeper than this: Chekhov in his own play is another Trigorin. The unhappy *affaire* of Nina and her middle-aged, middle-rank writer closely follows a well-known scandal involving two of Chekhov's own friends. Lika Mizinova, (probably out of a sense of frustration with Chekhov himself, who had flirted with her for years) ran off with Potapenko, a minor writer who was already married, and, like Nina, she too had a child which died; she, too, was abandoned by her middle-aged lover. Lika and Potapenko recognised their unhappy *affaire* in Chekhov's plot — indeed the resemblances were sufficiently obvious to all Chekhov's friends.[14]

Details from the life of yet another of Chekhov's close friends also found their way into the play. In July 1895 Chekhov had been summoned to the estate of A. N. Turchaninova, a lady with whom the artist Levitan was having an *affaire*. Levitan, a close friend of Chekhov, had attempted to shoot himself because of the rivalry for his affections between Turchaninova and her daughter. It is easy to see here the elements which in Chekhov's play were to become transmuted into a mother–son–lover rivalry leading to attempted suicide. The Turchaninova estate also had a lake and this too has found its way into *The Seagull*, as has Levitan's shooting of a woodcock (perhaps even a seagull). This is not the first instance of Chekhov's plagiarism from the life of his friend. Earlier Levitan had almost challenged him to a duel because of the use Chekhov had made of another of the artist's love affairs in the story *The Butterfly (Poprygun'ya)*.[15]

An even more curious refurbishing of real life is to be found in Act III. Nina gives Trigorin a medallion with an inscription referring him to a line in a volume of his own collected works. On looking it up, Trigorin finds that it reads: 'If ever you need my life, come and take it'. An ardent female admirer, Lidiya Avilova, had presented Chekhov himself with a similar pendant, inscribed with a page and line reference to the master's own works. It led to the story *Neighbours* and to the very same statement used by Chekhov for Trigorin's medallion. Indeed in the St Petersburg production Avilova's pendant was actually used on stage.[16]

Some eight months or so before the first performance of *The Seagull*, but after the gift of the watch pendant, Avilova claims to have encountered Chekhov by chance at a masked ball. In speaking to him she strove to preserve her anonymity, but when she asked him if he knew who she was, he promised to answer her from the stage. It was with great excitement that Avilova watched *The Seagull* on its opening night, and immediately recognised the plagiarism in the scene with the medallion, but although the message was the same, the page and line reference quoted on stage differed from her original. Page 121, lines 11 and 12 appeared to make no sense as a key to Chekhov's works; but applied to her own, it yielded the sentence: 'It is not proper for young ladies to go to masked balls.'[17]

Although many critics are justifiably suspicious of many aspects of Avilova's account of *Chekhov in My Life*, there is, nevertheless, enough evidence here to show that Chekhov was not above using art as the vehicle for a private joke. The medallion, referring to text and context outside the play itself, has a parallel in the Maupassant quotation in Act II with its oblique

reference back to the passage which has preceded it. This could
well be another of Chekhov's private jokes, warning friends and
lady acquaintances, who might feel flattered to have their own
pet author, that, nevertheless, there is a price to pay. Chekhov
appears not to have taken the 'passions' and the 'tragedies' of
Mizinova, Potapenko, Levitan, Turchaninova, Avilova et al. as
seriously as they obviously did themselves. When, on the first
night of *The Seagull*, it seemed probable that Potapenko might
occupy a box adjacent to Lika Mizinova, Chekhov observed
that this would 'just serve Lika right'.[18] It is the comment of an
author who could designate as comedy a play which ends in
suicide.

Trigorin, the author, not merely consumes the lives of others
— his own life, he feels, is itself consumed in this process:

> TRIGORIN. and I can't get any rest away from myself. I feel as though I'm
> devouring my own life, that for the sake of the honey I give to all and
> sundry I'm despoiling my best flowers of their pollen, that I'm plucking
> the flowers themselves and trampling on their roots. Am I out of my
> mind?

Trigorin feels that the exigencies of his career have left him with
no youth. He confesses to Nina: 'During those years, the best
years of youth, my writing career was one endless torment',*[19]
and in Act III he tells Arkadina what Nina's love means to
him: 'I've never yet known a love like that . . . In my youth I
never had time. I was always hanging around on editors' doorsteps, struggling with poverty. Now it's here, that love; it has
finally come, it beckons . . .' Here then is a second reason for
Trigorin's *affaire* with Nina — it is an attempt to catch up with
life. But the *affaire* is short-lived; the destructive artist within
him cannot be tamed, and life, as always, is sacrificed to art.

The theme of lost youth has relevance for Chekhov himself —
he, too, as a young man had 'hung around editors' doorsteps'
and had expended his enormous energies in gaining himself an
education and professional qualifications, whilst at the same
time supporting his family and laying the foundations of his
literary career. In middle age he was to realise that tuberculosis
had deprived him of a future (his brother Michael noticed the
first serious decline in his health in August 1895 — shortly

before serious work on the play began).[20] It is not difficult to see
that, like Trigorin, he felt in some sort of trap: self driven, yet
also driven by others — like a 'fox badgered by the hounds'.
The temptation of finding his youth through a younger woman
must have had its attraction, but he was able to watch the
romance of Potapenko and Lika with complacent fascination,
and feel that, but for the tyranny of art, there went he. Three
years before his death he succumbed to the temptation, and
married the young actress Olga Knipper.

Tolstoy recognised some of Chekhov's own traits in Trigorin.
Not only does he share his creator's passion for fishing, but the
techniques by which Trigorin achieves the effect of moonlight,
as related by Treplev in Act IV, are those of Chekhov himself.
These techniques are advocated by Chekhov in a much quoted
letter to his brother Alexander (10 May 1886) and put into
practice in the short story *The Wolf*, which also dates from that
year.[21]

At the same time there is also self-identification with the
younger writer Treplev, who like Chekhov himself is searching
for 'new forms' in the theatre. Trigorin's account of Treplev's
apparent success in the two capital cities, and the mystery he
creates with his pseudonyms, recalls Chekhov's own position
some ten years' earlier, when he too was a young writer on the
point of establishing a career.

The artistic 'duel' between Trigorin and Treplev is the reflection of an argument within Chekhov himself. Trigorin is a man
of mid-to-late thirties. (Chekhov's own age at the time of writing *The Seagull*). He is an author whom the world sees as
successful; he writes 'charmingly and with talent', but he fears
that his epitaph will be: 'here lies Trigorin. He was a good
writer but not as good as Turgenev'. He is concerned at the
thought that, as a writer, he will be assessed merely for his
powers of description:

TRIGORIN. But you see, I'm not a mere landscape painter, I'm also a
citizen of my country; I love it, I love its people. As an author, I feel I'm
in duty bound to write about the people, their sufferings, their future —
and about science, the rights of man, and so on, and so forth. And I
write about everything in a great hurry while I'm being prodded and

urged on from all sides and people keep getting cross with me, so that I
dash about from one side to the other like a fox badgered by the hounds.
I see science and society forging ahead, while I drop further and further
behind, like a peasant who's just missed his train, and in the end I feel
that all I can do is to paint landscapes, and that everything else I write
is a sham — false to the very core.

In the context of writing the term 'citizen' (*grazhdanin*) has the
specific connotation of an artist who devotes himself to social
questions. Trigorin proceeds to outline such issues: the people
(i.e. the peasants — *narod*); their present conditions (i.e.
'sufferings'); and their future role; the question of human rights,
which is linked to this; and the progress of science (a much
broader term in Russian, which may include philosophy, both
social and political). All these areas were difficult to write about
in the late nineteenth century. Yet his public expects Trigorin,
as a serious writer, to raise these issues, while editors and
censors strive to mute and mutilate, thus he feels driven from all
sides and his serious themes all turn out false. Chekhov, too,
was often criticised, quite unjustly, for what was seen as a lack
of social commitment. Given this orientation in the Russian
public, he could seem a lesser figure than Tolstoy, Turgenev
and Zola — the three writers with whom Trigorin is compared
to his detriment.

Treplev is twenty-five when the play opens; an age at which
Chekhov himself had not realised his full potential as a serious
writer. Treplev shoots himself at the age of twenty-seven, and
this age seems to have been one of crisis in Chekhov's own life;
for between the years 1886 and 1887 Chekhov had seemed prey
to the new demands placed upon him as a serious writer, and
the need to have a philosophy of life.[22]

Nevertheless, the artistic argument is not just a confrontation
between the author's past and his present; it also implies a duo-
logue on the future, which centres on new forms versus old
routine; aestheticism versus social commitment and poetic allegory versus life-consuming realism. Treplev stands for a more
abstract art, not rooted in the problems of the moment, but
concerned with the eternal and the future; an art of symbols
and poetic diction; an art, not of reality, but of dreams. His

mother sees this as 'decadent', and it may indeed be related to the *fin de siècle* avant-garde. Nevertheless, in extreme form, it does contain the basic elements of Chekhov's own new forms for the theatre: the apparent lack of action (Nina comments 'But there's hardly any action in your play, there are only speeches'); the insistence on that which is natural having, at the same time, symbolic value;[23] an orientation towards the future; the world as a 'dream' (projecting sub-conscious elements in human motivation, such as the three sisters' 'dream' of Moscow).

At the same time, of course, Treplev's aesthetic ideas are rooted in the period. Rejecting the routine theatre, in which his mother sees herself as a priestess, he likens his flight from such vulgarity to that of Maupassant from the Eiffel Tower. The reference is to the opening chapter of the latter's autobiographical work *La Vie Errante*. For Maupassant, the Eiffel Tower, built as a symbol of *L'Exposition Universelle* of 1889 (which in itself was commemoratively symbolic of the Revolution, a hundred years before) seemed to stand for a new age of commercialism and applied science: it marked the death of art and literature, the triumph of 'l'aristocratie de la science ou plutôt de l'industrie scientifique'.[24] Indeed, Maupassant's reactions to the Eiffel Tower are curiously similar to those of Dostoyevsky to the Crystal Palace in 1862, but Maupassant's flight was essentially from Paris and its materialism ('mais on dirait que le cours de l'esprit humain s'endigue entre deux murailles, qu'on ne franchira plus: l'industrie et la vente')[25] to Florence and art. Throughout Europe (and Russia was certainly no exception) literary movements were turning from the real world towards aestheticism and a world of myth, poetry and symbol. Treplev's play is in keeping with the experiments of the avant-garde symbolists of the 1890s, and it is significant that his 'villain', the devil, is identified with materialism — 'the father of eternal matter'; on the other hand his 'heroine', the 'world soul' seems to owe something to the fashionable philosophy of Vladimir Solovyev.[26]

That a writer, so conscious of the real world and its problems as Maupassant, should feel the need to escape to 'art' is indicative of the times. It is this pull within himself, to which

Chekhov (who has more in common with Maupassant) gives expression in Treplev. Thus while Trigorin/Chekhov is complaining that his writing is valued merely for aesthetic reasons (his landscapes) when he himself is striving to found a reputation as a civic writer, the art of Treplev/Chekhov, by contrast, flees the real world for an aesthetic construct of symbols and eternal essences.

Dorn, who has Chekhov's other profession of doctor, is the only character to take Treplev's play seriously, and it is significant that he, too, sees artistic creation as a flight from the material world:

> DORN. But if it had ever been my lot to experience the exaltation an artist feels at the moment of creative achievement, I believe I should have come to despise this material body of mine and all that goes with it, and my soul would have taken wings and soared into the heights.

He also adds a word of caution: Treplev's writing must have a clear and defined idea. Unfortunately Konstantin does not listen; his thoughts are full of Nina. Dorn is still Treplev's champion in Act IV, but again he repeats his view of the need for direction in his work:

> DORN. Well, I believe in Konstantin Gavrilych. He's got something! He certainly has! He thinks in images, his stories are vivid, full of colour, and personally I'm deeply moved by them. But it's a pity he doesn't set himself any definite goal. He makes an impression, that's all, but an impression alone doesn't take you very far.

Dorn now seems more able to appreciate the new art of impressions and images, having just returned from the West; his experience of merging with the crowd on a Genoese street makes Treplev's 'world soul' seem a possibility. Nevertheless, his insistence on definite goals (literally 'specific tasks' — *opredelennyye zadachi*) is just as relevant for Trigorin, the would be civic writer, as it is for the avant-garde aestheticism of Treplev.

Chekhov himself was often accused of lacking such goals. What struck the audience of his day was the apparently formless naturalism of his plays: '"Everything is as it is in life" — for a long time, right up to the present day, this formula has been the commonplace of articles and books about Chekhov.'²⁷ Yet, despite the 'naturalness' of the play, it must be obvious that *The Seagull* has an equally striking symbolic content. The very title calls attention to a symbol which will dominate the action.

In Act I Nina tells Konstantin that she is drawn to the lake like a seagull and in Act II Konstantin lays a gull, which he has shot on this same lake, at her feet (the effect of an echo is strengthened in both cases by Treplev's need to be assured that they are alone). When Trigorin and Nina are alone towards the end of Act II, the dead seagull inspires the older writer with his 'plot for a fairly short story', and this moment is echoed and further developed in Act III, when, after receiving Nina's all-revealing medallion, Trigorin promises to remember her as she was on that day:

> TRIGORIN. a week ago, when you were wearing that light-coloured dress . . . we talked . . . there was a white seagull lying on the seat.
> NINA [*pensively*]. Yes, a seagull.

By Act IV Trigorin already seems to have forgotten, or to wish to forget. When Shamrayev twice calls his attention to the original seagull, which has been stuffed on Trigorin's orders, his reaction on both occasions is to claim that he does not remember (followed in each case by a second, more pensive: 'I don't remember'). This act also reveals that after Trigorin has abandoned her, Nina signs letters to Treplev as 'the seagull', and in their final scene together she constantly refers to herself on stage as 'the seagull'. We can see from all this that the seagull motif is developed in a patterned echo-like effect, but a double resonance lies at the heart of the symbol itself: it has validity both for Nina and for Treplev.

Both come from similar backgrounds. Nina has a wilful father and a stepmother, neither of whom we see, but there is a hint of a sexual rivalry between father and daughter similar to the relationship between Treplev and his mother. Nina is attracted to older men, only marginally to Dorn, but irrevocably to Trigorin (there is even an obverse reflection of such an attraction in Sorin who comments: 'She was a most charming girl, I said, Councillor Sorin was actually in love with her for a time').

In Act II Dorn, who shortly before has been singing to himself a popular love song: 'Tell her, my flowers' (*rasskazhite vy yey
tsvety moi*) is presented with freshly picked flowers by Nina;
almost at once they are destroyed by the jealous Polina. The
motif of love and jealousy expressed through flowers seems to
echo Treplev's guessing game in Act I, but flowers and the seagull theme become linked in a further echo, when, immediately
after presenting flowers to Dorn, Nina herself is presented with
Treplev's dead seagull, as though in answer to her own earlier
self-identification.

Nevertheless, Treplev's explanation of the gesture is explicit
— he has himself in mind: 'soon, I shall kill myself in the same
way'. When Nina accuses him of talking recently in symbols:
'and now this seagull here is apparently another symbol',
Treplev responds by linking her change of feelings to his own
artistic failure: 'my play wasn't liked. You despise my kind of
inspiration, and now you think I'm commonplace and insignifi-
cant just like all the rest . . .' The implications of Treplev's
symbolic gesture are acted out; between Acts II and III, he
does, indeed, turn a gun on himself, but as in art, and as in
love, he is unsuccessful even here. Significantly his symbol had
already been appropriated by his arch-rival and adapted to his
own ends; for towards the close of Act II Trigorin had reinter-
preted the seagull to Nina as a symbol of herself sacrificed to his
own art and to his own love. With appalling insensitivity he
even has the bird stuffed, perpetuating it as an exhibit in a way
which parallels his 'rat-like' behaviour as a writer. Yet if the
seagull is assimilated to the aesthetic procedures of Trigorin,
whose 'taxidermic' art lends his victims a showcase *life*, the
death of a symbolic bird derives, nonetheless, from Treplev's own
aesthetic system, and could well have figured among the list of
extinct creatures with which he opens his play.

There are other thematic symbols which derive from the 'play
within the play'. When the curtain opens for Act I the lake is
not visible; it is obscured by the curtain of Treplev's own stage,
and is only revealed when that curtain, too, is drawn. The lake
is Treplev's backdrop and central image of his play. Nina has

already confessed that she is drawn to the lake like a seagull and the lake seems closely bound with her ambitions to be an actress:

> NINA. My father and stepmother won't let me come here. They say this place is Bohemian . . . they're afraid of my going on the stage. And I am drawn to this place, to this lake, as if I were a seagull . . . [My heart is full of you.*][28]

Although these words are spoken to Treplev, it seems more likely that the 'you', which fills Nina's heart, is the artistic community itself. Thus Nina is immediately uneasy after uttering this apparent admission, and looks round. Treplev assures her that they are alone, and manages to steal a kiss, but the parallel is with Act II, when Nina again escapes from her parents, and embracing Arkadina says: 'I'm so happy! Now I belong to you.'

The reflecting mirror of the lake seems to stand for art itself. Treplev's playlet projects the lake into the future — a cold symbolist future devoid of all real life. His mother rejects such art. At the beginning of Act II she confesses that she has made it her rule never to look into the future. As an actress conscious of her age, she associates the lake with the past, a time some ten to fifteen years ago, when she was in her late twenties, and almost every night there was singing and music. There were also 'romances' in which Dorn was 'the male lead'. This ageing Lovelace still sings throughout the play, and Arkadina's choice of vocabulary: *romany* ('love affairs/novels') and *jeune premier* ('male lead') seems consciously to confuse the terms of art with those of love (but in her reminiscences of the lake there is also the ominous mention of shooting). Act I ends with Dorn asserting the bewitching quality of the lake: 'How distraught they all are! How distraught! And what a quantity of love about . . . It's the magic lake!'

In interrupting his play, Treplev drops the curtain on his rudimentary stage, and once more obscures the lake. It is Dorn who suggests that it should be raised, and this renewed view of the lake seems to stimulate discussion of the fragment of the play they have just seen. Trigorin compliments Nina on her acting and praises the background: TRIGORIN. 'and the scenery

was beautiful. [*Pause.*] There must be a lot of fish in this lake.'
With this latter remark the lake's significance appears to have
been shifted to a different plane, but the discussion has not, in
fact, abandoned the theme of art:

> TRIGORIN. I'm very fond of fishing. As far as I'm concerned, there's no
> greater pleasure than to sit on the bank of a river in the late afternoon
> and watch the float . . .
> NINA. I should have thought that for anyone who'd experienced the joy of
> doing creative work no other pleasure could exist.

Trigorin seems consciously to be deflating Treplev's elevated
symbol, but throughout the play fishing and art are closely
associated. Treplev had set the theme at the beginning of Act I
in his condemnation of the contemporary theatre, and of those
writers who 'fish out' (*vyudit'*) some petty, useful moral from
vulgar scenes and phrases.[29] It is this which makes Treplev
wish to flee — like Maupassant from the Eiffel Tower. The dif-
fering attitudes of Treplev and Trigorin to the lake reflect, in
their own way, Maupassant's apposition of poetic and prosaic
in his contrast of the nature of the poet to that of the novelist.

In Act II the lake becomes a 'hunting ground' for the two
writers: Treplev with his gun; Trigorin with his rod and line.
Arkadina confesses that her son is spending whole days on the
lake, and Masha comments that his soul is troubled. It is on the
lake that Treplev shoots the seagull; and, in presenting it to
Nina, he tells her that her coldness has made him feel as though
he has woken up to see that the lake has suddenly dried up or
has drained away into the ground. The image of Treplev con-
fronting Nina with gun and prey stands in visual contrast to
Trigorin who earlier had crossed the stage with fishing tackle
and pail, summoned from his activities by a distraught
Arkadina. Yet towards the end of the act Trigorin will return to
the lake to capture the heart of Nina, as predatory artist and as
potential lover.

Act III marks Treplev's all-round humiliation. He seems to
have failed as artist, lover, son — even as self-destroyer. The
lake is not mentioned; we merely learn that Trigorin, when
leaving, wants to take his fishing tackle, as he still has use for it:
his books, on the other hand, he is prepared to give away.

The lake figures prominently again in Act IV, but in a different mood and as a presence sensed off-stage. At the opening Masha announces that there are huge waves on it, and Medvenko appears to link this with Treplev's old stage, which he considers should be broken up; it stands like a skeleton with its curtain flapping. He even thinks that he heard someone crying in it (later, of course, we learn that Nina has returned and is wandering round the lake).

When Trigorin appears, the idea of fishing on the lake prompts him to think of Treplev's play, and the use he can make of it for his own writing. Nevertheless, shortly afterwards he claims that if he lived in such a house by the lake, he would overcome his passion for writing, and spend his time catching fish. But Trigorin, as we know, is compulsively driven to write, and this implied deflation of the artist's elevated calling is also meant for Treplev: it not only echoes Trigorin's earlier reaction to the younger writer's symbolic use of the lake in Act I, but can be seen as the continuation of opinions he has just voiced on Treplev's lack of talent. It is in this sense that Dorn picks him up:

TRIGORIN. Just to catch a perch, or a ruff — how delightful it is!
DORN. Well, I believe in Konstantin Gavrilych. He's got something! He certainly has!

The lake, like the symbol of the seagull, has a double resonance: for the emotional aspirations of the chief protagonists it is both 'art' and 'love'. Such ambiguity is hardly surprising, given a play in which art and love are so inextricably fused, yet it is as a metaphor for art that the lake assumes its chief symbolic role. For Nina it is a source to which she is drawn like a seagull; for Arkadina its real associations are in the past; her son seeks to project it into the future, and it is he who has consciously elevated the lake to the level of symbol. But, whereas the prosaic Trigorin fishes his prizes from the element itself, the poetic Treplev, in a gesture of self-destruction, can only kill the white bird which soars above it.

All Treplev's inspiration comes from 'above'. He introduces his play with an invocation to the shades which pass above the lake at night to send sleep and let his audience dream what it will be like in two hundred thousand years' time. His other symbol, the moon, is suspended above the lake, as a cold eternal body of sleep and sole illumination for an art which shuns living people and seeks inspiration in dream: TREPLEV. 'Living characters! We don't have to depict life as it is, or as it ought to be, but as we see it in our dreams.' The stage directions for Act I make it plain that the sun has just set, and we see that Treplev is at pains to time his play to catch the rising moon ('We'll raise the curtain at exactly half past eight, when the moon rises'). Nina in her haste to arrive on time is aware of the red sky and knows that the moon is beginning to rise: she drives her horse on. Treplev looks constantly at his watch, but the timing is right. When the little curtain is raised to reveal the lake, the stage directions tell us that the moon is above the horizon, and that it is reflected in the lake.

The stage directions for Act II aim at a complete contrast. Not only is it midday and hot, but the lake is visible from the start and it is not the moon but the sun which it now reflects. The new symbol, in Treplev's mind at least, is identified with Trigorin, as he reveals in bitter words to Nina when he sees Trigorin approach: TREPLEV. 'The sun hasn't come near you yet, but you're smiling already and your eyes are melting in its rays. I won't inconvenience you further.' [*Goes out quickly.*] Undoubtedly, it is the presence of such a 'sun' which makes him feel that the lake has 'dried up'.[30]

All the signs in Act II point to Trigorin's growing usurpation, of everything to which Treplev lays claim. In Trigorin's intimate conversation with Nina, he even asserts that the symbol of the moon is also his — it is a mark of his compulsion to write:

TRIGORIN. You know what it is to have a *fixed idea*, for instance when a man keeps on thinking about the same thing day and night, about . . . let us say, the moon. Well, I, too, have a kind of moon of my own. I'm obsessed day and night by one thought: I must write, I must write, I just must.

By the end of the act Trigorin's usurpation is confirmed. It is not Treplev's dreams, which Nina is destined to act out, but those of Trigorin. The curtain falls on one word, picked out for special emphasis:

> [*Trigorin goes into the house.*]
> NINA [*advances to the footlights; after some reflection*]. '[It's] a dream!' [*Curtain.*]

If in Act I Treplev had greeted Nina as his enchantress and his dream (*Volshebnitsa, mechta moya*) by Act III it is for Trigorin that she has become, not only a dream, but the source of dreams, as he confesses to Arkadina:

> TRIGORIN. Sometimes people go to sleep on their feet, and that's just the state I'm in as I talk to you — all the time I feel as if I were asleep and dreaming of her. I'm possessed by sweet and wonderful dreams. . . . Let me go.

He continues:

> Young love, enchanting, poetical — love that carries you off into a world of dreams — it's the only thing that can bring happiness on this earth!

By these words, and from what follows, Trigorin demonstrates that he is capable of a feat well beyond Treplev's powers: at one and the same time he can hold the affection of both Arkadina and Nina. This exchange, with Arkadina imploring her lover on her knees, begs comparison with the earlier scene of the quarrel which breaks out between mother and son as she bandages his head.

Two years have elapsed between Acts III and IV. Treplev now seems reconciled to his situation, and has actually gained some notice as a writer. Yet the stage directions of Act IV call for disturbing sounds: the noise of trees and the wind howling in the chimney. The lake reflects neither moon nor sun: it is tossed by storm. There is, moreover, the banging of the watchman (always an oppressive sound in Chekhov).[31] It does not seem to augur well that the watchman is heard immediately after Masha's comment on the more comfortable conditions which Treplev now has for his work, and the easier access the room affords to the garden. Indeed, not long afterwards we learn from Treplev himself that such guards have been placed by Nina's father and stepmother to keep her away from their house.

The presence of Trigorin increasingly unsettles him. Although the older writer arrives with a journal which has printed one of Treplev's stories, Trigorin has read his own contribution in it, but the pages of Treplev's story remain uncut. His own mother confesses that she has never had time to read any of his stories, but the admission is made as she is playing lotto.

Treplev is still at odds with the routine lives of his mother and her lover. He doesn't eat when they eat,[32] and the introspective isolation of his artistic nature is expressed in the wistful strains of the piano which he plays off stage, while on stage his mother, Trigorin and the others play their game of lotto. Needless to say, Trigorin wins; Arkadina comments: 'This man's a lucky fellow always and everywhere.'

It has been strongly argued that the game of lotto in Act IV parallels in function and basic features the abortive play produced by Treplev in Act I.[33] As the game is being laid out Trigorin reveals a possible intention of turning the fiasco of this play into a theme for his own art. In its turn, this suggestion echoes the offer of a fitting subject for Treplev himself made by his uncle in circumstances heavily tinged with irony. Dorn is singing one of his continual snatches of song: 'The moon floats through the night sky' (*Mesyats plyvet po nochnym nebesam*), and mention of the moon seems to trigger a memory:

> SORIN. You know, I'd like to give Kostya a subject for a novel. I'd call it: 'The Man Who Wished'. *'L'homme qui a voulu'*. Long ago in my young days I wanted to become a writer — and I didn't; I wanted to be a fine speaker — and I spoke abominably [*mimicking himself*] — 'and all that sort of thing, and all the rest of it, and so on, and so forth'. . . . When I tried to sum up my argument, I'd go plodding on and on until I broke into perspiration. . . . I wanted to get married — and I didn't, I always wanted to live in town — and here I am finishing my life in the country, and all that sort of thing.

'The Man Who Wished' is not so much a title for a novel as a title for Treplev's life.

When the others have finished their game of lotto they go to eat, leaving Treplev behind to work. He is already disillusioned with what he has written: 'I used to talk such a lot about new forms in art, and now I feel I'm slipping into a rut myself little by little.' It is not merely that he is prey to the values he so despises in others, he also realises that his arch-rival is master of the symbol, which Treplev regards as his own:

> TREPLEV. The description of the moonlit evening is too long and rather precious. Trigorin has worked out his own methods — it comes easily to him. . . . He would just mention the neck of a broken bottle glistening on the dam and the black shadow of a mill-wheel — and there you'd have a moonlit night. But I have to put in the tremulous light, the soft twinkling of the stars, and the distant sounds of a piano, dying away in the still, fragrant air. . . . It's excruciating!

Equally disturbing for Treplev are constant reminders throughout Act IV of Trigorin's appropriation of his other symbol: the seagull. Thus immediately after Arkadina's confession that she has not read her son's writing, he enters to hear Shamrayev informing Trigorin about his stuffed seagull. Shamrayev's phrasing even seems significant: 'Your thing, Boris Alekseyevich, has remained with us' (*A u nas, Boris Alekseyevich, ostalas' vasha veshch'*).[34] Treplev's reaction is to throw open a window, and to listen attentively, as he says: 'How dark it is! I can't understand why I'm feeling so restless.' It is as though 'Trigorin's seagull' has given him some premonition of Nina's presence outside, and shortly afterwards, just as Treplev is expressing his disillusionment with 'new forms', she appears at the window. In the scene which follows Nina repeatedly identifies herself with the seagull, yet confesses that, in spite of everything, she will always love Trigorin. Her presence reminds Treplev, not only of his own failure in love, but also of his failure in art — his art of new forms and dreams:

> TREPLEV [*sadly*]. You have found your right path, you know which way you're going — but I'm still floating about in a chaotic world of dreams and images, without knowing what use it all is. . . . I have no faith, and I don't know what my vocation is.

Nina's hasty departure leaves Treplev alone to his final moments on stage:

> TREPLEV [*after a pause*]. It won't be very nice if someone meets her in the garden and tells Mamma. It might upset Mamma. . . . [*He spends the next two minutes silently tearing up all his manuscripts and throwing them under the table, then unlocks the door at right and goes out.*][35]

It is significant that his very last words do not show concern for Nina, but concern for his mother. The tearing of petals in Act I (behind which lies Treplev's anxiety about his mother's attitude to himself and to his art) receives its final answering echo in this tearing of manuscripts, but it takes a full two minutes of stage time: he is not merely destroying his writing — he is tearing up his life.[36]

Close on Treplev's departure, the others return on stage. Shamrayev is showing Trigorin his stuffed seagull with the words: 'This is what you ordered' (*vash zakaz*) and Trigorin repeats: 'I don't remember! I don't remember!' when the shot rings out. Treplev has re-established the primacy of the seagull image for himself, in the only way he can: 'Soon I shall kill myself in the same way.'

* * * * * * * * *

The minor characters often appear to contribute to the play an element of the spontaneous, the random, the natural. Chekhov, however, judges his effects well, and closer examination reveals that the secondary characters, each in his own way, provide a commentary for main themes of the play.

Masha, despite her permanent black dress ('in mourning' for her life) has many attributes of a comic character: her snuff-taking; her vodka-drinking; her foot which goes to sleep in Act II. She is a visual reminder of the mixed elements from which Chekhov constructs his 'comedies', and it seems significant that she serves as an introductory figure for each act (though she is not always the first to speak).

Her comic remark about mourning at the beginning of Act I sets the tone of the whole play, and the effect is repeated in the opening exchanges of Act II, when she complains of dragging her life 'like a dress with an endless train'. Here, too, there is the theme of 'lost youth', which Trigorin will develop later in the act. The related theme of 'age and youth', and the sexual rivalry of the generations, is given visual expression, when in her opening words Arkadina, wearing a light coloured dress insists that Masha in her black dress should stand beside her to see who looks the younger. At the beginning of Act III Masha tells us of Treplev's suicide attempt, and by offering the details to Trigorin as a subject, relates the 'seagull' theme to that of the 'predatory artist'. In Act IV she sets the scene symbolically by her reference to the waves on the lake. In Act I Masha also has a closing role to play in the final scene with Dorn, where she reveals herself as a figure in parallel to Nina. She loves Treplev, but at the same time feels the attraction of a father figure in Dorn, to whom she confesses: 'I'm not really fond of my father . . . but I've a soft spot in my heart for you. For some reason, I feel a sort of deep affinity with you . . .' (In an earlier version it was actually disclosed that Dorn was her real father.) Masha's philosophy of bearing her cross provides yet another parallel with Nina (as we see her in Act IV).

Medvedenko,[37] who later becomes Masha's husband, is one of Chekhov's unflattering portraits of the provincial school-master and the Masha/Medvedenko relationship will later be refurbished in *The Three Sisters* as that of Masha/Kulygin. This schoolmaster is not a bearer of culture, he is both physically and spiritually the eternal 'pedestrian': 'Each day I walk six versts here and six versts back, and all I encounter is indifferentism.'*[38] Even in Act IV, when married to the daughter of a man with horses at his disposal, he still has to go on foot.

His use of the word 'indifferentism' characterises his pretensions to education; he is, in fact, a representative of regional philistinism and narrow materialism, concerned not with his work, but with his salary. We see him at the opening of the play unable to understand Masha's unhappiness in any terms other than financial, and Masha sharply reminds him: 'It's not a matter of money, even a pauper can be happy.'*[39] Such materialism, such concern for money, links him with Arkadina, who towards the end of the act sees the misfortune of Nina's family circumstances merely in the fact that her mother's money has been made over to her stepmother.

Medvedenko's materialism is also 'ideological'. He raises philosophical objections to Treplev's play: 'There's no ground for making a distinction between spirit and matter, because

spirit might consist of a combination of material atoms.' Such
ideas derive from the seminarist-educated young men of the
1860s (Chernyshevsky, Dobrolyubov et al.) but in the backward
provinces they obviously still subsist in the figure of
Medvedenko, and what he then goes on to say emphasises, not
only his obsession with himself and his own material conditions,
but reveals a view of literature which would reduce it to the
'denunciatory' social theme fashionable in the 1860s:

> MEDVEDENKO . . . [*With animation to* TRIGORIN.] But you know, someone
> ought to write a play describing how our sort of people live — I mean we
> teachers — and get it produced somewhere. It's a hard life, a very hard
> life!

These remarks have some significance for Trigorin himself. We
later learn of his own desire to be thought of as a writer with a
social theme.

Masha's father, Shamrayev, serves principally as a figure
commenting on Arkadina, but in him he has met her match.
Just as she has no money for her son, so he has no horses for
her, (or even for his own son-in-law). He tells Arkadina: 'My
dear lady! Forgive me, I have the greatest admiration for your
talent, I'm prepared to give ten years of my life for you — but I
can't let you have the horses.' Like Arkadina he is a capricious
despot with a certain 'style', who has a sensitive, but difficult
child (Masha) and a partner (Polina) who conducts an *affaire*
with another — to this extent the Shamrayev household
provides a comic reflection of the relationships of the main protagonists themselves.

Shamrayev's professed veneration of Arkadina's talent always
succeeds in devaluing it. He constantly asks her, not about herself, but about other actors — actors, moreover of the past,
whom he appears to think she must know. This hardly flatters
Arkadina's vanity about her age, and she retorts: 'You're
always inquiring about some old fossil or other. How should I
know?' The actors he praises are also provincial ones, thus his
first words in the play are: 'In 1873, in Poltava, at the fair, her
acting was stunning.'*40 The grand airs of Arkadina herself
should be seen in this perspective: when, for instance, in Act IV

she proclaims her delight with her reception in Kharkov. The trials of a provincial actress are brought out in Nina's words at the end of Act IV (the life has also been described much more starkly in Saltykov-Shchedrin's novel *The Golovlev Family*). There is, perhaps, not as much hope in Nina's career, as some critics wish to see.[41]

Shamrayev combines flattery with a complete lack of tact. Thus his gracious reception of Arkadina in Act IV obviously pleases her, yet it is he, who later in the act will remind Trigorin of the stuffed seagull. In Act I he tactlessly gives expression to the idea which seems to lie behind his praise of older actors:

> SHAMRAYEV. The theatre is in a decline, Irina Nikolayevna. We used to have massive oak trees, now we see nothing but stumps.
> DORN. It's true enough, there aren't so many outstandingly gifted people nowadays — on the other hand, the average actor is much more competent.
> SHAMRAYEV. I can't agree at all with you there. However, it's a matter of taste. *De gustibus aut bene, aut nihil.*

Shamrayev's misquoted tag is, in fact, apt. He wishes to say 'There's no disputing over tastes' (*De gustibus non est disputandum*) but at the same time he manages to imply: 'Speak only good of the dead or say nothing' (*De mortuis aut bene aut nihil*) — a true expression of his own attitude to actors of the past.

Shamrayev's theatrical tittle-tattle relates to the theme of art in a comic way, but at the same time it provides more serious indirect commentary. In Act I Nina tries to elicit Trigorin's reaction to Treplev's play. She is obviously in awe of the famous writer and Arkadina jokingly tells her not to flatter him, as praise causes him confusion. It is then that Shamrayev chooses to tell his story about the Opera Theatre in Moscow, and how the famous bass Silva was praised for a low note by a rural church chorister in a voice a whole octave lower. The story implies that an unknown provincial is capable of outshining the acclaimed professional. The relevance of this to the artistic rivalry of Treplev and Trigorin is further underscored by Chekhov's treatment of the story almost as another 'play within the play'. Not only does Shamrayev act out the chorister's words but his own final comment: 'the theatre just froze'[42] produces an awkward pause on the stage itself. It is only broken by Dorn's pointed remark: 'The angel of silence has flown over us!'

Nevertheless Shamrayev is obviously pleased with his story. Shortly afterwards, he recalls it again, and in circumstances which seem strangely to anticipate the theme of 'writer-rats' Shamrayev has just refused to untie the dog which keeps Arkadina awake at night: it is, he suggests, a deterrent to thieves who might steal millet from his barn.

As Arkadina and Trigorin are preparing to leave in Act III Shamrayev tells them another theatrical tale about an actor who fluffed his lines and said something approaching: 'We're taught in a cap' (*My popali v zapandyu*) instead of: 'We're caught in a trap' (*My popali v zapadnyu*). The combined elements of muddle and trap have direct relevance for the events which flow from the circumstances of Trigorin's departure, and at the same time Shamrayev's unfaithful wife, Polina, offers them 'sweet' fruit (plums).

When in Act III Trigorin and Arkadina return as though nothing had happened, Chekhov provides another ironic commentary on the parallel situation of these two couples through the 'inappropriate' laughter of Shamrayev: Dorn, Polina's lover, mocks Sorin's improbable infatuation with Nina, but the laughter which follows, not only comes from the man whom he himself has deceived — it heralds the arrival of Trigorin and Arkadina:

> SORIN. She was a most charming girl, I said. Councillor Sorin was actually in love with her for a time.
> DORN. The old philanderer!
>   [*Off-stage* SHAMRAYEV *can be heard laughing.*]
> POLINA. I think they've arrived from the station.

Dorn, himself, is a man of reason and common sense, a role which Chekhov ascribes to many (but not all) of his doctors. He is a mediator and a counsellor, and it seems significant that Dorn is absent throughout Act III, when the other characters fall into 'the trap'. In his relationship with Polina he is far from showing himself the man of passion. Nevertheless all the women in the play seem drawn towards him. Musical motifs are constantly associated with Dorn. Thus singing from across the lake (not called for in Chekhov's stage directions, but apparently heard by Arkadina and Polina) evokes for Arkadina memories of the lake as it was ten or fifteen years ago, when Dorn was the 'male lead' in all the romances.

Dorn's own snatches of song are used to ironic effect. On his first appearance in Act I Polina scolds him for not taking care of himself and he replies by singing: 'say not your youth was ruined'. Then as a retort to Polina's jealousy over Nina and her accusation: 'You're so anxious to prostrate yourselves before an actress. Every single one of you', he sings: 'Again I stand before you' adding the explanation: 'It's in the nature of things for people to admire artists and treat them differently from . . . well, let us say, tradesmen. It's a sort of idealism.'

Thus Dorn, too, is given words in Act I which seem to look forward to the Maupassant quotation of Act II. In this case, however, he is talking of the performing artist. The connotations surrounding Dorn's first use of this scrap of song should, perhaps, be borne in mind; for when he next sings it (in a slightly fuller version: 'Again I stand before you, enchanted') he has just found Treplev's body, but wishes to reassure the assembled company that all is right.[43]

A 'musical' commentary is also provided by Sorin, who, as he goes off to summon the audience for his nephew's play, sings a snatch of Schumann and adds:

> I remember I once burst into song like this and the Assistant Public Prosecutor said to me: 'I say, your Excellency, that's a powerful voice you've got.' Then he thought a bit and added: 'And an offensive one too.' [*Laughs and goes out.*]

A similar formula of vitiated approval is contained in that other musical assessment: Shamrayev's story about Silva. Indeed Sorin's parting anecdote might be read as a premonition of the audience's reaction to his nephew's play, much as Shamrayev's story obliquely refers back to it. For, if Shamrayev's remarks throughout the play form an indirect commentary on Arkadina and Trigorin, the words of Sorin provide a similar commentary on the inadequacies of Treplev. In their first conversation in Act I Sorin tells his nephew that the tragedy of his own life is that women did not love him, and he develops the theme slightly later:

> years ago there were just two things I wanted passionately. One was to get married and the other was to be a novelist. I haven't managed to pull it off either way. Yes, even to be a minor writer must be rather nice, when all is said and done.[44]

Although Sorin takes Treplev's part against his mother, and defends his play even before he has heard it, he nevertheless falls asleep at significant moments. In Act II his snoring interrupts discussion of the play by the rivals, Masha and Nina, and in Act IV Arkadina notices that her brother has again fallen asleep after Trigorin has just dismissed her son's literary talent.

In Act III Sorin tries to argue his nephew's case with Arkadina, pointing out that he needs money for clothes and even for a trip abroad. He is obviously agitated and tries to conceal the fact by whistling, but Arkadina refuses to give money. Sorin has an attack on stage.[45] The association between uncle and nephew is even stronger in Act IV, but it seems ominous that Sorin, who constantly talks of his own failure and imminent death, should now have moved his bed into the room where Treplev works at his writing. Ominous too is the theme which Sorin wishes to bequeath him: 'L'homme qui a voulu'.

Sorin's constant regret that he lives in the country and his desire to move into the town seems, in embryo, to look forward to a dominant motif in *The Three Sisters*, [46] and in the ebullient Arkadina and the feckless Sorin we have a brother and sister relationship, which in certain essential features anticipates that of Lyubov Andreyevna and Gayev in *The Cherry Orchard*. In *The Seagull* the Chekhovian play has not yet found its fullest expression. The sub-plotting is not as spare as in the later plays, the symbolism is a little heavy and the dramatic ending on a suicide seems to look backwards rather than forwards. Nevertheless all the essential elements are there: the creation of mood and special effect through literary reference, through music, sounds, and pauses; and the use of subtle juxtapositions, and skilful deployment of secondary characters, to suggest an indirect commentary on the main themes of the play.

2

UNCLE VANYA

THE MOSCOW ARTS THEATRE staged *Uncle Vanya* in October 1899. When the play was written is not entirely clear, but it is an obvious reworking of *The Wood Demon* (*Leshiy*), written ten years earlier, and first produced at Abramova's theatre in Moscow in December 1889.[1] *The Wood Demon* was not a success, and Chekhov would later write: 'I am unable to read *The Wood Demon*. I hate that play and try to forget about it.' The earlier play, it is true, lacks real coherence: there are too many characters, and the suicide of Uncle Georges (the Uncle Vanya of the later play) provides a tragic climax in Act III, which gives the more light-hearted final act the sense of a postscript (an impression Act IV of *The Seagull* might also give, if it did not end with suicide). The central character on the evidence of the title, *The Wood Demon*, must be Dr Khrushchev, who in his passion for nature conservancy is the direct forerunner of Dr Astrov. One of the play's weaknesses was seen to lie in the fact that Khrushchev was not so much the main protagonist as a secondary character in the action. Chekhov seems to have realised this himself; for in reworking the play he gave the title role to Voynitsky (Uncle Vanya), who is now no longer cast in the Ivanov and Treplev mould of a weak character who ends in suicide. Instead he attempts to shoot his tormentor, and at the end of the play has found a new stoicism.

It was inevitable that the weaknesses of *The Wood Demon* should be ascribed by at least one reviewer to the attempt of a well-known author of short stories to 'tell a tale from the stage'. Chekhov's devices for portraying life more naturalistically were also a source of perplexity; the same critic saw all the action confined by eating: 'Feasting takes place and during it conversations are conducted.'[2] The reference is obviously to the opening act of *The Wood Demon* where the action centres round a lunch table, but the hospitality of Zheltukhin's table has not the same dramatic relevance for the main themes of the play, as the tea-drinking which replaces it in Act I of *Uncle Vanya*, and it is significant that, in tightening the whole structure of his play and endowing it with a new life as *Uncle Vanya*, Chekhov gives added point to his naturalistic devices by making them also bear structural and symbolic weight.

There is very little real action in Act I of *Uncle Vanya*, but the repetitive event is the drinking of tea. In the opening stage directions a table set for tea figures prominently; the other props mentioned are benches, chairs, a guitar and a swing. All these have a role to play as the act unfolds, but the focal point is the tea-table and its chief prop is the samovar, presided over by the old nurse Marina, who opens the action of the play by pouring a glass of tea. The first words are hers too: 'Here, drink it, dearie' (*Kushay, batyushka*). In reality the verb *kushat'* does not mean to drink, but to eat and it is in this sense that Marina will use it shortly afterwards, in a third offer of hospitality to the doctor: 'wouldn't you like something to eat?' (*Mozhet ty kushat' khochesh'?*) Food, as we shall see, has an associated, but secondary, symbolic function in Act I.

When the chief character, Uncle Vanya, comes in (having had a nap after lunch) his first speech is concerned with the great changes which have taken place in the household. The old life was one of work; the new life is one of sleeping, eating and of course, drinking:

> VOYNITSKY. . . [*Yawns.*] Since the professor and his consort came to live here, our usual routine has been completely upset. . . . Now I sleep at the wrong time, I eat the wrong kinds of food at dinner and lunch, I drink wine . . . it's all bad for my health! In the past I never had a free moment — Sonya and I used to work like Trojans. . . . But now only Sonya works while I just sleep, eat, and drink. . . . It's a bad business!

At this Marina shakes her head in disapproval: 'such goings on!' (i.e. *poryadki*: 'what sort of order!') Marina is the only character in the play whose prototype is not to be found in *The Wood Demon*, and given that Chekhov's rewriting involved the shedding of characters, the addition of Marina is clearly germane to the new direction the play has now taken. She represents the traditional values of the Voynitsky/Serebryakov household. The opening directions describe her as 'slow-moving' (i.e. 'not mobile' — *malopodvizhnaya*). The sense is physical, but it also has psychological implications — Marina is against change. Voynitsky has identified the old order as work and the new order as one of sleeping, eating and drinking. Marina is always working; she is constantly knitting socks on stage, and, after shaking her head at Voynitsky's contrast of the old with the new, she goes on to criticise the new ways which have come about since the advent of the professor and his young wife. Significantly her criticism is framed in terms of the central 'action' of Act I — the serving of tea:

> MARINA [*nods her head disapprovingly*]. Such goings-on! The professor gets up at midday, but the samovar is kept boiling the whole morning waiting for him. Before they came we always had dinner soon after twelve, like everybody else, but now they are here we have it after six in the evening. The professor spends the night reading and writing, and then suddenly, past one o'clock, the bell rings. . . . My goodness, what is it? He wants some tea! So you've got to wake people up to heat the samovar. . . . Such goings-on!

These general criticisms have pointed relevance for the particular situation of 'tea-drinking' in Act I; for Marina tells us that the samovar has already been on the table for two hours, but that the professor and his wife have decided to go for a walk with Sonya and Telegin. In this way the trivial domestic occupation of tea-drinking throws into relief a much larger domestic situation.

At the same time the taking of tea has a structural function in Act I. Through it we are introduced, one by one, to all the characters of the play, and the way in which each receives and drinks his tea affords an insight into that character's personality and attitudes. It is a Chekhovian 'tea-ceremony' in which patterned ritual effects the social introductions.

Astrov is the first to be offered tea, and his refusal, might seem in retrospect to be the unwillingness of a positive man of work to associate himself with the new unsettling ways. However, Marina goes on to suggest that he might prefer vodka instead of tea and, although he retorts that he doesn't drink vodka every day, it is clear that he is being driven to find such consolation, because of the conditions of his work:

> ASTROV. Yes. . . . In ten years I've become a different man. And what's the cause of it? I've been working too hard, Nanny. I'm on my feet from morning till night — I never have any peace. At night as I lie under the blankets I feel afraid all the time that I may be dragged out to see a patient.[3]

Later in the act when he is 'dragged off' by a workman to see a patient in the local factory, his first request is for a glass of vodka. Astrov is disillusioned with his life, he feels that he is growing old to no avail, and he has on his conscience the recent case of a patient who died under chloroform. The reasons behind his apparent preference for vodka prepare us for his drinking in Act II.

Work is the reason for Astrov's presence on the estate in Act I; he has been summoned by Yelena to attend to her husband's rheumatism. Yet when he returns from his walk, Serebryakov pays as little attention to the doctor as he does to the tea which has been waiting two hours for him. He refuses to drink tea in the garden and asks for it to be sent to him in his study. Thus his demanding and capricious nature, his aloofness, his isolation and his need to hide behind 'work' as an excuse are all brought out through Serebryakov's attitude to tea.

Telegin is the next to be offered tea. He approaches the table with a speech about the bliss of being alive, which reads like the parody of a well-known poem by Pushkin, written in a completely different key (it is about the presentiment of death).[4] The inappropriate optimism and sentimentality of Telegin's character is heavily underscored in the act of taking tea itself, when he says: 'we all live here in peace and harmony — what more do we need? [*Taking the glass she hands him.*] Thank you kindly.' (Literally 'Sentimentally grateful — *chuvstvitel'no vam blagodaren.*)

Voynitsky's mother, Mariya Vasilyevna, comes in with a book. The stage directions read: *She sits down and reads; tea is put before her; she drinks it without looking up.* Her whole character is

summed up in such oblivious consumption. Throughout the rest
of the play we see her engrossed in her pamphlets on female
emancipation, unaware of everything around her. She is the
professor's uncritical admirer, and the expression of any opinion
culled from her voracious reading is bound to annoy her son.
When she makes an unexpected exclamation (because she has
forgotten to tell the professor about a pamphlet in which the
author refutes his former convictions), Uncle Vanya retorts that
that there is nothing terrible in this and that she should continue to drink her tea — it is clear that he, too, has had a
similar change of heart.

When Sonya enters she takes charge of the samovar, telling
Marina to attend to the peasants who have come on estate
business, saying that she herself will pour the tea (*a chay ya
sama*). The exchange of roles is not gratuitous: it highlights
Sonya's divided loyalties between the new erratic obligations of
hospitality and the duties of work and the estate. These can
now be relegated to Marina (a point further emphasised by
Marina's concern for the chickens on her return); for in spite of
Uncle Vanya's earlier view, that since the arrival of the professor and his wife it is only Sonya who continues to work, the
fact is that she, too, is letting things slide, as she herself will
later confess.[5] Her function in the 'tea-ceremony' graphically
conveys this change: she has relinquished her role as regulator
of the estate affairs, for that of dispenser of inopportune
hospitality.

Nevertheless the fact that the presence of her father and his
wife has turned the old values upside down appears to afford
Sonya the opportunity of offering something more substantial
than tea to the man she secretly loves:

> SONYA. Marvellous. It's so rare that you spend the night here. I bet you
> haven't had any lunch.
> ASTROV. No, I've not had lunch.
> SONYA. Well, how fortunate that you will be able to have lunch. We lunch
> now after six o'clock. [*She drinks.*] Cold tea!*[6]

This sudden, deflating discovery acts as an indirect commentary on Sonya's hopes. It is ironic that the same inconsiderate
behaviour of her father, which makes her offer of lunch possible,

is also responsible for Sonya's 'cold tea'. She can expect no benefits from the new disorder: Astrov is called away to the factory before the end of the act.

The tea of Yelena (Hélène) is also cold, and her readiness to drink it indicates indifference and a certain coldness within herself. In contrast to the knitting of socks, the studying of pamphlets, and the act of pouring tea itself, the associations for Yelena's tea-drinking seem those of futile pleasure: she drinks her cold tea sitting on a swing, yet the swing is the visual symbol of her own emotional attitudes. There are three men in the play who claim some amorous relationship with her: her elderly husband; her middle-aged admirer, Uncle Vanya; and Dr Astrov. For each of these, to different degrees, she appears to entertain a wavering affection.

In reality Yelena is indifferent to people. She reveals this in a soliloquy in Act III, where those who surround her (and Sonya) are seen, in terms of the play's recurrent motif — they are mere 'consumers':

> YELENA. I understand the poor girl so well. In the middle of all this desperate boredom, with just grey shadows wandering around instead of human beings, with nothing but commonplace tittle-tattle to listen to from people who do nothing but eat, drink, and sleep, he appears from time to time — so different from the rest of them.

Although her words indicate a view that Astrov stands out from among the others, even he is capable only briefly of warming her cold indifference.

The cold tea which appears to chill Sonya's own hopes in respect of Astrov in Act I is given added bathetic emphasis by Telegin before it is then taken up by Yelena:

> TELEGIN. There's been a big fall in the temperature of the samovar.
> YELENA. Never mind, Ivan Ivanovich, we will drink it cold.

But in seeking to associate Telegin with her readiness to drink 'cold tea' Yelena further betrays her basic indifference to those around her. Telegin does not in fact bear that most banal of Russian names, Ivan Ivanovich, he is Ilya Ilyich. He reminds Yelena that he is nicknamed after an item of food — 'waffles', and feels that she should know him, if only as a consumer: 'if you would be pleased to note, I lunch with you every day'. Sonya, too, rushes to his defence, describing Telegin as: 'Ilya Ilyich, our helper and right hand [man].' She offers him a second glass of tea (presumably still cold): an ironic token of acceptance of this 'helper' whose name and patronymic is synonymous with laziness itself,[7] a 'right hand' whose only activity in the play is the strumming of a guitar. Thus throughout Act I the 'tea-ceremony' provides an antithetical commentary on the theme of real work, whilst at the same time behind its banal ritual of hospitable communion lurk passions and frustrations, which shatter Telegin's naive view of what should be: 'We all live here in peace and harmony — what more do we need?'

One of the most potent forces for dissension flows from the cold inaccessible beauty of Yelena. The negative power of beauty is a Dostoyevskian theme, but Chekhov has also made it his own, particularly in the story The Beauties (Krasavitsy). In Uncle Vanya he presents feminine beauty as a destructive force and almost as a mythological theme. Thus in Yelena there are overtones of that other Helen, whose beauty 'launch'd a thousand ships, And burned the topless towers of Ilium'.[8] Voynitsky's name is derived from voyna — 'war', and Telegin seeks a distant sense of kinship through a 'spartan' — Lakedemonov — the brother of his brother's wife. The Homeric reference in The Wood Demon was even more explicit. In Act IV Dyadin, the prototype of Telegin, tells Serebryakov: 'It is I who have abducted your wife, as a certain Paris at one time abducted the beautiful Helen!'[9]

The Wood Demon also has strongly developed elements of native mythology: the wood demon (leshiy); the water spirit (rusalka); and even a reference to the house spirit (domovoy). There are traces of such mythology in the theme of destructive beauty as it is portrayed in the later play. The water spirits were maidens who seductively lured men to their deaths, and Voynitsky tells Yelena that such blood flows in her veins too. Nevertheless, the name Yelena suggests the root len' — 'laziness', and Chekhov seems to be playing with the idea, when he makes Voynitsky see the beauty of Yelena's movements as stemming from her laziness: 'she walks about staggering with sheer laziness' (*khodit i ot leni shatayetsya* i.e. 'she walks about and sways from laziness'). Once more the image of the swing seems relevant to the presentation of Yelena.

The tea, which the thoughtless behaviour of the professor has allowed to go cold, is closely connected with the central theme of the play — waste.[10] The point is underscored linguistically in the outcome of Sonya's substitution of her role as mistress of the estate for that of dispenser of cold tea; for when Marina returns and is asked what the peasants want, she replies: 'The same as before — they are still going on about the waste land.' Her reference to *pustosh'* (waste land) anticipates both linguistically and thematically the important speech by Astrov which follows shortly afterwards (*opustoshayutsya zhilishcha zverey i ptits*):

ASTROV. . . . the homes of animals and birds are being laid waste, the rivers are getting shallow and drying up, wonderful scenery is disappearing for ever — and all this is happening just because people are too lazy and stupid to stoop down and pick up the fuel from the ground.

Astrov identifies the cause of 'waste' as man's laziness, and significantly he addresses the continuation of his speech to Yelena (the beauty whom Voynitsky will shortly accuse of being too lazy to live — *kakaya vam len' zhit'! Akh, kakaya len'*).

ASTROV [*to Yelena*]. Isn't it so, Madam? Anyone who can burn up all that beauty in a stove, who can destroy something that we cannot create, must be a barbarian incapable of reason. Man is endowed with reason and creative power so that he can increase what has been given him, but up to the present he's been destroying and not creating.

In laying waste the forests man is also destroying life. Animals and birds are used symbolically to emphasise this theme. In Act III Astrov will call Yelena an animal of prey, a beautiful, fluffy weasel (literally 'polecat') and, in this context, refer to himself as 'a wise old sparrow'. Birds, in particular, form a constant motif illustrating the theme of waste. Thus when Marina returns from attending to the peasants and the 'waste land', she enters with a cry used for calling birds. The speckled hen has gone off with her chicks, and Marina is frightened that they might fall prey to the crows. Such concern not only reinforces the change of role from dispenser of hospitality to guardian of the interests of the estate, but the motif of crows related to the theme of waste seems linguistically to echo Voynitsky's view of his own life, wasted in the service of the professor: 'I lie awake, night after night, in sheer vexation and anger — that I let time slip by so stupidly' (*tak glupo provoronil vremya: vorona* = 'crow').

The call: 'chook, chook, chook' in itself may be seen as an oblique commentary on Voynitsky.[11] In the conversation which precedes it, he has just called the professor a 'writing *perpetuum mobile*', much to the annoyance of the 'old jackdaw' his own mother.[12] An argument is about to break out, but Yelena, in embarrassment starts talking about the weather:

> YELENA. What a lovely day! . . . Not too hot either.
>   [*A pause.**]
> VOYNITSKY. It would even be pleasant to hang oneself on a day like this.
> [TELEGIN *tunes the guitar.* MARINA *walks to and fro near the house, calling the chickens.*]
> MARINA. Chook, chook, chook![13]

An onomatopoeic verb for a bird call (*pogogochut* = 'they will cackle') is used again by Marina in Act III. It appears to be a comment on the foolishly violent behaviour of Voynitsky in attempting to shoot the professor:

> MARINA. Never mind, child. The ganders will cackle a bit — and then they'll leave off. . . . They'll cackle and leave off.

On yet a third occasion Voynitsky's drive towards destruction elicits the 'cackle' itself (*go-go-go*). At the beginning of Act IV he has stolen a bottle from Astrov's bag and intends to poison himself. He wants no one watching over him and tells both Marina and Telegin to leave. Marina's bird-call commentary is now quite explicit: 'Gander: go-go-go!'[14] Throughout the play Marina's attitude to Uncle Vanya is obliquely critical, and in this Voynitsky is an exception; for Marina readily offers her sympathy to Sonya, Telegin, Astrov and even Serebryakov, yet in Act I there is the barest minimum of exchange between Marina and Voynitsky, and he, of all the assembled characters, is the only one not to be offered tea.

Act II further illustrates the theme of the 'new ways' — the *poryadki* of which Marina had complained in Act I. The professor and those around him are turning night into day. Again, the point is made by Marina through 'tea'. When Sonya advises her to go to bed, she retorts: 'the samovar hasn't been cleared away. I can't very well go to bed!' The setting for such wayward 'consumers' is the dining room, but there is a whole new shift of atmosphere: we have left the garden for the more claustrophobic atmosphere of indoors, and there is a thunderstorm brewing. The window bangs and has to be closed by Yelena, and another intermittent sound comes from outside: a peasant watchman announces his presence by banging on metal — a sound, which, as we see from *The Seagull* and from many of the stories, is frequently used by Chekhov to heighten a sense of claustrophobia.

Serebryakov seems oblivious to the storm. At first, he forbids Yelena to close the window; he is more concerned with his gout. On the other hand, the storm for Voynitsky seems full of symbolic importance: it will bring fresh life to nature, but he alone will not be freshened by it; yet, if he were married to Yelena, he could comfort her in the night and quell her fears about it. The thunder and the rain have woken the hard-working Astrov from his much needed sleep, and he turns to drinking. Yet the storm passes and when towards the end of the act Yelena, announcing its departure, comments on the quality of the air and opens the window which the storm had forced her to close, it seems a portent for the 'clearing of the air' that is about to take place between her and Sonya.

The mood of Act II had been set by the closing words of Act I, which were spoken by Yelena: 'This is torture' (*eto muchitel'no*). This device — the end of one act anticipating the mood or themes of the next — is a noticeable feature of *Uncle Vanya*. It is one of the means used by Chekhov to give greater structural coherence to his reworking of *The Wood Demon*'s looser form.

The scarcely veiled torment which lies behind the tea-drinking of Act I is further developed within the claustrophobic dining room of Act II. Its chief source is Serebryakov, whose

capricious and wayward behaviour is evident from the very
opening of the act. He does not want to go to bed in spite of
tiredness and gout, and on learning that it is twenty past
twelve, he demands that his wife should find him the works of
Batyushkov in the morning (a poet with the unjustified reputation of an elegant sybarite).[15] It is Serebryakov who sets the
theme of claustrophobia by complaining of the stuffiness of the
room and of his inability to breathe. His illness, which does not
seem entirely genuine, is the pretext for petty tyranny. He sees
his plight in 'literary' terms ('They say Turgenev got *angina
pectoris* from gout'), and complains about everybody, while
demanding sympathy for himself.[16] Even when he is taken off to
bed by Marina, his presence can still be felt inhibiting the
behaviour of the others. Indeed throughout the whole play
Serebryakov who is a character more frequently off-stage than
on it, contrives to be a constantly felt presence.

Astrov has been summoned to see him as his doctor, but
here, as in the first act, Serebryakov will not allow him near
him. The professor represents a wayward and largely dis-
credited 'authority' and in refusing the ministrations of Astrov
it is as though he is refusing to acknowledge the authority of
another; refusing to admit that there is anyone who has power
over him.

The portrayal of Serebryakov as a bogus, stifling authority,
enfeebled, wayward and narrow-minded carries more than a
hint at the political situation of the 1880s and early 1890s.
Stanislavsky, commenting on Chekhov's reaction to an account
of a provincial production of *Uncle Vanya* saw the 'chief idea' of
the play as:

> The naturally gifted Astrov and the poetically tender uncle Vanya go to
> seed in a provincial backwater, whilst the blockhead of a professor bliss-
> fully thrives in St Petersburg, and along with others like him governs
> Russia.*[17]

During the reign of Tsar Alexander III, the arch-reactionary K.
P. Pobedonostsev, who had been a professor of law, ruled as
virtual prime minister in his capacity as Procurator of the Holy
Synod. Serebryakov, too, has an ecclesiastical background: 'The
son of a common sexton, trained as a priest [i.e. a seminarist] he

somehow managed to get university qualifications and a profes-
sorship; later he became "your Excellency" and the son-in-law of
a senator, and so on, and so forth.' Nevertheless, Serebryakov's
church origins and education lend an equivocal political significance to this background: they were typical of the radical intelligentsia of the 1860s. Such figures as N. A. Dobrolyubov, N. G.
Chernyshevsky and N. G. Pomyalovsky came from a similar
background, and the word seminarist was often synonymous
with the term 'nihilist'. This view of Serebryakov is further
strengthened by the fact that Mariya Vasilyevna, his staunch
admirer in the play, is obsessed by the problems of women's
rights. Indeed V. Ya. Lakshin sees the prototype for
Serebryakov in the progressive teacher and populist S. N.
Yuzhakov.[18] On the other hand Serebryakov's interest in art is
not in keeping with the anti-aestheticism of the 'men of the
sixties'.

Another source for the character of Serebryakov has been
seen in M. O. Menshikov, who visited Melikhovo in August
1896 and inspired the following entry in Chekhov's notebook:
'M. in dry weather walks about in galoshes, carries an
umbrella, in order not to perish from sunstroke, he is frightened
of washing in cold water, and complains of his heart missing a
beat.'*[19] This description may be compared with the words of
Voynitsky in Act I: 'It is hot and stuffy, but our great scholar is
wearing an overcoat, galoshes, has an umbrella and gloves.'
Such details are strongly reminiscent of a story of 1898, *The Man
in A Case* (*Chelovek v futlyare*) in which the central character
Belikov is given similar characteristics as the mark of a con-
servative and repressive pedagogue, with obvious implications
for the society of his day. The role of Serebryakov in the play is
certainly that of a stifling dead authority, but it was obviously
advisable to present him with a certain degree of political
ambiguity. Indeed the Theatrical Literary Committee, it was
rumoured, had rejected Chekhov's play because of the figure of
Serebryakov.[20]

The identification of the interests of Serebryakov and those of
the state is made at a comic level through Telegin's reaction to
the cynical remarks of Voynitsky on Yelena's faithfulness:

TELEGIN [*tearfully*]. Vanya, I don't like it when you say these things. Come, really! . . Anyone who can betray a wife or a husband is an unreliable person who might betray his own country, too!

The political overtones of a stagnating present come out more strongly when taken in conjunction with Astrov's hopes for future generations.[21] Serebryakov's fruitless aesthetic labours are the complement of his wife's idle beauty; both are contrasted to the values of useful work. In reply to Sonya's query about his attitude to her stepmother, Astrov quotes from Pushkin alluding to the beautiful but destructive stepmother of the Snow White tale: 'She is beautiful, there's no denying that' (*ona prekrasna, spora net*).[22] He goes on to contrast Yelena's life as a mere 'consumer' with the 'purity' of useful work:

> but . . . she does nothing but eat, sleep, go for walks, charm us all by her beauty . . . nothing else. She has no responsibilities, other people work for her. . . . Isn't that so? And an idle life can't be virtuous.

Both she and her husband are directly implicated in the disease of 'laying waste' (*opustosheniye*), as Astrov tells Yelena in Act IV:

> You two infected all of us with your indolence. I was attracted by you and I've done nothing for a whole month, and in the meantime people have been ill and the peasants have been using my woods, my plantations of young trees, as pasture for their cattle. . . . So you see, wherever you and your husband go, you bring along destruction with you. . . . I'm joking, of course, but still . . . it *is* strange. I'm convinced that if you'd stayed on here the devastation would have been immense.

In the repressive atmosphere of Act II Voynitsky and Astrov seek escape in drink, but Astrov's attempts at merriment have to be muted, because as Telegin keeps reminding him, everyone else is asleep. He is put to flight by the arrival of Sonya. She remonstrates with her uncle, whose only defence is his sense of a wasted life: 'When people have no real life, they live on their illusions. Anyway, it's better than nothing.'

The return of Astrov, now properly dressed, allows Sonya to make some amends for the offer of hospitality frustrated in Act I.[23] Yet even here her father is still a presence:

> SONYA. I like having little snacks at night. I believe there's something in the sideboard. They say he's had great success with the women, and he's been spoilt by them. Here, have some cheese.

In this context the offer of cheese could well be another of those private jokes to which Chekhov seemed so prone in *The Seagull*. Thus the unfortunate Lika Mizinova wrote to Chekhov about another of his supposed *amours*: 'Tell her a fellow-sufferer sends her regards; I once stupidly acted as the cheese you refused to eat', to which Ronald Hingley adds the following comment: 'Of "cheese", a symbol for love-making in his correspondence, Chekhov understood nothing, jeered Lika. "You only look at it from afar, even when you're hungry: not eating it . . ."'[24] Of course the offer of cheese to Astrov, who is a vegetarian, is quite natural. At the same time it is also clear that the undercurrent behind this transitory bond established by the late night snack is undoubtedly the question of love and the nature of Astrov's affections.

In revealing her admiration for him, Sonya binds him to an oath. Astrov promises her to stop drinking from that moment on. Yet there is another person with an amorous interest in Astrov — Sonya's own stepmother. There is therefore particular irony in the fact that when, later in the act, the two women pledge reconciliation, they drink from the same glass a toast of '*brüderschaft*' in the wine which Astrov has been forbidden to drink:[25]

> YELENA. . . [*Seeing that the sideboard is open.*] What's this?
> SONYA. Mikhail Lvovich has been having supper.
> YELENA. There's wine too. . . . Let's drink to our friendship. [i.e. '*brüderschaft*'.*]

The omens for this reconciliation are not good. When Sonya confesses her love for Astrov, Yelena replies by her own positive evaluation of his character and his ideals, which suddenly turns into self-pity. The gulf between the two women is only too apparent:

> YELENA. Really, Sonya, when you come to think of it, I'm a very, very unfortunate woman. [*Walks about in agitation*]. There's no happiness for me on this earth. None! Why do you laugh?
> SONYA [*laughs, hiding her face*]. I am so happy . . . so happy!

Yelena's reaction is a sudden desire to play the piano, as a release for her emotions ('I shall play and cry . . . cry like a

foolish girl'). Before she can do so, she must first ask he
husband. Sonya goes off to seek his permission, and through he
he gives his inevitable reply in the final word which closes th
Act: *Nel'zya*! ('It is forbidden/it is impossible', or as Miss Fe
translates it: 'We mustn't!')

Act III develops the implications of the closing word of Ac
II. It reveals the *impossibility* of the whole situation: the veto o
the tentative amorous relationships of Sonya and Astrov, c
Astrov and Yelena, of Yelena and Voynitsky; and the ac
reaches its climax by demonstrating the *impossibility* fo
Serebryakov and Yelena of remaining any longer in the house
hold. This is the dramatic highpoint of the whole play. It show
great mastery in the handling of dénouement and climax; fo
the three potential amorous relationships are all frustrated in
single scene, and significantly the background for this i
Astrov's illustrated lecture on man's capacity to lay waste
Yelena has asked to see Astrov's pictorial maps as a pretex
(within a pretext) to question him about his intentions toward
Sonya. Astrov admits that he might have considered marryin;
Sonya before the advent of Yelena herself, and then proceeds t
embrace his disingenuous interrogatrix, only to be caught in th
act by Voynitsky, who has come to present Yelena with a sym
bolic bouquet of roses.

All potential liaisons are dashed in a single blow. Sonya ha;
lost Astrov — has lost him for ever, for Yelena has engineerec
her into the promise that, if Astrov's response is negative, h(
must never come to the house again. If Yelena herself is abou
to fall to his advances (and in this she shows her 'wavering'
thus she tells Astrov to leave her alone, but lays her head on hi;
chest) then the fact that she has been caught out by Voynitsky
decides the matter: there can be no further question of an illici
relationship which is known to her persistently tormenting
middle-aged admirer. Voynitsky, in his turn, has his own hope;
dashed when they are most buoyed up with romantic sym
bolism: the presentation of his autumn roses ('exquisite, mourn
ful roses'; 'as a token of peace and harmony'). Astrov, for hi;
part, vents his annoyance by addressing the intruder in pro
vocative commonplaces about the autumn weather — a devic(

to cover up embarrassment which Yelena had earlier used in Act I.

It is ironic, in view of the events which follow, that Yelena should beg Voynitsky to use his influence to get her husband to leave with her that very day. Almost immediately, too, Sonya is made aware of her own position through Yelena's non-verbal confirmation of her fears. In the dramatic scene which follows Voynitsky, Yelena and Sonya are already overwrought, and the silly literary joke with which the professor introduces his radical proposal is entirely in the wrong key.[26] Voynitsky, already in a state of angry disillusionment, now receives his second hammer blow: his brother-in-law wishes to sell the estate.

Beside himself in fury and despair, Voynitsky exits saying that Serebryakov will have cause to remember him. The professor is persuaded to follow him out to talk to him, and when a shot rings out off stage, the audience might well think that Voynitsky has committed suicide and thus taken the way out of Ivanov, Treplev and his own forerunner in *The Wood Demon*, but the stock situation has taken a new twist: the inadequate hero has shot instead at his tormentor, and the point is reinforced when Voynitsky pursues Serebryakov back on stage and attempts to shoot him a second time in front of the audience.

The family council summoned by Serebryakov is announced at the very opening of Act III, but when Yelena suggests that her husband must have in mind some business (*delo*), Voynitsky gives the word a semantic shift — denying that the professor can have any business in a phrase which suggests that he really does nothing at all (*nikakikh u nego net del*). This linguistic motif of *delo* ('deed', 'business') and its verb *delat'* — 'to do' is developed throughout the opening exchanges of the act, and bears a clear relationship to the twin themes of 'laziness' and 'laying waste'.

Yelena complains of not knowing what to do; Sonya has plenty of advice on what there is to be done, but none of it appeals to Yelena. Sonya replies that idleness is contagious, and that under Yelena's influence she, Uncle Vanya and Dr Astrov have all ceased to be active.

The sense of waste clearly lies behind Voynitsky's violent

rebellion at the family council itself.[27] He accuses the professor
of having ruined his life, and because of this is his worst enemy
Sonya, too, in her distress blurts out that she and her uncle
have always worked hard, they are not mere consumers: 'We
have not eaten bread for free. No I don't mean that. I don't
mean that.'* (cf. Fen: 'We really did earn our daily bread! I'm
saying it all wrong — all wrong.')

Unenlightened consumption had been the burden of Astrov's
'lecture' in the earlier scene with Yelena:

> ASTROV. Here we have a picture of decay due to an insupportable struggle
> for existence, it is decay caused by inertia, by ignorance, by utter irre-
> sponsibility — as when a sick, hungry, shivering man, simply to save
> what is left of his life and to protect his children, instinctively, uncon-
> sciously clutches at anything which will satisfy his hunger and keep him
> warm, and in doing so destroys everything, without a thought for
> tomorrow.

Yet, shortly after this Astrov will offer himself up to be
consumed by the 'beautiful weasel' (polecat) to whom this
speech is addressed:

> ASTROV. A beautiful, fluffy weasel. . . . You must have a victim! Here I've
> been doing nothing for a whole month. I've dropped everything, I seek
> you out hungrily — and you are awfully pleased about it, awfully. . . .
> Well, what am I to say? I'm conquered, but you knew that without an
> interrogation! [Crossing his arms and bowing his head.] I submit. Here I am,
> devour me!

The family council brings the mounting sense of frustration at
useless consumption and idle waste to its dramatic climax. It is
only Voynitsky's mother who takes the professor's side. As
always, she sees in him the infallibility of authority:

> MARIYA VASILYEVNA. Jean, don't contradict Alexandre. Believe me, he
> knows better than we do what's good for us and what isn't.

Yet in spite of this it is to his mother that Voynitsky turns for
sympathy, almost as a small child; whereas Sonya makes
repeated calls on the emotional support of Marina. It is with
such a cry that Act III ends: SONYA [quietly]. 'Nanny!
Nanny!'*[28] As with previous endings, this one repeated word
looks forward to the next act: the final one, in which the old

values of order and work represented by Marina herself, will once more be re-established.

The opening stage directions for Act IV are more detailed than for the other three acts. We are in Uncle Vanya's study which also serves as the estate office. There is evidence of work all around: in the estate ledgers and various other papers. Very soon Marina is to reassure us that the old order is about to return:

> MARINA. We'll be living again as we used to — in the old way. Morning tea soon after seven, dinner at twelve, and in the evening we'll sit down to supper. Everything as it should be, just like other people . . . like Christians. [*With a sigh.*] It's a long time since I tasted noodles, sinner that I am!

With the return of order to tea-drinking and meals, the affairs of the estate can be dealt with properly. Marina will no longer be called on to attend to the peasants — they will have direct access to Uncle Vanya in his study-cum-estate office, as the opening stage directions make clear: [*In front of the right-hand door there is a mat to protect the floor from mud off the peasants' boots*]. No peasants are in evidence in Act IV, but Chekhov is stressing a point through one of his extra-theatrical directions — for the benefit of a reader, if not for an audience. The set also has two other props of symbolic importance, and for one of these there is again an extra-theatrical direction: [*on the wall is a map of Africa, obviously unnecessary for anyone here*].[29] The map of a distant, exotic land, as Chekhov suggests, is out of place for people who have returned to their old way of life, and are entrenched in the narrow niche of provincial Russia with winter approaching. It is Astrov who calls attention to its incongruity. He inspects it before leaving and says: 'I suppose down there in Africa the heat must be terrific now!' Astrov's comments on the map of a distant continent seem all the more pointed as he has just removed his own local maps from the house — never, perhaps, to return. Yet 'terrific heat' suggests passion, and that, too, for this household is now elsewhere, is exotic and inaccessible. After seeing the play in Nizhniy Novgorod, Gorky told Chekhov: 'In the last act of *Vanya*, when the doctor after a long pause, speaks about the heat in Africa, I began to tremble in delight at your talent, and in fear for people, for our colourless, beggarly life.'*30

In the opening directions for Act IV the wider horizons indicated by the map are preceded by the mention of another prop, which is its emotional antithesis: a caged starling. We have already seen that such domestic birds as hens and geese are linked, not only with the theme of 'laying waste', but also more specifically with Voynitsky. This domesticated wild bird carries on the motif, and hints at the loss of personal freedom. In Act III Yelena had expressed the desire to escape like a free bird:

> YELENA. To fly away, free as a bird, away from all of you, from your sleepy faces and talk, to forget that you exist at all — everyone of you!

In *The Wood Demon*, with its different emphasis, it had been Yelena herself who felt trapped in the final act, yet had become reconciled to her old life. There the symbol of the caged bird was applied directly to her:

> DYADIN. But you, why did you run away? You see, looking at the matter honestly, there's no happiness for you anywhere. A canary is expected to sit in a cage and look at other people's happiness. Well, then, sit there, for the whole of your life.
> YELENA ANDREYEVNA. But perhaps I am not a canary, but a free sparrow!
> DYADIN. So that's what you think! You can tell a bird from its flight, my dear lady . . .*31

By Act IV of Uncle Vanya Yelena does indeed fly away leaving behind her in Voynitsky's study a caged bird which is neither a canary nor a sparrow, but a bird noted for its contentiousness and noise — a starling. Thus between *The Wood Demon* and *Uncle Vanya* identification with a caged bird has passed from Yelena to Voynitsky, and in the process verbal metaphor has been concretised into visual symbol. It is Uncle Vanya who must reconcile himself to the old life, sitting in his study-cum-estate office with work as his only consolation and only escape, since the wider horizons represented by the map of Africa are: 'obviously unnecessary for anyone here'.

Work, routine and domestic, opens the action of Act IV. Marina has enlisted the 'right-hand' Telegin for the winding of

wool. When he compains that in the village he is called a
scrounger, a 'hanger on' (*prizhival*), Marina's reply underlines
the relevance of his position for the central characters
themselves:

> MARINA. You take no notice, my dear. We are all hangers on with God.
> Whether it's you, or Sonya, or Ivan Petrovich — nobody sits about
> without work. We are all toiling. All of us.*[32]

On the other hand, Serebryakov's words of parting are full of an
unconscious and uncomprehending irony: he advises his erst-
while hosts to do something useful.[33] Yet, just as his arrival on
stage had initiated the belated tea-drinking of Act I, so in Act
IV his departure signals the onset of work. Voynitsky refuses to
see them off, plunging instead into work as a form of therapy.
One by one the other characters return after taking their last
farewells of the professor and his wife; each, in turn comments
on the fact of the Serebryakovs' departure: 'they've gone'; each
then immediately takes up an activity. Just as in Act I the
characters had introduced themselves through their tea-
drinking, they now take their leave engrossed in work. Astrov,
alone, is not caught up in this process, but the parallelism with
Act I is maintained for him too. In Act IV he is also summoned
away by a workman and again offered vodka with the invitation: '*kushay*'. This second departure, like that of the
Serebryakovs, is greeted by the repeated comment: 'he's gone'
(from Marina and Sonya) and the calculations made by
Voynitsky as he works on the accounts. In this way the parallelism of exits echoes Act I's patterning of entrances. The play
ends with Telegin strumming his guitar, Mariya Vasilyevna
writing in the margins of her pamphlets, and Marina knitting
socks — all the elements of Act I, with one essential difference:
the new mood is no longer the indolence of tea-drinking, it is
work.

The estate accounts appear to have received little attention
since early spring; they are for commodities purchased for Lent
(a time from which the recent decline of Astrov also appears to
stem — a patient died under chloroform in Lent). All the characters on stage are picking up the threads of their former life,
left so loose and tangled by the presence of the professor and his

wife. It is the well-known round of daily work, to which they now turn — one which contains both the reassuring familiarity and the soulless boredom of a routine. The return to the old 'order' makes Marina feel more relaxed; using a nursery word (*bain'ka*) she says that she feels sleepy, and Astrov is almost lulled into staying by the cosy atmosphere of monotonous activity.

Nevertheless before Sonya and Uncle Vanya there stretches an endless vista of work, not for themselves but for others. This is the positive message of the play: amidst a constant process of wastage man's one salvation lies in work — work which may seem dull and futile, but work which is not for oneself but for others, building for the generations to come. The only respite from these labours, which Sonya can promise her uncle, appears to be death: the play ends on the ambiguously reassuring note: 'We shall rest!' The ending is undoubtedly powerful, yet it is created out of nothing. No solution of the play's dramatic tensions is put forward other than resignation (the philosophy of a Dostoyevsky or a Schopenhauer, whose equal Uncle Vanya, in an absurdly comic admission, feels he might have become). The ending owes its effect to the ambiguity of response it evokes in the audience: to the contrast between Sonya's elevated words, and the banal background of routine work against which they are set; to the note of claustrophobia (and the reference back to Act II), in the banging of the peasant watchman as Sonya first asserts: 'We shall rest!'; and to the ultimate realisation that the promise of rest from their labours is in reality death.[34]

A similar ambiguity inheres in Voynitsky himself, whose character exhibits a typically Chekhovian ambivalence of tragedy and comedy. By calling his play *Uncle Vanya* Chekhov is clearly singling Voynitsky out for the central role. At the same time 'uncle' betokens a relationship: Voynitsky is only 'uncle' in his relation to Sonya, so that she too is obliquely implied in Chekhov's title, and it is on these two figures that the spotlight falls at the end. Nevertheless the appellation 'uncle' (*dyadya*), when used colloquially has the meaning of 'a grown up chap' or 'fellow': its overtones are comic.[35]

In Act III Yelena uses 'uncle' in this way when she says: 'That Uncle Vanya suggests that the blood of a water spirit flows in my veins.'*[36] But Yelena, in recalling the remark, appears to be thinking of a relationship, not with Voynitsky, but with Astrov. A similar use of the word is also made by Astrov when he takes his leave of Yelena in Act IV: 'While there's no one here — before Uncle Vanya comes in with a bunch of flowers allow me . . . to kiss you . . . good-bye . . . yes?'

Thus for both Yelena and Astrov, when talking of love and feelings they might have for one another, Voynitsky is just '*dyadya*', just a middle-aged chap — someone, indeed, claimed by another relationship. There is, after all, something essentially comic about the love of this middle-aged man with his 'autumn roses', for the young and beautiful Yelena. His aspirations here seem almost as misplaced as his claim to the career of a Dostoyevsky or a Schopenhauer. Such incongruity between reality and aspiration is implied in the stage directions for Voynitsky's first entrance: on the one hand he has a 'dishevelled' (squashed) look (*pomyatry vid*), yet on the other hand he is wearing a 'smart' (dandified) tie (*shchegol'skoy galstukh*).

In Act IV Astrov calls Voynitsky a clown:

ASTROV. It's an old story. You're not mad, simply an eccentric, a clown. At one time I too considered every eccentric to be ill, not normal. But now I am of the opinion that the normal condition of man is to be an eccentric. You are completely normal.*[37]

Thus, like everything else in the play even the 'eccentricity' of Voynitsky is reduced to the level of the ordinary and everyday. Astrov, too, at the beginning of the play identifies himself as eccentric, and comments on his stupidly long moustache.[38] The gibe of Serebryakov that Astrov knows as much about medicine, as he himself knows about astronomy, may not be fair, but it is suggestive. Astrov's name is derived from the Latin word for 'star' (*astrum*) and whatever qualms he may have about his practising of medicine he is, nevertheless, guided by a higher light of idealism. He is a preserver of life — a vegetarian who has a passionate interest in the forests and the local flora and fauna. He is, in a modern sense, a conservationist.[39] In his job as a doctor he works tirelessly to cure and help people, but unfortunately he no longer likes the human race: he has become a misanthropist.

Metaphorically he sees his position as that of one who is lost among his beloved trees, without a guiding light (the light implied in his own name) to show him the way ahead:

> ASTROV. You know when you walk through a forest on a dark night and you see a small light gleaming in the distance, you don't notice your tiredness, nor the darkness, nor the prickly branches lashing you in the face. . . . I work harder than anyone in the district — you know that — fate batters me continuously, at times I suffer unbearably — but there's no small light in the distance. I'm not expecting anything for myself any longer, I don't love human beings. . . . I haven't cared for anyone for years. [i.e. For a long time now there has been nobody I have loved.*]

Although Yelena sees Astrov as a bright moon on Sonya's horizon, this confession to her augurs badly for any future relationship between them, and Astrov's loss of 'love' and 'light' stands in contrast to the confession which Voynitsky makes to Yelena earlier in the act. Through similar images one rejects love, while the other solicits it:

> VOYNITSKY. I have no past — it has all been stupidly wasted on trifles — while the present is awful because it's so meaningless. My life, my love — look at them — where do they belong? What am I to do with them? My feeling for you is just wasted like a ray of sunlight falling into a well [literally 'a pit'*] — and I am wasted too.[40]

Voynitsky's image of lost light is egocentric, self-pitying; Astrov's light is idealistic, beyond the self, but the sense of its lack drives him to seek consolation in vodka. In Act II Sonya makes him solemnly swear that he will stop his drinking, but it is a promise which he obviously does not regard as binding. Before he leaves the house for ever, in Act IV, he accepts a glass of vodka from Marina, refusing to eat the bread that is offered with it, saying: 'No, that'll do for me' (i.e. I'll have if just as it is' — *net ya i tak*): a phrase which implies a need to drink for its own sake, and suggestive of the way in which Astrov might spend his lonely misanthropic life in the future.

Astrov appeals to both women because, despite his apparent pessimism and cynicism, they recognise the idealist in him. In

Act I Sonya is only too ready to interpret his enthusiasm to Yelena: his idea that trees ameliorate the climate and improve the quality of life and civilisation. Yelena, for her part, endorses the tribute in Act II when she tells Sonya what has impressed her about Astrov:

> YELENA. He plants a tree and wonders what will come of it in a thousand years' time, and speculates on the future happiness of mankind. Such people are rare, and we must love them.

Thus she declares her own interest in Astrov, and some instinct seems to drive her on to scheme against Sonya's happiness. Hence her suggestion that she herself should cross-question Astrov about his feelings for her step-daughter, and the promise she exacts that Sonya must never admit him to the house again if Astrov should say that he has no love for her (even though Sonya herself has mixed feelings about such an undertaking: 'No, ignorance is better . . . At least there is some hope'). Despite the muddled outcome of her 'interrogation', Yelena tries to clinch Sonya's fate by reminding Astrov in Act IV that he has promised to leave. This promise, unlike the forswearing of drink made to Sonya in Act II, has not been exacted before the audience, yet it appears more binding: Astrov removes his maps and departs — after a farewell glass of vodka. The rupture, however, might not be final, he indicates that he may see Sonya the following summer, if not called to visit them sooner in his capacity of doctor.

Nevertheless, Yelena, too, is one of life's victims. That wastage to which Astrov points in Russia's natural resources is seen by her not as it is seen by others: as a parallel for her own behaviour, but as an analogue of the way others behave towards her, in particular, Voynitsky:

> YELENA. This sympathy for me — oh, how well I understand it! As Astrov said just now: you go on destroying the forests senselessly, and soon there won't be anything left on the earth. Just in the same way you senselessly ruin human beings, and soon, thanks to you, there will be no loyalty, no integrity, no capacity for self-sacrifice left. Why can't you look at a woman with indifference unless she's yours? Because — that doctor is right — there's a devil of destruction in every one of you. You spare neither woods, nor birds, no women, nor one another.

Yelena, like nearly every other character in the play, sees herself as a tragic figure, an 'episodic figure' who, 'if one thinks about it is very unhappy'. Yelena's view of the tragedy of human life and all that laying waste that is going on around her is central for the play itself. She tells Voynitsky:

> You, Ivan Petrovich, are educated and intelligent, and I think you ought to understand that the world is being destroyed, not by bandits, not by conflagrations, but by hatred and enmity, by all these trivial, petty unpleasantnesses . . .*41

This indeed is the nature of the tragedy which lurks beneath the surface of *Uncle Vanya*. It is not brought about by grand events, by major forces of evil: it results from the trivial and petty unpleasantnesses of day-to-day living.

3

THE THREE SISTERS

CHEKHOV began work on *The Three Sisters* in August 1900. It was the first play he wrote specifically for the Moscow Arts Theatre after their earlier successes with *The Seagull* and *Uncle Vanya*. The play received its premiere on 27 January 1901, with Olga Knipper, soon to be Chekhov's wife, playing the role of Masha. *The Three Sisters* is described as a 'drama in four acts'.

In Act I of *Uncle Vanya* Chekhov exploits the banal pattern of tea-drinking both to introduce his characters and to suggest a psychological dimension to a domestic situation. The central event in the first act of *The Three Sisters* is the name-day celebration of Irina, and we shall see later that the ritual of this occasion, the giving of presents, provides a similar framework for the illumination of situation as well as for the presentation of character.[1] As with *Uncle Vanya*, Act II is built around frustrated merry-making but the passions which erupt in Act III of *Uncle Vanya* are presented more obliquely in the third act of *The Three Sisters*, allegorically reflected in the all-consuming fire outside. The symbolic heat of elsewhere (as in the 'map of Africa') now forms the backdrop for an entire act. Like *Uncle Vanya* Act IV is centred on departures, but the shooting has now been moved from the previous act to provide a point of climax near the end. Given these formal similarities between the two plays, *The Three Sisters*, nevertheless, marks an advance in the Chekhovian technique of wringing symbol from apparent naturalism. The play is regarded by many as the high point of Chekhov's theatre.[2]

The play's opening is so saturated with thematic significance that it is worth dwelling on at some length. Thus the opening stage directions immediately present us with a series of visual

contrasts. The stage is divided in two, between a drawing room
and a large reception room which is being used as a dining
room. There is yet a third dimension — the sense of 'off-stage':
[*outside it is sunny, gay**],³ directions, which as we have already
seen hint not so much at the tangible or the readily perceptible,
but at mood. Three female figures occupy the foreground — the
sister themselves, each of whom is differentiated and contrasted
through dress and movement. Irina is in white for her name-
day; Masha, like that other Masha of *The Seagull*, in mourning
for her life, is in black; Olga is in the blue uniform of a school
mistress. Masha is sitting; Irina is standing; Olga is standing
and walking about. One is reading; one is marking; the other is
lost in thought. A further contrast is provided by three male
figures who appear in the background: Tuzenbach, Chebutykin
and Solyony. They are in the far room beyond the columns and
are conducting their own conversation.

Olga's opening speech also appears to be 'setting the stage',
to be merely the conventional résumé of the events which have
led up to the actions we are about to witness. It is, in fact, far
more than this:

> It's exactly a year ago that Father died, isn't it? This very day, the fifth of
> May — your Saint's day, Irina. I remember it was very cold and it was
> snowing. I felt then as if I should never survive his death; and you had
> fainted and were lying quite still, as if you were dead. And now — a year's
> gone by, and we talk about it so easily. You're wearing white, and your
> face is positively radiant.

Thus the opening action is set very precisely in time, but it is a
day which, like the visual contrasts on stage, looks two ways: it
is full both of grief and of happiness; it looks to the past and the
death of the father, but as the name-day of the youthful Irina it
also appears to look forward to a bright future. Like the contrasting dresses of Masha and Irina it is both 'black' and
'white'.

Olga's speech is interrupted by the auditory intrusion of time:
the clock strikes twelve — very protracted by the yardstick of
stage time and thus very emphatic. The naturalism of presenting things as they are thus takes on symbolic significance and
Olga calls our attention to the echoing of time: 'The clock

struck twelve then, too.' She goes on to recall the details of her father's funeral, which with its shooting and its music seems uncannily to anticipate that other military departure which will end the play, and such circularity is further underlined by the fact that Act IV will also begin at twelve midday.

If the warm weather of Irina's name-day is in contrast to the cold and snow at the time of their father's death,[4] there is yet a third emotional dimension to the echoing significance of this day: eleven years ago, at this very time of year, the three sisters left Moscow, but then everything was in bloom, was warm and was bathed in sunlight. Around this theme, too, the past the present and the future are all united in Olga's mind:

> yet I remember everything about it, as if we'd only left yesterday. Oh. Heavens! When I woke up this morning and saw this flood of sunshine, all this spring sunshine, I felt so moved and so happy! I felt such a longing to get back home to Moscow!

This is the first mention in the play of the all important theme of Moscow, and it is significant that the divided stage at once underlines its ambiguity. The apparent naturalism of a snatch of overheard conversation from the men in the other room serves as a comment on the symbol of Moscow, so rooted in the past and yet so full of hope for the future: CHEBUTYKIN. 'The devil you have!'[5] TUZENBACH. 'It's nonsense, I agree.'

The indirect commentary is taken up also by the black figure on the fore-stage: Masha quietly whistles (whistling was often considered a bad omen — it could raise the devil).[6] Olga reacts sharply to this third negative 'comment', and her instinctive response is that of the school mistress: 'Masha, do stop whistling! How can you?' From this she goes on quite naturally to complain of her own life and the job which seems to draw all energy and youth from her. To set against this she has only a dream, which Irina now puts into words: 'If only we could go back to Moscow! Sell the house, finish with our life here, and go back to Moscow.' Olga takes up the refrain: 'Yes, Moscow! As soon as we possibly can', while in the commentary conversation from the other room, Chebutykin and Tuzenbach laugh.

Irina thinks that Masha will be the only one to remain behind, but Olga holds out the hope that even so she will be able to spend the whole summer in Moscow every year. Masha's sole response is to whistle her song. The final comment from the men coincides with Olga's regret at not being married. When, after a pause, she says 'I would have loved a husband',[7] Tuzenbach says to Solyony in the other room: 'Really you talk such a lot of nonsense, I'm tired of listening to you.' He then joins the three sisters on the fore-stage, shortly to be followed by his two companions.

This, however, is not the end of indirect commentary in the play. Having thus marked out the device in an emphatic manner at the outset, Chekhov will use similar effects, though less obtrusively, throughout the course of *The Three Sisters*. The play's effects are rich and concentrated; they create mood not by direct assertion but through ambivalence and allusion. Here, as in *The Seagull*, literary quotation is particularly important.

Visually, Masha in black is the antithetical figure to Irina in white. Irina on her name-day is buoyed up; Masha, although not absolutely silent, is morose and pensive and does not actually speak until well into the act. When she does at last speak, her words are a quotation from Pushkin's 'Prologue' to his poem *Ruslan and Lyudmila*:

> A green oak grows by a curving shore,
> And round that oak hangs a golden chain

The words seem strange, incantatory and without real meaning, yet taken in context they are another form of indirect commentary: it is Masha's oblique response to the presentiment voiced by her sisters of an inappropriate gift to Irina on her name-day (Chebutykin's silver samovar). There are indications that Masha's black mood stems from the whole occasion, from her awareness of Irina's youth and happiness and the conflicting memories she has of former name-day parties. She prepares to leave, much to Irina's displeasure and the shocked surprise of Tuzenbach: 'To leave a name-day party!'* (cf. Fen: 'What! Going away from your sister's party?').

Masha decides to stay after all, but it is only because of the impression created by a new arrival — Vershinin. Nevertheless at the celebration lunch itself she quotes the Pushkin verse once more, adding tearfully: 'Why do I keep on saying that? Those lines have been worrying me all day long!' The quotation springs to Masha's lips at the presentation of a humming top, the last of Irina's gifts, which in marked contrast to Chebutykin's silver samovar emphasises Irina's girlish immaturity.

If throughout Act I the quotation is associated with Masha's 'black mood', it is significant that it does not recur until the final section of Act IV, and then more of it is revealed, though in a garbled form. The verses are a commonplace of the Russian cultural tradition, and Chekhov could count on every member of his audience having them by heart and knowing that the four lines to which Masha refers are (literally translated):

> Near the curved seashore is a green oak tree.
> On this oak tree is a golden chain.
> And day and night a learned tomcat
> Keeps going round and round on the chain.

Masha's quotation is a barely conscious symbolic statement of her own position. The oak tree is a symbol of strength; its greenness shows vigour and a capacity for life (Tolstoy had used the green oak tree in a similar way in *War and Peace* to parallel the emotional change in Prince Andrey, before and after his visit to Natasha).[8] But the oak tree is in a provincial backwater (*lukomor'e*) in direct symbolic contrast to Moscow, moreover it is attached by a golden bond (marriage) to a 'learned tomcat' (the pompous schoolmaster Kulygin) who with his prattle and fussing round and round her constantly hems her in.[9]

In Act I Masha herself seems puzzled by the significance of the lines which come involuntarily to her lips, but the more extended quotation in Act IV brings their meaning nearer the surface. It is on the departure of Vershinin that she falls back on them in desperate incantation, almost as though they are a talismanic formula against the old encirclement which Kulygin once again is offering her:[10]

KULYGIN [*embarrassed*]. Never mind, let her cry, let her. . . . My dear Masha, my dear, sweet Masha. . . . You're my wife, and I'm happy in spite of everything. . . . I'm not complaining, I've no reproach to make — not a single one. . . . Olga here is my witness. . . . We'll start our life over again in the same old way, and you won't hear a word from me . . . not a hint.

MASHA [*suppressing her sobs*]. 'A green oak grows by a curving shore, And round that oak hangs a golden chain.' . . . 'A golden chain round that oak.' . . . Oh, I'm going mad. . . . By a curving shore . . . a green oak.

OLGA. Calm yourself, Masha, calm yourself. . . . Give her some water.

MASHA. I'm not crying any more.

KULYGIN. She's not crying any more . . . she's a good girl.

[*The hollow sound of a gun-shot is heard in the distance.*]

MASHA. 'A green oak grows by a curving shore, And round that oak hangs a golden chain.' . . . A green cat . . . a green oak . . . I've got it all mixed up. . . . [*Drinks water.*] My life's messed up. . . . I don't want anything now. . . . I'll calm down in a moment. . . . It doesn't matter. . . . What *is* 'the curving shore'? Why does it keep coming into my head all the time? My thoughts are all mixed up.

[*Enter* IRINA.]

OLGA. Calm down, Masha. That's right . . . good girl! . . . Let's go indoors.

MASHA [*irritably*]. I'm not going in there! [*Sobs, but immediately checks herself.*] I don't go into that house now, and I'm not going to.

At this dramatic high point much that is suppressed, or only half understood by the characters themselves, comes nearer to the surface. Kulygin reveals what so far he has not openly expressed: that he is aware of the relationship between his wife and Vershinin. Masha reacts to his suggestion of returning to the old life, by revealing more of the elements of her allegorical self-image and compulsively repeats its formula as though to exorcise a returning ghost. A shot rings out. Masha, after her earlier conversation with Chebutykin, must be aware of its significance — subconsciously at least: it signals the end of Irina's hopes for escape. Masha reacts with renewed poetic exorcism. Nevertheless, there can be no return to the old life, as her refusal to set foot in the house again makes plain. Thus as Masha seeks psychological refuge in her half-understood literary quotation, she is aware at various levels of three irreversible defeats: her own loss of future happiness; Irina's loss of a future with Tuzenbach; and their collective loss, as three sisters, of their home and their past.

Masha's Pushkinian quotation, like the references to *Hamlet* in *The Seagull*, offers the audience an added dimension of psychological insight. At the same time, through this garbled and not fully comprehended self-reference Masha makes a banal, rebarbative truth aesthetically acceptable to herself by projecting it in eternal, poetic form. It is a formulaic surrogate for unpalatable reality which acts both as its filter and as its potential instrument of exorcism, and in as much as it allows her to come to terms with what she does not wish to hear it bears on a central theme in the play — the condition of psychological deafness.

If Masha's use of literature to grasp her own position is barely conscious, Solyony seeks self justification in literature in a way which seems almost premeditated. He thinks that he looks like Lermontov, the romantic poet notorious for his picking of quarrels, who died in a duel with a 'friend' in 1841. Solyony believes that he has Lermontov's character and throughout the play behaves in a rude challenging way to all around him. He quotes significant lines from Lermontov's poem *The Sail:*

> And he, rebellious, seeks a storm,
> As if in storms there were tranquillity.'

and even his quotation from Griboyedov's *Woe from Wit* evokes a Lermontovian motif: 'I am strange, but who's not so?'[11] Given such a model, a duel with Tuzenbach seems an inescapable part of the literary programme. Solyony's second speech in the play is almost a prophecy:[12] 'In twenty-five years' time you won't be alive, thank goodness. In a couple of years you'll die from a stroke — or I'll lose my temper with you and put a bullet in your head, my good fellow.' Immediately after these words he sprinkles scent on his chest and hands, just as he will do before his duel with Tuzenbach, claiming that his hands smell of dead bodies. Solyony's attitude to his friend recalls that of Pechorin to Grushnitsky in Lermontov's novel *A Hero of Our Time.* Pechorin, too, has a premonition of their future conflict and, whether consciously or unconsciously, sets about to engineer it. Towards the end of Act II Solyony makes a threat to Irina that he will kill any rival for her hand; in Act III he objects that Tuzenbach is allowed in to the sisters' room, but that he is not and again he sprinkles scent on his hands. By Act IV a chal-

lenge has already been issued — a challenge which Chebutykin
sees in Lermontovian terms: 'Solyony imagines he's like
Lermontov. He actually writes poems. But, joking apart, this is
his third duel.' If Solyony casts himself in the role of a
Lermontovian hero, he seems rather to view his friend as Aleko,
the hero of Pushkin's poem *The Gipsies*. When Solyony calls him
'Aleko' in Act II, Tuzenbach is mystified, but shortly afterwards he repeats the appellation, and adds the quotation:
'Away, away with all your dreams!'[13] The identification now
seems clearer; for Solyony is commenting on Tuzenbach's intention to resign his commission in order to go off and engage in
simple physical work. The hero of Pushkin's poem also thought
he could make a romantic gesture, and escape from civilisation
to live the simple life of a gipsy, but the reality proved far
different from the dream. Yet allusion to *The Gipsies* also hints at
another theme: sexual jealousy as a motive for murder — the
motive of Solyony himself. We shall also see that there are other
oblique, but no less important allusions to *The Gipsies* throughout Chekhov's play.

Oblomovism, that spineless laziness, which seems to lurk within
many of Chekhov's characters, may also be sensed as a literary
presence in Tuzenbach's description of his upbringing as a
spoilt child in a noble St Petersburg family. His capricious
behaviour with the lackey who used to take off his boots is
strongly reminiscent of a similar incident between Oblomov and
his servant Zakhar. Tuzenbach claims that his family tried to
shield him from work, but that they were not successful. Indeed
he now appears to have turned into something nearer to
Oblomov's antithesis: the half-German 'man of action' —
Shtolts.

> TUZENBACH. Yes, we must work. I suppose you're thinking I'm a
> sentimental German. But I assure you I'm not — I'm Russian. I don't
> speak a word of German. My father was brought up in the Greek
> Orthodox faith. [*A pause.*][14]

Although neither Oblomov nor Shtolts is mentioned in the text,
it nevertheless seems significant that in commenting on
Tuzenbach's ideas and opposing to them his own incapacity for

work, Chebutykin should cite the chief critic of Goncharov's novel and populariser of the term 'Oblomovism' to illustrate his own fecklessness: 'For instance, here. . . . I know from the paper that there was a person called Dobrolyubov, but what he wrote about I've not the faintest idea. . . . God alone knows.'[15]

The play is full of references, both direct and oblique, to the classics of Russian literature, but references abound which are classical in another sense. There is, for instance, Kulygin's constant use of Latin tags. Provincial schoolmasters in Chekhov's works are not usually portrayed sympathetically (e.g. Medvedenko in *The Seagull* and Belikov in *The Man in a Case*). Belikov, in particular, is portrayed as a repressive force in local society, and it is no accident that such a figure should be presented as a teacher of classical languages; for in the latter part of the nineteenth century knowledge of Latin and Greek was used as a repressive government policy to restrict educational opportunity.[16] Kulygin is a teacher of Latin, but he is not the sort of police spy at which Chekhov hints in his portrait of Belikov, nevertheless his veneration of authority is expressive, and the story he tells about a fellow schoolboy who could not learn the Latin grammatical construction *ut consecutivum* and had therefore to be content with a lowly paid job has pointed social relevance. Not only is there irony in the Latin construction thus singled out (the indicator of consequences and results of actions) but the way in which Kulygin gloats over his comrade's fate, still calling him by the school nickname of '*Ut Consecutivum*', tells us much about his own insensitivity.

Kulygin enters late in Act I. Like the three sisters he is characterised by his clothing: he is wearing a formal tailcoat. He also brings his own interpretation of occasion to this day which looks in so many directions; he points out that it is Sunday, a day of rest from his labours as a schoolmaster, but then proceeds to list the household tasks which must be done in preparation for the summer:

> The Romans enjoyed good health because they knew how to work *and* how to rest. They had *mens sana in corpore sano*. Their life had a definite shape, a form. . . . The director of the school says that the most important thing about life is form. . . . A thing that loses its form is finished — that's just as

true of our ordinary, everyday lives. [*Takes* MASHA *by the waist and laughs.*] Masha loves me. My wife loves me. Yes, and the curtains will have to be put away with the carpets, too.

Kulygin's love for Masha is mere form — a domestic arrangement, which like the spring cleaning has its allotted role. In fact he would be just as happy married to Olga, as he himself appears to admit near the beginning of Act III, or even perhaps to Irina (he compares Irina to Masha in Act IV).

When Kulygin makes one of his formal declarations of his love for Masha in Act III not long after the nonsense communication between her and Vershinin ('*Tram, tam, tam; tra, ra, ra,*' etc.*)[17] Masha angrily responds by conjugating the verb 'to love' in Latin. Her intention is obvious: she is parodying his own pedantic, formalistic view of love. Kulygin, however, is delighted, regarding it as the revelation of unsuspected depths in his wife, but his words: 'I am content, I am content, I am content!' receive an immediate mocking echo from Masha: 'I am fed up, I am fed up, I am fed up.' Kulygin's parting words as he leaves Masha in Act III are again: 'I am content, I am content, I am content.'[18] Yet, just as Masha's formal conjugation of 'love' for Kulygin is to be seen in the context of her formless declaration to Vershinin: '*Tram, tam, tam.*' etc., so too the exchange of thrice repeated sentiments between her and Kulygin is echoed later in the act in Masha's confession to her sisters: 'I love, love, love that man' which in itself is an echo of Vershinin's words to her in Act II: 'I love, love, love . . . Love your eyes, your movements . . .'[19] In matters of love, Masha has her own sense of form.

Kulygin has a Latin tag for every occasion: for the history which he has written of the school — '*feci, quod potui, faciant meliora potentes*'; for the Shrove-tide party which does not take place — '*O, fallacem hominum spem!* Always use the accusative case in exclamations'; for the drunkenness of Chebutykin — '*in vino veritas*'; for his own self-sufficiency — '*omnia mea mecum porto*'; for being clean-shaven in imitation of his headmaster — '*modus vivendi*, you know'. Besides the Latin pedantry there is also the authentic voice of a fatuous provincial schoolmaster, who pretends to award marks for behaviour both to his wife and to

Chebutykin, and who, to divert his wife after the departure of Vershinin, can put on an artificial beard and moustache confiscated from a pupil.

If, because of the figure of Kulygin, there is much classical allusion in the play, there is also a hint of 'classicism' at a structural level. From the very opening we were aware of a stage divided by columns, behind which the men seem to act as a chorus commenting on the central action. Such commentary, of course, is indirect and it is also brief, but 'indirect commentary' in one form or another is carried on throughout the play by different characters and through a range of devices. By beginning the play with a 'chorus' associated with columns, Chekhov appears to be calling his audience's attention to the ancient dramatic principle from which his own indirect commentary has developed.[20]

Here, too, as in a classical tragedy, no violent action is permitted on stage. Act III is played against a catastrophe, of which the audience is constantly aware but never actually allowed to see. Most of the town is on fire and, although the Prozorov house seems to be the hub for relief operations, all the drama takes place off-stage, and the still centre of Olga's and Irina's bedroom is disturbed only by off-stage sounds of alarm and reports brought in from outside. In Act IV Tuzenbach is killed, but this violent deed only reaches the stage as a distant muffled shot, and as an oral report brought by a messenger (Chebutykin).[21]

The unities of place and time are not, of course, strictly observed by Chekhov. Nevertheless all the action takes place in or around the Prozorov's house, and although the late spring of Act I has at the end of the play turned into the autumn of Act IV, a certain temporal unity is at least suggested through the time of day (midday in both cases). The actual fabric of the play, with its suggestive naturalism and its everyday symbolism seems far removed from classicism, yet despite this, certain elements of structure and tightness of form, the shunning of direct action and an overall sense of restraint, all point to a pre-romantic and more ancient concept of theatre.

The motive force for classical drama is fate, and the concept has central importance in *The Three Sisters*. The title alone seems significant with its allusive evocation of the three Parcae of classical mythology, or Shakespeare's 'three weird sisters', a resonance further strengthened by the surname Prozorov (from *prozorlivyy* — 'perspicacious', 'able to see into the future'). Visually, too, Chekhov singles out the three sisters as a group, giving particular symbolic emphasis to them as a triad both at the beginning and the very end of his play. Yet the suggested identification of the three sisters with the Parcae can only be made with heavy irony: Chekhov's sisters are not in control of fate — they are rather its victims.[22] Indeed fate, which so easily passes over into age-old Russian fatalism, is treated here as it is in many of the stories: 'The fault, dear Brutus, is not in our stars, but in ourselves . . . '[23]

The sisters link their fate and their future with Moscow, but this symbol has its own inbuilt inertia; for, as we have seen, Moscow is also their past. Critics of a realistically literal turn of mind have pointed out that there is no reason why Olga and Irina, at least, should not just get up and go to Moscow.[24] The sisters, however, do not see 'Moscow' as attainable by mere action — only by fate: through omen and portent. Yet, the omens are against them. When Moscow is first mentioned in the opening sequence of the play, there is immediate choric commentary from the three men, who respond with 'devils', 'nonsense' and with laughter. The choric laughter is carried on throughout the rest of the play by the comically deaf Ferapont, who in each subsequent act makes some absurd comment about Moscow. If such choric effects suggest ridicule, other omens are no less favourable. In Act II Fedotik shows Irina a new way of playing patience. Secretly she treats it as a game of prediction and, thinking that it is about to come out right, declares that they will go to Moscow. But Fedotik points out that she has made a mistake; the cards are against a successful outcome: 'That means, you won't go to Moscow.'[25]

In Act III, when the rumour of the regiment's departure is being discussed, Irina asserts: 'We'll go away, too!', but at this point Chebutykin drops and breaks a valuable clock, with the comment: 'smashed to smithereens!' (*Vdrebezgi*). Indeed, by Act

IV Irina seems reconciled to the inevitability implied by such
omens: 'I have decided: if it is not decreed for me to be in
Moscow, then let it be. It means that it is fate, you can't do
anything about it . . . Everything is God's will. That is true.'*[26]
Yet in this act fate has decreed a second shock for Irina — the
death of her fiancé. For this, too, there are ominous presenti-
ments which run through the play, particularly Solyony's
repeated quotation: 'He did not even have time to say "Akh"'
before the bear fell on him.'[27]

In Act II Tuzenbach refers to his decision to leave the army
as: 'the die is cast', but his gaming metaphor has as its background Irina's own game of patience and her pensive repetition
of: 'Balzac's marriage took place at Berdichev'[28] — their two
futures seem haphazardly linked by omens of change. The
beginning of Act II sees the burgeoning of an amorous relationship between Masha and Vershinin, but it is marked by a bad
omen:

> MASHA. What a noise the wind's making in the stove! Just before Father
> died the wind howled in the chimney just like that.
> VERSHININ. Are you superstitious?
> MASHA. Yes.

Given Masha's predisposition, it is inevitable that she should
view her repeated quotation of the lines from Pushkin as something unfathomable, almost Delphic, rather than as a poetic key
to her own psychology. For Masha fate is not in herself but in
her stars. As she tearfully repeats her Pushkin lines at the end of
Act I, her husband suddenly notices that there are thirteen at
table for Irina's name-day lunch.[29] Natasha, who had joined the
party with extreme diffidence (and thinking that Olga was criticising her green belt, not as a lapse of taste, but as a bad omen)
rushes from the table, teased by Kulygin and Chebutykin who
assert that the unlucky number thirteen indicates the presence
of lovers. Andrey follows her out, and in comforting her makes a
declaration of love which is sealed with a kiss. Thus the omens
themselves forge the instrument of fate, which will finally bring
about the complete dispossession of the three sisters.

Confronted by such black portents of the future, the Prozorov family is at the same time haunted by ghosts from the past. Indeed, the play is remarkable for its wraith-like secondary cast of non-appearing characters. Two of these, the mother and the father, are in fact dead, but their influence is still very much alive for those on stage.

The father's death and funeral, even his posting to the provinces eleven years before, haunt the opening act and the fitful joy of Irina's name-day. The dark undercurrent is sensed in the black-clad figure of Masha, who wishes to leave because a name-day party is not what it was when her father was alive. The arrival of Vershinin, however, encourages her to stay. He comes like a messenger from the past; not only does he recollect the sisters as little girls, but his imagination can resurrect the dead: 'I remember your father, though, I remember him very well. All I need to do is to close my eyes and I can see him standing there as if he were alive.'

The lack of drive, which now besets the sisters and their brother Andrey, seems to stem directly from the death of their father. Olga says her father trained them all to get up at seven o'clock, and that although Irina still wakes at seven, she lies in bed thinking until nine. Irina, for her part, introduces her brother to Vershinin as a future professor: 'Papa was a military man, but Andrey chose an academic career.' to which Masha adds the pungent comment: 'at the wish of his father'.*[30] Later Andrey makes his own significant admission:

> Yes. My father — God bless his memory — used to simply wear us out with learning. It sounds silly, I know, but I must confess that since he died I've begun to grow stout, as if I'd been physically relieved of the strain. I've grown quite stout in a year. Yes, thanks to Father, my sisters and I know French and German and English, and Irina here knows Italian, too. But what an effort it all cost us!

Just as the opening of the play identifies painful memories with the father's death, so the happiness of Irina herself on her name-day is associated with her childhood and memories of her mother. If there is a hint that Masha might be attracted to the older, military man, Vershinin, through association with her father, there is an even stronger suggestion that Chebutykin feels a special attraction to Irina, because of the love he had for her mother. The present he gives her, the silver samovar, causes consternation: it is completely inappropriate as a name-day gift for a young girl and the sense that Irina is its recipient only by proxy appears to emerge from Chebutykin's mumblings of self-justification: 'My dear, my sweet little girl, haven't I known you since the very day you were born? Didn't I carry you about in my arms? . . . didn't I love your dear mother?' When, in Act I, Vershinin tells the sisters that he knew their mother, Chebutykin's immediate response is: 'She was a good woman, God bless her memory!', but, whereas Irina recalls that her mother is buried in that symbolic city — Moscow, Masha (as though in contrast to Vershinin's vivid recollection of her father) admits that she is already beginning to forget what her mother looked like.

There are strong indications that because of his love for her mother, Chebutykin does not wish to lose Irina. When he drops the china clock immediately after her words about leaving, it is, as we have seen, a commentary on the theme of Moscow; but at the same time it is also a commentary on Chebutykin's attitude to Irina: the clock was her mother's. The loss of Irina would also mean the shattering of something extremely valuable and fragile — a link through time with her mother.

Chebutykin seems glad that her fiancé is fighting the duellist Solyony,[31] and when Masha says that the duel should be stopped, he replies: 'The Baron's a good fellow, but what does it really matter if there's one Baron more or less in the world? Well, let it be! It's all the same.' The opening stage directions for Act IV are quite explicit about Chebutykin's state of mind in anticipation of the duel: [*Chebutykin, in a benign mood, which does not leave him throughout the course of the whole act, sits in an armchair in the garden, and waits to be called**].[32] The call he awaits is to attend the duel in his capacity as a doctor, yet in spite of these directions, his mood, on one occasion, does change: he becomes emotional when Irina discusses the preparations for her departure with the baron, comparing himself to an old migratory bird which cannot fly.[33] Significantly, it is in this act that Masha asks him about his love for her mother:

MASHA. Tell me something. Were you in love with my mother?
CHEBUTYKIN. Yes, very much in love.
MASHA. Did she love you?
CHEBUTYKIN [*after a pause*]. I can't remember now.

Perhaps Masha sees a parallel between Chebutykin's ill-fated
love for her mother and her own impossible love for Vershinin.
She goes on to ask: 'Is my man here?' referring to one of the
obstacles to that love — her husband Kulygin. The other
obstacle is yet another of that secondary cast of wraith-like
non-appearing characters; Vershinin's wife.

Tuzenbach, on first mentioning Vershinin's proposed visit in
Act I, tells us that he has been married twice, has two
daughters, that his wife is half-mad, that she philosophises (a
characteristic which she apparently shares with her husband)
and that she makes attempts at suicide.[34] Yet in the play she
and the daughters are only a presence exerting their influence
from off-stage. In Act II Vershinin tells Masha that he has been
quarrelling with his wife from seven o'clock until nine that
morning, that one of his daughters is ill, and that he has had
nothing to eat all day. In spite of this he is called away from the
Shrove-tide party without even having tea, in response to a note
telling him that his wife has again tried to poison herself.

In Act III we learn that Vershinin's family have suffered
from the fire, and that his wife and two daughters are actually
staying in the Prozorov house. They never appear on stage, but
we do have a graphic description of their plight from Vershinin.

Masha's life is also plagued by another presence from beyond
the wings — her husband's headmaster. Kulygin lives under his
shadow and expects his own wife to do the same. As we know
the headmaster regards 'form' as the most important thing in
life, and this too is the view of Kulygin. Even the most banal of
words uttered by this authoritarian figure are treasured by his
sycophantic subordinate:

KULYGIN. In spite of weak health, that man is certainly sparing no pains to
be sociable. A first-rate, thoroughly enlightened man! A most excellent
person! After the conference yesterday he said to me: 'I'm tired, Fyodor
Ilyich. I'm tired!' [*Looks at the clock, then at his watch.*] Your clock is seven
minutes fast. Yes, 'I'm tired,' he said.

Much to Masha's annoyance Kulygin has just told her that at four o'clock they must assemble at the headmaster's for a promenade of teachers and their families (the day is Sunday), then spend the rest of the evening at the headmaster's house.

Even charity must not be seen to contravene pedagogic dignity as prescribed by this petty tyrant. When Tuzenbach proposes a concert in aid of the victims of the fire, and praises Masha's skill on the piano, Kulygin is pleased that his wife is praised, but wonders whether it would be fitting for her to play at such a concert, as the headmaster has views on this sort of activity. He admits that it is none of the headmaster's business, but nevertheless feels that he ought to be consulted. By Act IV, Kulygin has been made Deputy Head and has shaved off his moustache to conform with the new fashion set by the headmaster.

There is yet another threat from the wings which never manifests itself in the flesh: Protopopov — Natasha's past, who dominates the Prozorovs' future.[35] In Act I there is talk of Natasha marrying Protopopov; instead she marries Andrey and by Act II Andrey has become Protopopov's subordinate. He is the secretary of the town council of which Protopopov is chairman. Natasha forbids Shrove-tide festivities in the house to the others, but at the end of the act goes off for a pleasure ride with Protopopov. In Act III Chebutykin tells the sisters that they are blind to the fact that Natasha is having an *affaire* with Protopopov, and by Act IV her lover seems to have made himself complete master of their house. He and Natasha are inside (she, ironically is playing him 'The Maiden's Prayer') whilst all the Prozorov family are outside in the garden. Andrey is pushing a pram, under his wife's orders, and there are clear hints that Sophie, the second child, is not really his. Even at this point when Protopopov seems in complete occupation of the house he does not appear on stage, but manifests his authority over Andrey through his constant emissary Ferapont, who brings papers for Andrey to sign as he pushes his pram at Natasha's command.

We have seen that the operation of fate in *The Three Sisters* is largely a projection of the innate fatalism of the characters themselves. Such fatalism easily passes over into nihilism, and its most explicit expression in the play is to be found in the attitude of Chebutykin. When Irina tells him in Act III that the china clock which he has just broken belonged to her mother, Chebutykin replies:

> Well, supposing it was. If it was your mother's, then it was your mother's. Perhaps I didn't smash it. Perhaps it only appears that I did. Perhaps it only appears to us that we exist, whereas in reality we don't exist at all. I don't know anything, no one knows anything.

Admittedly Chebutykin is drunk, but his philosophy is an attempt to justify his own inadequacy. He is a tireless collector of knowledge, yet it is merely a ragbag of disconnected facts gleaned from newspapers: that Dobrolyubov was a writer (he himself is an Oblomov-like reader); that smallpox has broken out in Tzitzikar (he himself is medically incompetent); that Balzac got married in Berdichev (he himself is a lonely old bachelor who still harbours love for Irina's mother). Ephemeral newspaper facts have replaced any body of professional knowledge which he once might have had and, as a qualified doctor, it is ironical that his first speech in the play should be the jotting down of an amateur cure for baldness published in a newspaper.[36] He would no more be able to help in Tzitzikar, than he is in the town on the night of the fire. Indeed, on that occasion, as Kulygin points out, the doctor has purposely got himself drunk. Nevertheless, Chekhov does not wish his drunkenness to be caricatured: Chebutykin enters [*without faltering, as though sober**],[37] but his first action is heavily symbolic — he washes his hands as he gloomily says:

> The devil take them all . . . all the lot of them! They think I can treat anything just because I'm a doctor, but I know positively nothing at all. I've forgotten everything I used to know. I remember nothing, positively nothing.

He has on his conscience the death of a woman whom he had attempted to cure, and a sense of guilt prompts his nihilism:

> Perhaps I'm not a man at all, but I just imagine that I've got hands and feet and a head. Perhaps I don't exist at all, and I only imagine that I'm walking about and eating and sleeping. [*Weeps.*] Oh, if only I could simply stop existing!

Chebutykin's preoccupation with a sense of inner tragedy, his withdrawal from involvement and responsibility, is merely an extreme form of a condition which to varying degrees affects all the characters in the play. There are facts about those close to them which they do not wish to hear. Yet drink stimulates Chebutykin's tongue (*in vino veritas*, as Kulygin says); after breaking the priceless clock, the doctor in his cups blurts out the truth about them all:

> Why are you staring at me? Natasha's having a nice little affair with Protopopov, and you don't see it. You sit here seeing nothing, and meanwhile Natasha's having a nice little affair with Protopopov.

Chebutykin's flight from involvement in Act III may be extreme, but it is only a matter of degree. Throughout the act the characters on stage are engrossed in their private preoccupations, while a tragedy is being enacted all around them, and although some of its victims are actually in the house, their presence is never allowed to intrude on stage. Fire alarms punctuate the conversation, but the fire itself cannot be seen from the bedroom of Olga and Irina. As Olga tells Natasha (with the characteristic stage direction: [*without listening to her*]): 'You can't see the fire from this room; it's quiet in here.' Shortly afterwards Irina will reinforce the point when she says to Vershinin and Tuzenbach: 'Let's sit down here for a while. No one will come in here.' Only when a door opens can a window be seen which reflects the red of the blaze outside. The three sisters seem to be cut off from the outside world, and this effect is further emphasised by the division of the set into areas of personal privacy: '*On the left and on the right are beds, surrounded by screens.*' *38

When the act opens Olga may be looking out clothes for the victims of the fire, but it is the elderly who are charged with delivering them — Ferapont and her old nurse Anfisa. When Natasha enters, Olga is more concerned with her sister-in-law's plan to get rid of Anfisa, than with the fire itself. Masha is angry, but instead of intervening, or attempting to support Olga, she takes up a pillow and leaves.

The charitable view is that the sisters are worn out after a

hectic night spent helping the victims of the fire;[39] but their
refusal to face up to problems, their own and others', is a
dominant motif of the play. In Act III it is merely seen in more
dramatic form and presented symbolically through the contrast
between the anguish and confusion outside and still centre of
the sisters' room with its inner refuges behind the screens.

Towards the end of the act, when Masha makes her open
confession of love for Vershinin to her sisters, Olga pointedly
goes behind her screen saying: 'Don't say it. I don't want to
hear it.' Masha carries on undeterred, but once again we hear
the voice of Olga: OLGA [behind the screen]. 'I can't hear it
anyway. Whatever nonsense you might speak, I just can't hear
it.'*[40] After Masha's confession Andrey comes in, obviously
seeking some showdown with his sisters. They seem annoyed at
his request for a key to a cupboard. Olga leaves the protection
of her screen to give it to him, but Irina immediately retires
behind her screen without addressing a word to him. Andrey
has his three sisters together and is alone with them; he wants
an explanation from them of their attitude towards him. Olga
says it can wait until the next day. Masha says that they are
tired; she goes behind the screen to kiss Irina, bids farewell to
Andrey and leaves, much as she had done earlier, rather than
confront Natasha over the dismissal of Anfisa. Olga retires once
more behind her screen, and it is now Andrey's turn to address
his 'confession' to the deafness of the screens. When finally left
to themselves the two sisters conduct the concluding conversation of the act from behind their respective screens, but peering
out, Irina gives expression to the fears and emotions which are
uppermost in her mind: rumours of the regiment's leaving; the
possibility of marrying; and the need to leave for Moscow.

Masha's flight from a confrontation with Andrey is all the
more remarkable given the fact that only shortly before she had
claimed that she was unable to get the thought out of her head
that Andrey had mortgaged the house which belonged to all
four of them and had given the money he had received to
Natasha. Masha had said that she could not keep silent. Her
husband reproaches her for such thoughts, which he apparently
does not wish to hear, just as at the end of Act II he had com-

pletely ignored Irina's statement that her brother had lost two hundred roubles at cards and that it was the talk of the town. But Masha herself is little concerned at this; earlier, she too had received Irina's information with indifference.

All the characters suffer from an unwillingness to listen. In Ferapont deafness is given a comic treatment, and it is his deafness which Andrey most prizes in him as a confidant. Failure of communication has long been identified as one of Chekhov's main themes; in *The Three Sisters* it has tragic proportions. It is because the sisters do not wish to know about their brother's problems, that progressively throughout the play they allow themselves to be dispossessed. The process begins in Act II. Natasha is now firmly in control as mistress of the house, and her position is thus the very reverse of her situation at the end of Act I, when she had fled from the name-day celebration as the unwanted thirteenth person at table. Natasha has a ready-made instrument for dispossession in her children. She suggests that Irina should move into Olga's room to make way for little Bobik. The child, too, is Natasha's excuse for cancelling the Shrove-tide celebrations, so eagerly anticipated by everyone else.

Act III presents us with a *fait accompli*; Irina is already sharing Olga's room, but now Natasha mounts another attack through her children. They already have their own nurse, she argues, what is the point of keeping on Anfisa, the aged nurse of the Prozorov children themselves? When Olga protests, she is told that school affairs are her concern, but that domestic matters are Natasha's own province.[41] At no point do the sisters seem willing to confront Natasha, nor yet approach their brother, either to offer, or to seek, family support. They stand by and let events take their own course.

Act IV marks the complete dispossession of the Prozorov family. Symbolically, as well as literally, they are all relegated to the garden, while Natasha and her lover occupy the house itself. Masha refuses to set foot inside, and we know that their home has been mortgaged without the sisters having been consulted. Olga, now a headmistress, is already living in official school accommodation, and Irina's impending departure is seen by Natasha as an opportunity to move yet another piece in her game. Little Sophie is to oust her husband from his room. He and his fiddle can take up the room vacated by Irina: 'He can saw away at it as much as he likes there.'

Out in the garden the dispossession of the brother and sister is complete. Not only, with the departure of the regiment, are they saying goodbye to the old life and established affections, but the garden itself seems scarcely theirs, even on a private occasion such as this. The stage directions read: [*From time to time people from the street pass through the garden to get to the river*]. The Prozorov's garden has become public property — the result of the permission which, in the preceding act, Andrey had given Protopopov's emissary Ferapont, allowing firemen access to the river. The new public nature of the garden is further emphasised by the wandering musicians who stroll through it and by Olga's comments: 'Our garden's like a public road. Everybody goes through it.' It is such a garden which is the only psychological background and space left to the four central characters on stage, yet even here the dispossessing hand of Natasha will soon be felt:

NATASHA. So tomorrow I'll be alone here. [*Sighs.*] I'll have this fir-tree avenue cut down first, then that maple tree over there. It looks so awful in the evenings.

Significantly, in spite of the fact that her husband is not leaving, Natasha can think of herself as about to be left alone. Yet Andrey, for his part, has exactly the same feeling:

ANDREY. Our house will seem quite deserted. The officers will go, you'll go, my sister will get married, and I'll be left alone in the house.
CHEBUTYKIN. What about your wife?

In this Chekhovian world every man is an island.

An even more tragic consequence of such indifference and psychological deafness is the way in which the duel between Solyony and Tuzenbach is allowed to take place. The incident which happened near the theatre is brought up by Irina and discussed in the presence of Tuzenbach by Kulygin and Chebutykin. Nevertheless Tuzenbach's desire not to hear anything further about it and the obvious reticence of Chebutykin do not sufficiently arouse Irina's suspicions for her to ask what really happened. The matter is again raised by Andrey in Irina's absence. Chebutykin tells him about the duel, and Masha seems sufficiently concerned to comment: 'My thoughts are all in a muddle. . . . But what I mean to say is that they shouldn't be allowed to fight. He might wound the Baron or even kill him.' Her brother adds: 'I think it's simply immoral to fight a duel, or even to be present at one as a doctor.' To these observations Chebutykin replies with his philosophy of nihilistic indifference, even though, as we have seen, he is secretly glad at the situation which has developed.

Although Masha and Andrey express their indignation at the duel, neither makes the slightest move to prevent it, nor yet does that upholder of official positions, Kulygin, even though he, too, appears to know about it. Chebutykin, perhaps for a not fully realised subconscious motive, will certainly make no effort to stop it, but the most interesting case of suppressed knowledge is Irina herself, who in spite of various hints and premonitions makes no real effort to find out the truth; nor, given Tuzenbach's obvious nervousness and confusion, does she press her suggestion that she should accompany him. Irina is not marrying the baron from love, and after his strange words of parting, asking that coffee be made for his return, she stands for a moment in thought. Then, in a gesture which links her with the wavering Yelena of *Uncle Vanya*, she sits on a swing. Later, when Chebutykin tells her of Tuzenbach's death, Irina quietly cries, saying: 'I knew it, I knew it.' but if Irina really did 'know', it can only be on that subconscious level at which most of the central characters achieve self-knowledge.[42]

Just as Chebutykin is the embodiment of their indifference, Ferapont the comic mirror of their 'deafness', so too Solyony is the gross caricature of their treatment of one another. Solyony's ill manners seem to counter Chekhov's own view that the officers posted to outlying corners of the Russian empire were the bringers of culture and civilised values.[43] Indeed, in Act II Masha tells Vershinin: 'Perhaps it's different in other places, but in this town the military certainly do seem to be the nicest and most generous and best-mannered people.' She goes on, shortly afterwards, to proclaim the delicacy of her own feelings:

> but there are such a lot of vulgar and unpleasant and offensive people
> among the other civilians. Vulgarity upsets me, it makes me feel insulted, I
> actually suffer when I meet someone who lacks refinement and gentle
> manners, and courtesy. When I'm with the other teachers, my husband's
> friends, I just suffer.[44]

Vershinin replies that he cannot see much difference between military and civilians, particularly in this town, and his criticism of the local intelligentsia is phrased in terms which amount to self-criticism. Given her avowed revulsion at bad behaviour, Masha could well be more self-critical herself. Her sullen attitude at the beginning of Act I is not in keeping with the name-day party of her younger sister, even less is her sudden decision to leave, which is greeted by dissatisfaction and surprise by the others. Ironically it is Vershinin's view of the worth of civilised, educated values for Russian society, and of the role played by culture-bearers such as the three sisters, which makes Masha stay for the name-day celebrations, not because his words have pricked her conscience but because they appear to justify her as a person.

Solyony reacts to the reasons which Masha gives for wishing to leave by making obscure but insulting remarks about women's philosophising. His insult is not as gratuitous as it may at first seem; for Masha in comparing the name-day party, with those given when her father was alive, is far from gracious to the present guests: 'And today — what have we got today? A man and a half, and the place is as quiet as a tomb.' Masha is quick to fall on Solyony for his counter remark on women's philosophising, and he replies by quoting from Krylov's fable on ingratitude, *The Peasant and the Workman*: 'He had no time to say "Oh, oh!" /Before that bear had struck him low' — words which later take on a more ominous significance for his relationship with Tuzenbach.

Solyony already seems to have been criticised and ridiculed in the opening commentary dialogue behind the columns, and his unexpected rudeness springs from extreme touchiness, as he himself confesses to Tuzenbach in Act II. Yet much the same could be said in defence of Masha: her apparent insensitivity derives from extreme sensitivity.[45]

In Act II, Masha, along with other members of the family, shows little consideration for Anfisa, their eighty-year old nurse, who is run off her feet once tea is served:

> MASHA. Bring it here, Nanny. I'm not coming over there.
> IRINA. Nanny!
> ANFISA. Comi-ing!

In serving the tea, however, Anfisa hands Vershinin a note about his wife's attempted suicide. He leaves immediately, and when Anfisa enquires where he has gone, Masha falls on her:

> MASHA [*flaring up*]. Leave me alone! Why do you keep worrying me? Why don't you leave me in peace? [*Goes to the table, cup in hand.*] I'm sick and tired of you, silly old woman!
> ANFISA. Why. . . . I didn't mean to offend you, dear.
> ANDREY'S VOICE [*off stage*]. Anfisa!
> ANFISA [*mimics him*]. Anfisa! Sitting there in his den! . . . [*Goes out.*]

The family's treatment of Anfisa is a touchstone of sensitivity which must be borne in mind in Act III, when the sisters are faced with Natasha's contemptuous hostility for their aged nanny.

Still angry, Masha rudely demands a place at the table where Irina is playing patience. She jumbles up the cards and tells the others there to go and drink tea:

> IRINA. How bad-tempered you are, Mashka!
> MASHA. Well, if I'm bad-tempered, don't talk to me, then. Don't touch me!

When Chebutykin tries to tease her he is called a sixty-year old man, who talks like a stupid child. It is left to the coarse, insensitive Natasha, with her pretentious French, to drive the point home:

> NATASHA [*sighs*]. My dear Masha, need you use such expressions? You know, with your good looks you'd be thought so charming, even by the best people — yes, I honestly mean it — if only you wouldn't use these expressions of yours! Je vous prie, pardonnez moi, Marie, mais vous avez des manières un peu grossières.

It is, of course, the impossibility of her relationship with Vershinin and her overall sense of frustration, which cause such behaviour, as she tells Chebutykin in Act IV: 'When you get happiness in snatches, a bit at a time, and then you lose it, like me, then little by little you become coarser, become evil tempered. [*She points to her breast.*] It boils in there.'*⁴⁶

Olga, too, shares Masha's 'sensitivity' and hatred of ill-mannered behaviour. Thus she cannot come to terms with Natasha's attitude to Anfisa:

> Please try to understand me, dear. . . . It may be that we've been brought up in a peculiar way, but anyway I just can't bear it. When people are treated like that, it gets me down, I feel quite ill. . . . I simply get unnerved. . . . Any cruel or tactless remark, even the slightest discourtesy, upsets me.

Despite this Olga herself has not always shown delicacy and tact in her dealings with Natasha. When Natasha, rather diffidently, had been about to join the other guests at Irina's name-day lunch in Act I, Olga had added to her confusion by criticising her green belt. The offence has sunk deep, and it is a mark of Natasha's complete self-confidence and sense of power in Act IV, that she can pass on the snub to Irina: 'My dear, that belt you're wearing doesn't suit you at all . . . Not at all good taste . . . You want something brighter to go with that dress.'

Irina, for her part, might not entirely have profited from that 'peculiar' and sensitive upbringing proclaimed by Olga. At least, Anfisa feels the need to warn her about her behaviour when Vershinin first visits the house, and in Act II Irina herself is conscious of her own insensitive attitude towards a bereaved mother who wishes to telegraph her brother in Saratov, but cannot remember his address.

The importance of educated, civilised values for present-day Russian society is passionately argued by Vershinin, and he links it with the future — a dominant motif in the play. We have seen that, from Act I, the contrast of past unhappiness and future hope is implicit in a present moment of time, but it is Tuzenbach who introduces a philosophical note into this theme:

> The time's come: there's a terrific thunder-cloud advancing upon us, a mighty storm is coming to freshen us up! Yes, it's coming all right, it's quite near already, and it's going to blow away all this idleness and indifference, and prejudice against work, this rot of boredom that our society is

suffering from. I'm going to work, and in twenty-five or thirty years' time every man and woman will be working. Every one of us!

These words mark an advance on the social theme of *Uncle Vanya*; they appear to ring out as a clear, unequivocal prophecy of the revolution to come — yet, perhaps all they reflect is a vague, chiliastic feeling among certain members of the Russian intelligentsia at the turn of the century. Tuzenbach (the Oblomov turned Shtolts) sees the future in terms of work: he will resign his commission to labour in a brickyard. Such a view of work is ideological and theoretical, as Kulygin comments in Act IV: 'All ideas and theories, but nothing really serious.' Irina, to whom these remarks are addressed, shares Tuzenbach's intellectual enthusiasm for work, but it is the dream of a girl who wakes at seven but does not get up until nine. Indeed her marriage to Tuzenbach is based on a sole passion — their shared enthusiasm for work in the abstract. She does not love him, and they have nothing else in common. Nevertheless, Irina's experience of work so far (in the telegraph office and in the town council) has scarcely been reassuring. She says of her first job: 'What I so wanted and about which I dreamed, was precisely what was lacking. It was labour without poetry, without ideas.'*47

For all Tuzenbach's fine phrases, his 'prophecy' of a revolution of work should be treated with caution: his ideas are inconsistent. In his argument with Vershinin, in Act II, about work and the future he appears to see no changes whatsoever:

And life will be just the same as ever not merely in a couple of hundred years' time, but in a million years. Life doesn't change, it always goes on the same; it follows its own laws, which don't concern us, which we can't discover anyway.

The play's chief philosophiser on the future is Vershinin. He first broaches his pet theme in commending the three sisters as bearers of culture:

So in two or three hundred years life on this old earth of ours will have become marvellously beautiful. Man longs for a life like that, and if it isn't here yet, he must imagine it, wait for it, dream about it, prepare for it, he must know and see more than his father and his grandfather did. [*Laughs.*] And you're complaining because you know a lot of stuff that's useless.

The proposition that man must 'dream' if such a life does not exist relates Vershinin's concept of the future to that other 'dream' for the future — Moscow; and it is significant that, when the Moscow theme is broached for the very first time, Olga introduces it as a dream (*mechta*) which she opposes to the grim reality of work:

OLGA. And indeed, during the four years that I have been working in the school, I feel that every day I am drained drop by drop of energy and youth. And the only thing which grows and gets stronger is a dream . . .
IRINA. To go to Moscow, To sell the house, Finish with everything here and go to Moscow.*48

Vershinin's view of the future is based on the spread of culture — that of Tuzenbach on the need to work, and when the baron attempts to add his own qualification to Vershinin's future, Vershinin changes the subject:

TUZENBACH. You say that in time to come life will be marvellously beautiful. That's probably true. But in order to share in it now, at a distance so to speak, we must prepare for it and work for it.
VERSHININ [*gets up*]. Yes. . . . What a lot of flowers you've got here!

Tuzenbach is not to be put off; he returns to the theme of work, and after a pause, Vershinin puts forward the idea that if everyone were given two lives he would not repeat the mistakes made in the first. When, however, in Act II Vershinin returns to his argument with Tuzenbach about the future, he seems strangely to have taken over the latter's ideas: 'We've just got to work and work. All the happiness is reserved for our descendants, our remote descendants.' It is now Tuzenbach's turn to quibble: he objects to Vershinin's attempt to deny to the present any feelings of happiness.

All this suggests that the arguments are not to be taken very seriously. Indeed the background for this discussion in Act II is the spontaneous, unmotivated laughter of Masha, which in itself not only provides a commentary motif for the argument as a whole, but even seems to belie Vershinin's contention that happiness is not to be found in the present. It is difficult to escape the conclusion that Vershinin is driven to speak not because of a philosophy, but because of a need to philosophise.

In Act III, caught between his concern about the future of his young daughters and his love for Masha, Vershinin once more launches into his pet subject:

> Oh, what a great life it'll be then, what a life! [*Laughs.*] Forgive me, I'm philosophising my head off again . . . but may I go on, please? I'm bursting to philosophise just at the moment. I'm in the mood for it.

For both Vershinin and Tuzenbach the need to philosophise is like the need for food. Solyony says: 'Don't feed the baron on porridge, just let him philosophise.'*[49] The same is true of Vershinin, for whom it is both a solace and a stimulant. Thus in Act II he has not eaten all day and would dearly like some tea, but as he has to wait before it can be served, philosophising becomes an acceptable substitute, he can talk of the future: 'Well, if we can't have any tea, let's do a bit of philosophising, anyway.' Philosophising once more comes to his aid in Act IV in the difficult task of making final farewells: 'What else can I tell you now it's time to say 'good-bye'? What shall I philosophise about now? . . .' [*Laughs.*] Again he embarks on the theme of the future, but it is punctuated by his concern for the present (he keeps looking at his watch). The end of this speech appears to strike a note of reconciliation, the synthesis of his own arguments and those of Tuzenbach: 'If one were, you know, to add to love of work education, and to education love of work.'*[50]

Like 'Moscow' the philosophy of the future presents a bright dream for those who feel themselves trapped in the present. Its appeal is even felt by Andrey:

> I hate the life I live at present, but oh! the sense of elation when I think of the future! Then I feel so light-hearted, such a sense of release! I seem to see light ahead, light and freedom. I see myself free, and my children, too, — free from idleness, free from *kvass*, free from eternal meals of goose and cabbage, free from after-dinner naps, free from all this degrading parasitism!

'Philosophy' of this sort is a crutch and not a key. Tuzenbach's arguments in Act II even challenge its value:

> TUZENBACH. Think of the birds that migrate in the autumn, the cranes, for instance: they just fly on and on. It doesn't matter what sort of thoughts they've got in their heads, great thoughts or little thoughts, they just fly

on and on, not knowing where or why. And they'll go on flying no
matter how many philosophers they happen to have flying with them.
Let them philosophise as much as they like, as long as they go on flying.

MASHA. Isn't there some meaning?

TUZENBACH. Meaning? . . . Look out there, it's snowing. What's the
meaning of that? [*A pause.*]

MASHA. I think a human being has got to have some faith, or at least he's
got to seek faith. Otherwise his life will be empty, empty. . . . How can
you live and not know why the cranes fly, why children are born, why
the stars shine in the sky! . . . You must either know why you live, or else
. . . nothing matters . . . everything's just wild grass. . . . [*A pause.*]

This exchange between Tuzenbach and Masha is the real clash
of philosophical argument in the play, and its resonances will
reverberate to the end. In refuting Vershinin's idealised future,
Tuzenbach has come round to a philosophy of the pointlessness
of life: there are only facts; there is no overall sense.[51] The self-
sufficiency of facts seems to be confirmed almost immediately
afterwards, by Chebutykin's 'random' discovery that Balzac
was married in Berdichev, and the compulsion he feels to note
this down. Yet it is Chebutykin who in the last two acts will
develop such nihilism to a point where even the existence of
facts themselves is challenged.

Masha refuses to see the migration of cranes and the falling of
snow as mere self-explanatory events. She needs to know the
meaning behind them, just as she feels there must be some
sense in her incomprehensible urge to quote Pushkin. Like her
sisters with their yearning for 'Moscow', Masha opposes *faith* to
the appalling absurdity of life's discrete factuality. In Act IV
she rejects the nihilistic philosophising of Chebutykin against a
background which echoes her earlier exchange with Tuzenbach:

Talk, talk, nothing but talk all day long! . . . [*Starts to go.*] Having to live in
this awful climate with the snow threatening to fall at any moment, and
then on top of it having to listen to all this sort of talk. . . . [*Stops.*] I won't
go into the house, I can't bear going in there. . . . Will you let me know
when Vershinin comes? . . . [*Walks off along the avenue.*] Look, the
[migrating*] birds are beginning to fly away already! [*Looks up.*] Swans or
geese. . . . Dear birds, happy birds. . . . [*Goes off.*][52]

The snow and the migrating birds do now appear to have found
a meaning for her, but as symbols of dispossession and depar-

ture. Tuzenbach also finds meaning in the migrating birds, but it is one which carries on a persistent literary echo in the play: Pushkin's poem *The Gipsies* (after murdering his mistress and her lover, Aleko is left behind by the gipsies, like a crane which has been shot and cannot join his fellows). It seems significant that Chebutykin's one change of mood before the duel should be manifested in words addressed to Irina, in which he seems to identify himself with Pushkin's image. It is as though, for all his comforting philosophy of the pointlessness of life, he senses his own guilt and his own rejection:

> CHEBUTYKIN [*moved*]. My dearest girl, my precious child! You've gone on so far ahead of me, I'll never catch you up now. I've got left behind like a [migrating*] bird which has grown too old and can't keep up with the rest of the flock. Fly away, my dears, fly away, and God be with you! [*A pause.*][53]

Ultimately, of course, the migrating birds are the officers of the regiment. When they have gone, the three sisters are left grouped together at the end of the play, proclaiming life and the ideas of Vershinin and Tuzenbach on the future and the need to work. We hear the brave words of Irina to which an echoing image, the blank pointlessness of threatening snow, adds more than a hint of doubt: 'winter will soon be here, and the snow will cover everything . . . but I shall go on working and working!' Similarly the words of Olga, which end the play, take up Masha's assertion in Act II of the need to know, but this last echo of the philosophical argument is a note of desperation: 'If only we knew, If only we knew' and its accompaniment is Chebutykin's absurd ditty: 'Tarara-boom-di-ay' and his repeated phrase: 'It makes no difference! It makes no difference!'[54] This ending, with its painful ambiguities, is a powerful climax. Nothing has been resolved, yet the mood is one of sombre elation: the poetry of life has triumphed over the meaning of life.

Nevertheless this ending and the discussion in Act II, to which it must be related, raise important questions about the nature of Chekhov's art. The endings of *Uncle Vanya* and *The Three Sisters* are comparable, yet the sense of spiritual elevation in *Uncle Vanya* is achieved through overtly religious sentiment and imagery. In *The Three Sisters* these trappings have gone, but a curious sense of preordained mystery still remains. There is a great paradox at the heart of Chekhov's treatment of life's factuality and its lack of ultimate meaning; the very fact that the examples used to illustrate the argument recur as images which have obvious symbolic content (the snow, the migrating birds) suggests that Chekhov's dramatic techniques strive to create order and sense out of the very lack of meaning put forward as that of life itself.

The everyday realism of the plays springs from the naturalness and apparent randomness of conversations, events and effects, yet such randomness is illusory. Chekhov, the artist, constantly gives point and meaning to seemingly discrete phenomena, and thus communicates a sense of shape and purpose. The disparate elements of naturalism and symbolism projected through the two theatrical stages of *The Seagull* are here more closely woven together, but in the process, particularly through such devices as omens, symbols and portentous sounds, naturalism appears to hint at the supernatural: it communicates a sense of immanent mystery and predestination. Nevertheless Chekhov's world is the world of the non-believer; a man is responsible for his own fate. Thus the three 'Parcae' are reduced to human proportions, and do not cut the thread of others, but their own. It is from this basic creative tension that the thrust of Chekhov's art is born; for it is not action, as it is normally understood, that provides the dramatic impetus for *The Three Sisters*. Each act derives its own inbuilt dynamism from the fact that it is centred on an event — a ready-made situation, which Chekhov exploits to full advantage.

Act I shows a name-day party but, as we have already seen, it is a day which looks in more than one direction. The happy event is marred, not only by the presence of thirteen people at table, but also by the fact that Irina's presents are all to varying degrees 'inappropriate'. Like the receiving of tea in *Uncle Vanya*, the gifts which Irina receives betray the character of the donor; how he is viewed in the family; and his attitude to Irina herself. The 'naturalism' of a name-day party is thus exploited for dramatic and symbolic effect.

The first present to be received on stage is Protopopov's cake. It is brought by his peasant emissary, Ferapont, and is also referred to (rather disparagingly) as a 'pie'.[55] It is clear that although the gift is just about acceptable, the donor is not, and he will not be invited to the party, or ever appear on stage. The next present is Chebutykin's silver samovar, which creates the reverse effect; for although Chebutykin is a person accepted in the house, his inappropriate present causes consternation. As J. L. Styan comments: 'The Doctor is making the anniversary of the father's death and the daughter's name-day into one of his own, an anniversary for the dead mother.'[56]

Andrey's present turns out to be a photograph frame which he has made himself. Irina shows it with some pride to Vershinin, but his obvious embarrassment suggests a comment on the amateurish nature of Andrey's skill. There is, moreover, something symbolically peripheral about such an object, which almost sums up his position in the household; for as Olga says, as Andrey retires in confusion: 'He's got such a bad habit — always going off like this'.

The brother-in-law's gift is another home-produced offering — it is the history which Kulygin has written of his own school. The present, in itself, would be enough to condemn the self-obsessed pedantry and insensitivity of its donor, even, had he not already given Irina the book as a gift on a previous occasion.

Finally Fedotik and Rodé arrive with a basket of flowers, and Fedotik produces a humming top. Irina's uninhibited delight in it shows that she is not as mature as her twenty years would suggest. Nevertheless, when in Act II Fedotik again gives her a present — of coloured pencils and a penknife, she responds: 'You still treat me as if I were a little girl, I wish you'd remember I'm grown up now'. However, the stage directions then read: [*takes the pencils and the penknife joyfully*], and this joy is expressed in the same words which she had earlier used about the top: 'How charming!' (*kakaya prelest'*).[57] Fedotik is an inveterate giver of small presents; in Act III, he had wanted to give Irina a notebook, but he has lost everything in the fire and that too had been burned. In Act IV he gives Kulygin a notebook and pencil as a token of remembrance.

Among the characters who are not seen to give Irina a present in Act I are her two sisters, Tuzenbach and Solyony. They are already on stage when the action opens. Vershinin arrives, but brings no gift, because he was unaware of the occasion. Most significant of all, Natasha is invited to the celebration lunch; she congratulates Irina on her name-day but appears to have brought no present with her.

Act II, like Act I, is also built round a festive occasion: Shrove-tide (*maslenitsa*). The word has also acquired the meaning of 'a happy, free and easy life', and such overtones are not without their significance for the frustration of *maslenitsa* which takes place in this act.[58] Whereas Act I had ended with Natasha's running away from the festive board, Act II opens with her very much in control of the household. Again, the opening stage directions are important: [*Off-stage, in the street an accordion is being played scarcely audibly!**].[59] As so often in Chekhov, a mood is evoked by sounds; it is a mood of festivity, but, significantly, it is [*Off-stage*]: it is someone else's celebration of *maslenitsa*. Tuzenbach thinks that he will be playing the piano all evening, and he declares his intention of getting drunk; but although singing, dancing, drinking and the playing of the piano do take place on stage, all this is soon stopped on Natasha's instructions, so that this second act is not unlike the second act of *Uncle Vanya* (or for that matter the revelry scene in Shakespeare's *Twelfth Night*).[60] Natasha's own pleasure, however, is not to be destroyed, she will go off for a ride with Protopopov, while her husband is once more forced out to the club with Chebutykin, where he will undoubtedly again lose money. The guests are dispersed and all possibility of unified conviviality is lost.

As we have seen, children are Natasha's chief emotional weapon against the Prozorovs. It it because Bobik is not well that the party must be broken up. Through off-stage sounds Chekhov gives symbolic expression to these two competing forces: revelry and Natasha's child. Thus before the first arrival of guests (Masha bringing in Vershinin), the stage directions read: [*singing is heard off-stage; a nurse is putting a baby to sleep*]. Similar directions mark the dispersal of the guests in disap-

ointment: [*The nurse sings to the baby off-stage*] but most signifi-
ant of all, the final words of the act are spoken against a background of the two competing auditory symbols: [*Someone is play-
ng an accordion in the street. The nurse sings in the next room*].

Shrove-tide is a time for indulgence in food and drink before
he rigours of the Orthodox Lent, but Natasha, who is con-
erned about a diet for her child, has also put her husband on
ne: 'For supper I have ordered yoghourt. The doctor says you
nust just eat yoghourt, otherwise you won't get slim'.*[61]
Vershinin has had nothing to eat all day; he is waiting impat-
ently for tea, but when it is finally served he is called away
before he can drink it. Everyone is looking forward to the arrival
of the mummers, and to enjoying *maslenitsa* to the full, but in
his they are frustrated: '*oh fallacem hominum spem*', as Kulygin
comments at the end, and his reminder that the case for such
exclamations is 'accusative' (*vinitel'nyy padezh*) has another
resonance besides that of mere pedantry.

Nevertheless, Natasha is not solely to blame for the destruction of *maslenitsa*. It is because of his wife that Vershinin has not
eaten all day, and also because of her that he is called away
from the tea. This happens at a moment dense with omen.
Vershinin's retreat is linked to the theme of Moscow, to happiness and to Solyony as the consumer of the 'sweets' of others:

VERSHININ. And in the same way, you won't notice Moscow once you live
    there again. We're not happy and we can't be happy: we only want
    happiness.
TUZENBACH [*picks up a box from the table*]. I say, where are all the
    chocolates?
IRINA. Solyony's eaten them.
TUZENBACH. All of them?
ANFISA [*serving* VERSHININ *with tea*]. Here's a letter for you, Sir.
VERSHININ. For me? [*Takes the letter.*] From my daughter.

This incident has been preceded by an even more revolting
projection of Solyony the 'consumer' — his outrageous response
to the Bobik-dominated prattle of Natasha: 'If that child were
mine, I'd cook him up in a frying pan and eat him.' This
bizarre threat is not just a gratuitous shock administered by
Chekhov to his audience, it is a verbal attack on the forces

hostile to *maslenitsa* in the play, but at the same time, through
the grisly image of the frying pan it contrives to pervert th
values of Shrove-tide itself. It is worthy of note that the argu
ments picked by Solyony throughout this act are all in som
sense linked to eating and drinking and as such are a series o
discordant notes in the Shrove-tide theme.

The stupid argument with Chebutykin over *chehartma* an(
cheremsha is a dispute about two distinct words, which might b
seen as further illustrating the 'deafness' the characters displa
to one another, but it is also significant that its ostensible sub
ject is exotic food. The quarrel with Andrey about the numbe
of universities in Moscow may be related to the city's symboli
role in the play and to the absurdity of Andrey's academic pre
tensions, yet its motivation derives from festive drinking
Tuzenbach has just proposed that he and Andrey should drin|
'*brüderschaft*' (a toast to a more intimate friendship permittin
them to address one another in the familiar 'thou' form)
Solyony can only feel excluded and slighted; for, shortly before
Tuzenbach had proposed a similar toast to him, but it was onl
to 'reconciliation' (even though Solyony considered that the
had not quarrelled). He had not suggested, as he now does t
Andrey, that they drink a toast sealing a greater intimacy an(
the right to address one another as 'thou'.

Act III uses the fire as a ready-made dramatic event agains
which to set the action on stage. The obvious drama is enactec
outside. Alarm and crisis are conveyed by noises from the
wings, whilst the room of Olga and Irina is a still centre ir
which the dominant feeling is escape.[62] Nevertheless it is agains
the background of off-stage alarms that the danger signals on
stage must be seen: Natasha's growing usurpation and he
affaire with Protopopov; Andrey's sense of failure and indif
ference to his fate; Solyony's jealousy and scarcely veiled mal
evolence; the ill-starred love of Masha and Vershinin. Each o
these private dramas is linked to the calamity which has struck
the town outside.

The destructive nature of the fire is associated with Natasha
When she walks across the stage with a candle, Masha com
ments: 'She goes about lookng as if she'd started the fire.' The

visual reference goes back to the opening of Act II, when Natasha with her candle makes her rounds of the house as its new mistress, but there is also a literary image in Chekhov's mind: he told Stanislavsky that she should walk across the stage like Lady Macbeth.[63]

Another undisclosed allusion seems to lie behind Andrey's indifference to the fate of the town; for Irina presents him almost as a second Nero, fiddling while Rome burns:

> The truth is that Andrey is getting to be shallow-minded. He's ageing and since he's been living with that woman he's lost all the inspiration he used to have! Not long ago he was working for a professorship, and yet yesterday he boasted of having at last been elected a member of the County Council. Fancy him a member, with Protopopov as chairman! They say the whole town's laughing at him, he's the only one who doesn't know anything or see anything. And now, you see, everyone's at the fire, while he's just sitting in his room, not taking the slightest notice of it. Just playing his violin.

The theme of 'saving the town' lurks behind another literary reference; for when Irina banishes Solyony from the room, he vents his annoyance against Tuzenbach by quoting the final lines of a Krylov fable: 'The thought could be further explained but I fear to tease the geese.'*[64] The quotation is from *The Geese*, and the 'thought' when 'further explained' points to the foolishness of claiming respect on the strength of the deeds of one's ancestors: 'But our ancestors saved Rome.' 'Just so, but what have you done like that?' The stupidity of geese is proverbial (one thinks of Marina's comments in *Uncle Vanya*). At the same time Solyony's innuendo casts a slur on the baron's social position as well as on his practical abilities, and, as with Andrey's fiddling, it suggests, yet again, an inability to save the 'eternal city'.

For Masha and Vershinin the background of fire suggests all-consuming passion. They express their feelings through nonsense words, but Fedotik intrudes in a state of totally absurd elation, which links their 'fire' to the events off-stage — to the repeated *tam* (i.e. 'there') in their nonsensical refrain:

MASHA. Tram-tam-tam.
VERSHININ. Tam, tam.

MASHA. Tra-ra-ra?
VERSHININ. Tra-ta-ta. [*Laughs.*]
[*Enter* FEDOTIK.]
FEDOTIK [*dances*]. Burned up! Burned up! Everything to a cinder!*[65]

The dramatic peg for Act IV is departure, which brings it
own emotions for the characters on stage, whilst the real drama
of irrevocable departure — the death of Tuzenbach, is enacted
off-stage. The act is full of ominous sounds. At the opening
Rodé twice shouts 'Gop! Gop!'* to evoke an echo, to which he
says farewell; the cry 'Ahoo!' is later used to summon Masha
but these two strange calls go like a refrain throughout the
whole act. They arouse in Irina some vague premonition: [*Off
stage, deep in the garden.*] 'Ahoo!, Gop, gop.' IRINA (*shudders*)
'Somehow everything frightens me today.'*[66] She is right to feel
uneasy; for when the cry is next repeated, Chebutykin
comments: 'That's Skvortsov, the second, shouting from the
boat. He can wait.' The next time the sound occurs Chebutykin
and Solyony leave for the duel, with Chebutykin ominously
quoting the Krylov phrase used by Solyony himself: 'He had
not time to say "Oh, oh!" Before that bear had struck him low.'
The cry again interrupts Tuzenbach's farewell to Irina: it calls
him to the duel too.

'Ahoo!' is a cry used to establish contact between people lost
in a forest, as such its constant repetition has a poignant relevance for the lack of communication exhibited by the characters
throughout the play. But 'Ahoo!' also has an idiomatic usage
which means 'it's all up', 'it's done for'.[67] Kulygin, Irina and
Anfisa use this call, when trying to find Masha who is lost
somewhere in the garden. The double significance of this haunting cry has particular relevance for Masha, but its refrain
echoing throughout the final act invokes a mood which
embraces the strivings and the shortcomings of all the
characters.

Other sounds punctuate the drama of departure. Most telling
of all is the muffled off-stage shot announcing the death of
Tuzenbach, but music is particularly important, and at the
simplest level it is Chebutykin's repeated humming of 'Tarara-
boom-di-ay. . . . I'm sitting on a tomb-di-ay.' This nonsense

refrain is the musical motif of Chebutykin's nihilism.[68] It suggests a view of the ultimate absurdity of things and an attitude of indifference, which characterises his own (and others) connivance at the death of Tuzenbach.

The theme of dispossession has its music too: the ludicrously inappropriate 'Maiden's Prayer' which denotes the occupation of the Prozorov home by Natasha and Protopopov, whilst the uprooted life of the Prozorovs themselves is reflected in the wandering musicians who stroll through their garden playing a harp and a violin. The violin is Andrey's own instrument and these sounds are first heard in the distance, just before Andrey talks of the town becoming deserted. Time also has its music. The striking of Chebutykin's watch is an echo of the striking clock in Act I; more ominously, too, it is a reminder of his shattering of time — the clock he broke in Act III.

The full poignancy of departure is communicated by the band playing as the regiment marches off at the end of the play. Some of the same ambivalence of mood of the opening act is caught in these sounds; for the occasion is sad, but the music, as Olga points out, is happy: 'How cheerfully and jauntily that band's playing — really I feel as if I wanted to live!' Yet as this music fades it yields place to Chebutykin's 'Tarara-boom-di-ay.'

The music and the sounds on stage contrast with images of 'silent instruments' applied to the characters themselves. Irina tells Tuzenbach that she is marrying him without love, even though she dreams of love day and night: 'but somehow my soul seems like an expensive piano which someone has locked up and the key's got lost'. Masha sees her brother as an eternally muted bell; 'thousands of people haul a huge bell up into a tower. Untold labour and money is spent on it, and then suddenly it falls and gets smashed. Suddenly, without rhyme or reason. It was the same with Andrey.'

The chief visual symbols of Act IV are the trees. The avenue of firs and the forest beyond the river are prominent features of the stage set, but the trees of the garden take on human attributes in the symbolic role they play in the central theme of farewell. Rodé says goodbye to the trees near the the beginning of the act, and later Tuzenbach, worried that Irina says that she

cannot love him, asks her to say something before he goes off to
the duel:

> TUZENBACH. Tell me something.
> IRINA. What? Everything around is so mysterious. The old trees stand and
> are silent. [*Lays her head on his shoulder.*]*⁵⁹

The mysterious silence of these trees reflects the silence of the
couple themselves on the one issue that matters — the
impending duel. Yet it is these same trees which dispel
Tuzenbach's forebodings. Their beauty seems to promise life:

> TUZENBACH. Really, I feel quite elated. I feel as if I was seeing those fir-
> trees and maples and birches for the first time in my life. They all seem
> to be looking at me with a sort of inquisitive look and waiting for some-
> thing. What beautiful trees — and how beautiful, when you think of it,
> life ought to be with trees like these!
> > [*Shouts of 'Ah-oo! Heigh-ho!' are heard.*]
> I must go, it's time. . . . Look at that dead tree, it's all dried-up, but it's
> still swaying in the wind along with the others. And in the same way, it
> seems to me that, if I die, I shall still have a share in life somehow or
> other. Good-bye, my dear. . . . [*Kisses her hands.*]

Thus despite Tuzenbach's thirst for life, the summons to the
duel reminds him of death and he seizes on the image of the
withered tree which, although dead, can somehow still take part
in life. A different tree comes into Masha's mind at her parting
with Vershinin — the green oak tree in chains: the recurrent
motif of her Pushkin quotation. As in *Uncle Vanya* (and more
clearly in *The Cherry Orchard*) change is associated with the destruction of trees. In words which seem like a negative echo of
those of Tuzenbach, Natasha states her intention, once everyone has left, of felling the firs and cutting down a maple tree
which she considers ugly. From all we have seen above, it is
obvious that *The Three Sisters* gains structural density through
the coherent way in which image, sound, significant juxtaposition and allusion reflect the ready-made 'event' on which each
act is centred, and that the play achieves overall coherence, less
from actions, than from the recurrence and development of such
motifs from act to act. The central symbol of Moscow is a striking example.

   In Act I the ambiguity of the festive occasion, looking both to

:he future and to the past, is further reflected in that Moscow recollected at the beginning of the act which was bathed in sun- shine and full of blossom when the sisters left it eleven years ago, opposed to the Moscow of the present, rapturously wel- comed in the unexpected arrival of Vershinin, but soon to be shown as a dark counter image to the sisters' actual present:

> VERSHININ. At one time I lived in the Niemietzkaya Street. I used to walk from there to the Krasny Barracks, and I remember there was such a gloomy bridge I had to cross. I used to hear the noise of the water rushing under it. I remember how lonely and sad I felt there. [*A pause.*] But what a magnificently wide river you have here! It's a marvellous river!
>
> OLGA. Yes, but this is a cold place. It's cold here, and there are too many mosquitoes.
>
> VERSHININ. Really? I should have said you had a really good healthy climate here, a real Russian climate. Forest, river . . . birch-trees, too. The dear, unpretentious birch-trees — I love them more than any of the other trees. It's nice living here.

Act II embroiders the theme of Shrove-tide and, correspond- ingly, the concept of Moscow is centred on eating and drinking. Andrey, on his diet of yoghourt, tells Ferapont: 'I don't drink and I don't like going to pubs, but my word! how I'd enjoy an hour or so at Tyestov's, or the Great Moscow Restaurant!' To which the deaf Ferapont responds with a story which places the motif of Moscow even more specifically in the context of Shrove-tide and the eating of rich pancakes: 'The other day at the office a contractor was telling me about some business men who were eating pancakes in Moscow. One of them ate forty pancakes and died. It was either forty or fifty, I can't remember exactly.'

The keynote of the Shrove-tide theme of Act II is, indeed, the denial of happiness. This too is linked to 'Moscow'. Masha claims that if she lived there she would be indifferent to the seasons, but Vershinin counters that if she were to live in Moscow it would be Moscow that she would cease to notice: 'We're not happy and we can't be happy: we only want happiness.'

In Act III the central theme of the fire is also linked to Moscow, and again through an apparently inconsequential remark of Ferapont: 'Moscow was burned down in 1812 just the same. Mercy on us! . . . Yes, the French were surprised all right.' In Act IV, where the set for the first time visibly proclaims Vershinin's antithesis to Moscow (the trees and the river, which he had so praised in Act I), Ferapont's absurd gossip not only seems to reflect Olga's objections to the coldness of this setting, and with comic exaggeration apply them to Moscow (or is it St Petersburg?) but his words are also a commentary on the related theme of the future in this exchange with Andrey:

> FERAPONT [*hands him the papers*]. The porter at the finance department told me just now . . . he said last winter they had two hundred degrees of frost in Petersburg.
>
> ANDREY. I hate the life I live at present, but oh! the sense of elation when I think of the future! Then I feel so light-hearted, such a sense of release! I seem to see light ahead, light and freedom. I see myself free, and my children, too — free from idleness, free from *kvass*, free from eternal meals of goose and cabbage, free from after-dinner naps, free from all this degrading parasitism!
>
> FERAPONT. They say two thousand people were frozen to death. They say everyone was scared stiff. It was either in Petersburg or in Moscow, I can't remember exactly.
>
> ANDREY [*with sudden emotion, tenderly*]. My dear sisters, my dear good sisters! [*Tearfully.*] Masha, my dear sister!

The coldness of Act IV is the loss of an ideal; the bleakness of separation; the prospect of a cheerless future: 'It's autumn now, winter will soon be here, and the snow will cover everything . . . but I'll go on working and working!' These are the last words of Irina, whose fiancé, now senselessly killed, had earlier denied all meaning to the falling of snow. Masha, in that argument had stressed the need to know in order to live, but now she merely asserts the need to live. Olga had opened the play by remembering the snow and the cold at her father's funeral. It is she who has the final words: 'If only we knew, if only we knew!'

4

THE CHERRY ORCHARD

CHEKHOV'S last play was written, with great pain and difficulty, in the year before his death. Yet despite the author's own tragic circumstances, he himself thought of the play as a comedy. The idea of writing a four-act vaudeville, or a comedy, for the Moscow Arts Theatre goes back to 1901[1] and his own formulation of: 'a funny play, where the devil would go about in a whirlwind'[2] seems to hint at the sort of naive slapstick comedy associated with the early Gogol of *Evenings in a Village near Dikanka*, as though Chekhov, at the end of his life, felt the need to go back to his own comic roots. Unlikely as it may seem, the influence of Gogol can certainly be detected in the play.

As *The Cherry Orchard* was nearing completion, Chekhov forewarned Stanislavsky's wife (M. P. Lilina) in a letter of 15 September 1903: 'Not a drama but a comedy has emerged from me, in places even a farce.'[3] The first person to read the play in Moscow was its recipient, Olga Knipper, but in the telegram she sent to her husband expressing her delight with the play, she mentioned the tears it evoked in her. That very same day (18 October) Nemirovich Danchenko read the play to a group of members of the Moscow Arts Theatre company. By the fourth act they were in tears. The following day the manuscript was given to Stanislavsky. The first act he dutifully read as a comedy, but described himself as forcibly caught up by the second act, in a sweat in the third, and by the fourth he, too, was blubbering. In a letter to the author, he challenged the view which Chekhov had advanced to Lilina: 'This is not a comedy or a farce, as you wrote, it is a tragedy, whatever way out you may have found for a better life in the last act.'[4]

The emotion which actors and producers alike felt in the play

was further reinforced by the circumstances of its first performance. The *première* took place on 17 January 1904, a date
which coincided with Chekhov's forty-fourth birthday, and was
further marked out as a jubilee celebrating a quarter century of
his career as a writer. At the end of the play, despite the fact
that he was a terminally sick man, the author was called on
stage to receive the tributes proper to such an occasion.
Chekhov's ordeal was not lightened by the fact that the play
had not only been badly acted but produced in a way contrary
to his own intentions. The happy comedy which he had envis-
aged had turned into a valediction of tears. In a letter to Olga
Knipper of 10 April, Chekhov complained:

> Why is it that in posters and newspaper announcements my play is persist-
> ently called a drama? Nemirovich Danchenko and Stanislavsky see in my
> play something absolutely different from what I have written, and I am
> willing to stake my word on it that neither of them has once read my play
> through attentively. Forgive me, but I assure you, it is so.[5]

This fundamental disagreement about the interpretation of *The
Cherry Orchard* is one of the most intractable, yet intriguing problems in Chekhovian scholarship. It suggests, as a general issue,
some irreconcilable cleavage between an 'author's theatre' and
a 'producer's theatre' the implications of which go beyond the
staging of Chekhov's own plays, yet, on a particular plane, it
raises fundamental questions about the nature of Chekhov's
humour. In spite of the tears that it evoked in those who first
read and performed it, Chekhov defiantly sub-titled his play 'A
comedy in four acts' (*komediya v chetyrekh deystviyakh*). Is it possible 'to read the play through attentively' and find out why?

At first sight it appears to be Chekhov himself who calls for
tears from his actors: his own directions indicate that many of
the speeches are to be delivered 'through tears'. Nevertheless as
rehearsals were under way, Chekhov clarified his intentions in a
letter to Nemirovich Danchenko (23 October) stressing that
these 'tears' were not to be taken literally — they were merely
an indication of mood.[6] Yet this prescription for a mood which
patently runs counter to the laughter expected of a 'comedy' has
its own resonance in the traditions of Russian literature: it
suggests Gogol's well-known formula 'laughter through tears'.

Nátional perceptions of what is comic vary significantly. Russian humour often appears to have a dark, cruel side, when compared with the blander, more good-natured view of comedy found in English writers. The humour of Dostoyevsky is a case in point; indeed one of Dostoyevsky's minor comic characters, Dr Gertsenshtube in *The Brothers Karamazov*, asserts that Russians very frequently laugh where one ought to weep.[7] There is perhaps something typically Russian in the concept: 'laughter through tears'. Chekhov, who once proclaimed Gogol the greatest of Russian writers, showed a Gogolian sense of humour in many of his early stories.[8] Thus in *The Death of a Civil Servant* he invites his readers to laugh at the circumstances which bring about the death of a figure traditionally treated as deserving compassion — the poor civil service clerk.

This does not, of course, explain why Chekhov's compatriots in the Moscow Arts Theatre did not find the play 'comic'. National attitudes to humour are but a partial explanation of the problem. Thus it is a commonplace that laughter and tears are closely associated; they are merely different physical vehicles for the release of emotional tension. The mixed elements of laughter and tears can be seen at the most fundamental level of the comic in the traditional figure of the clown, who not only exploits comedy and pathos in turn but often contrives to blend them for sharper artistic effect. The skilful admixture of the pathetic to the comic catches an audience 'between the wind and the water'; the presence of pathos in a situation which is principally perceived as funny intensifies the comic effect, in as much as the audience's awareness of another, and contrary, pull towards 'tears' produces a divided response, and a corresponding heightening of tension. If the comic prevails, such tension can only find its resolution in greatly intensified laughter. By the same token, an audience's awareness of comic elements in a situation of basic pathos sharpens the pang and can produce real tears. Shakespeare knew of this and made 'comic' detail tell in his account of the death of Falstaff in *Henry V* (the dying Falstaff compares a flea on Bardolphe's nose to a black soul burning in hell).

No situation is unequivocally comic in its own right. The

basic device of 'slapstick' contains pain and humiliation as well
as comedy, so that a clown can exploit a fall either in the direction of laughter or the direction of pathos. Chekhov spoke of his
last comedy as 'in places almost a farce' and it is true that it
contains pronounced elements of 'slapstick': an insensed and
indignant Trofimov falls downstairs; Varya, wishing to hit
Yepikhodov with a stick, hits Lopakhin instead: Yepikhodov
crushes a hat box, and has boots which squeak as he walks.
Nevertheless these stock ingredients of farce are not as straightforward as they might at first seem. When in Act I Lopakhin
pokes his head round the door and makes an unexpected
mooing noise at Varya, her reaction is to threaten him with her
fist, but Chekhov's accompanying directions read: [*through tears*].
When in Act IV Varya takes up an umbrella rather too
violently and Lopakhin feigns fear that he is about to be beaten,
the audience is aware not only of Varya's threatened fist in Act
I (and the actual beating in Act III) but also of the poignancy
of Lopakhin's non-proposal that preceded it and has injected its
own tension into this second non-event. This final act, where
the Moscow Arts Theatre saw only tears, is in reality packed
with comic detail. Even Lopakhin's failure to propose to Varya
has its Gogolian antecedents in the ludicrous behaviour of those
reluctant bridegrooms Shponka and Podkolesin (*Ivan Fedorovich
Shponka and his Aunty*, and *Marriage*) and overt comedy persists
until the end in such details as the unexpected onset of
Yepikhodov's comic voice.[9]

Throughout *The Cherry Orchard* Chekhov places the action on
a knife edge between laughter and tears; but he intends no
neutral balance. He expects pathos to weigh on the side of the
comic, not against it, and comedy, thus reinforced, to tilt decisively
in favour of laughter. The expectations of Stanislavsky were
entirely different, and with equal ease he was able to incline the
play's delicate mechanism in a contrary direction.

The 'tearful' interpretation of the play derives almost entirely
from a particular focus on a single character: Lyubov
Andreyevna. At the very beginning, before her entry on stage,
Lopakhin characterises her as: 'a good person, easy to get on
with, a person without affectation'* (*khoroshiy ona chelovek. legkiy,*

rostoy chelovek).[10] Once on stage she easily captures an audience's sympathy; she is warm, full-blooded, romantic, generous (though some of these qualities, particularly the latter, may also be flaws). She can be seen as a tragic figure, who has suffered both in life and in love. Happy and excited though she is, in Act I, to return to the place of her birth, there is nevertheless a sadness which she cannot conquer: 'If only one could take off this heavy stone from my breast and shoulders, if only I could forget my past.'*[11] Later in Act III she will be more precise about the nature of this stone — it is her lover in Paris from whom she has parted: 'I love, love . . . this stone round my neck. I am going down to the bottom with it, but I love this stone, and cannot live without it.'*[12] The fact that the image here is one of drowning (*ya idu s nim na dno*) suggests yet another identification for this 'stone' of the past — the grief and guilt associated with the drowning of her young son; a punishment, she feels, for having taken up with a lover.

It cannot be doubted that Lyubov Andreyevna is at the very centre of the play, and the conflict for possession of the cherry orchard might be interpreted as an opposition of her values to those of Lopakhin: the romantic and the generous opposed to the prosaic and the mercenary; the cultured and the vulnerable in hopeless combat with the philistine and the successful; the ancient and aristocratic ranged against the plebeian and the new. Conflict within the play, however, is not as straightforward as this.

Another possible opposition exists between Lyubov Andreyevna and the 'eternal student' Trofimov — a conflict between a depth of feeling which stems from a tragic past and a naive superficial optimism about the future, which shuns all emotion. Trofimov is the play's chief advocate for a complete break with the past. He successfully woos Anya, the representative of the younger generation of landowners away from all attachment to the cherry orchard, yet such wooing seems essentially ideological. Her mother mocks Trofimov for saying that he is 'above love' castigating his smugness as lack of experience:

You're able to solve all your problems in a resolute way — but, tell me, my
dear boy, isn't that because you're young, because you're not old enough

yet to have suffered on account of your problems. [Literally 'suffered a single problem through to the end'.*]

This choice of verb: 'to suffer through' (*perestradat'*) is typical o Lyubov Andreyevna's emotional attitude to life with it emphasis on 'love' and 'suffering' (it seems significant that he very christian name Lyubov' actually means 'Love'). He emotionalism is in obvious contrast to Trofimov's purely intell ectual attitude to life and its problems.

It cannot be denied that the play ranges Lyubov Andreyevn against Lopakhin and Trofimov, but it does not do so in an crude diagrammatical way. If comic elements, which are a fea ture of the way her two 'opponents' are presented, seen excluded from the portrayal of Lyubov Andreyevna herself, w should not necessarily assume that she is the only serious char acter in the play, and that her attitude to life is the only on endorsed by the author himself. A further point remains to b made about the legacy of 'laughter through tears'.

The 'tears' of Gogol's world hint at the serious intention which lie behind his comic artistry, yet paradoxically Gogo singularly failed in his portrayal of serious characters and posi tive ideas in Part II of *Dead Souls* precisely because he divorce them from humour. His successors, notably Goncharov an Dostoyevsky, learned the lesson. In an often quoted lette Dostoyevsky discusses the value of humour in portraying th positive hero,[13] and throughout his writing such preposterou figures as Stepan Trofimovich Verkhovensky, 'the undergroun man' and 'the ridiculous man', are often mouthpieces for idea close to the author's heart. Chekhov is frequently admired fo his sane objectivity and his refusal to preach at his readers, bu the serious ideas he presents in many of his short stories (suc as those of Gromov in *Ward No. 6*, of Poleznev in *My Life*, c Ivan Ivanovich in *Gooseberries*) are made more objective throug authorial self-distancing, using the device of humour. The fac that Chekhov calls *The Cherry Orchard* a comedy does not pre clude a serious intention. Quite the contrary — by giving comi overtones to the portrayal of both Trofimov and Lopakhi Chekhov makes this intention more credible.

If it were not for the figure of Lyubov Andreyevna, no producer would hesitate to present the play as a comedy. She is surrounded by a retinue of genuinely comic characters, as well as by more serious figures who nevertheless are not allowed to escape implications of the comic. Lyubov Andreyevna seems above all this, and yet the comedy is centred on her in a very real sense; for in those who surround her can be glimpsed traits and attitudes of Lyubov Andreyevna herself — but parodied and exaggerated to the point where they become comic. The most obvious example of this is to be seen in her brother who acts a comic *alter ego*. Brother and sister share many attitudes and assumptions in common, but in Gayev they are taken to ludicrous extremes. It is because of this exaggeration that the oppositional relationship of both Lopakhin and Trofimov is, as we shall see, even more pertinent for Gayev than it is for Lyubov Andreyevna herself.

The opening stage directions of Act I make clear the emotional and symbolic setting for Lyubov Andreyevna's homecoming: [*A room which used to be the children's bedroom and is still referred to as the 'nursery'*]. The Russian is even more piquant: the word: *detskaya* — 'nursery' is derived from an adjective which can also mean 'childlike', 'infantile'. Lyubov Andreyevna's first utterance in the play is this one word *detskaya* in the form of an exclamation. Her next remarks develop the theme: 'The nursery, my dear, my beautiful room! . . . I used to sleep here when I was little. . . . [*Cries.*] And now I feel as if I were little again' (*i teper' ya kak malen'kaya*). The ambiguity of this last statement, which could also mean '*even* now I am like a small girl' seems significant. It is followed by her twice kissing her brother Gayev, who is in essence a child, and by once kissing Varya — the most adult member of the household.

The nursery as the setting for Act I is thus highly suggestive: both Lyubov Andreyevna and Gayev have the characteristics of children incapable of looking after themselves or of living in any other world than that of make-believe. But it is in Gayev that the characteristics of the child are most pronounced — with his constant sucking of sweets (he jokes of having consumed his estate in the form of sweets); with his imaginary games of billiards; but above all through the way in which he allows Firs to fuss over him, and scold him for not wearing the right clothes.

The tendency towards romantic effusion, evident in Lyubov Andreyevna's opening speeches on the nursery, is taken to comic excess in Gayev. Towards the middle of Act I he causes embarrassment by his comically inappropriate declamation honouring the centenary of a family bookcase. Yet only shortly before this, his sister had addressed it, even kissed it: 'You can laugh at me, I'm foolish. . . . My dear bookcase! [*Kisses bookcase.*] My own little table!' In spite of her invitation to laugh at this exhibition of emotion (indeed perhaps because of it) such an unsympathetic response from the audience is effectively blocked. We are merely allowed a glimpse of irony, when it is later discovered that this emotional symbol of the past has been guarding the telegrams from her lover in Paris, summoning her return.[14]

When Gayev opens the window on to the cherry orchard in Act I he is permitted his one moment of poetry:

> GAYEV [*opens another window*]. The orchard is all white. You haven't forgotten, Lyuba? How straight this long avenue is — quite straight, just like a ribbon that's been stretched taut. It glitters on moonlit nights. Do you remember? You haven't forgotten?

This, however, is merely the prelude to a much longer speech from Lyubov Andreyevna in her most exalted and poetic manner:

> LYUBOV ANDREYEVNA [*looks through the window at the orchard*]. O my childhood, My purity! In this nursery I slept, looked from here out of the window at the orchard, Happiness awoke along with me every morning. Even then it was exactly the same, nothing has changed. [*Laughs from happiness.*] All, all white! O, my orchard! After a dark rainy autumn and a cold winter, you are again young, full of happiness. The heavenly angels have not forsaken thee . . .*[15]

Here in spite of the moments of potential bathos (the middle-aged Venus regretting lost 'purity'; the 'heavenly angels') Lyubov Andreyevna's speech is not comic. Indeed one may argue, in view of what has already been said on the mixed nature of the comic and the pathetic, that the audience's awareness of potential bathos serves in effect to heighten the pathos. Yet what is possible for Lyubov Andreyevna is not allowed her brother: his apostrophising of Nature in Act II is treated as yet another absurd embarrassment:

> GAYEV [*in a subdued voice, as if reciting a poem*]. Oh, glorious Nature, shining with eternal light, so beautiful, yet so indifferent to our fate . . . you, whom we call Mother, uniting in yourself both Life and Death, you live and you destroy.

Much the same is true in Act IV. Gayev is once more silenced when he begins to talk in a rhetorical manner about his feelings on leaving the house, whereas earlier in the act his sister had been allowed to pour out her elevated feelings on the same subject, and even to personify the house as 'old grandfather' (*staryy dedushka*): 'Good-bye, dear house, old grandfather [house]. Winter will pass, spring will come again, and then you won't be here any more, you'll be pulled down. How much these walls have seen!'

If Gayev is an obvious comic shadow for the childlike and naively romantic aspects of Lyubov Andreyevna, it can also be seen that similar functions are carried out by other characters who surround her. Simeonov-Pishchik is the embodiment of her fecklessness over matters of money and estate affairs. When Lyubov Andreyevna drops her purse in Act II the incident seems tragically symbolic (even though comedy is possible in the actions of Yasha crawling around the stage to pick up her scattered gold). Nevertheless, the comic counter-weight comes in Act III, when Pishchik, who is similarly faced with the need to make mortgage repayments suddenly thinks he has lost his money, but finds it again in the lining of his coat. Lyubov Andreyevna's incompetence in money results in the loss of her estate, but such fecklessness in Pishchik has the happy outcome of comedy. For Pishchik, something always turns up: Englishmen find china clay deposits on his estate, and at the end of the play he has money to pay everyone back.

The means by which Pishchik is saved is yet a further commentary on Lyubov Andreyevna's romantic attitude to her estate and her cherry orchard. He is prepared to come to terms with modern commercial interests, be it the railway he allows to pass through his estates, or the mining of china clay. The business proposition put to her by Lopakhin is dismissed as 'vulgar'.

Pishchik is a comic deflator of such pretentiousness. In Act I he interrupts the discussion of former gastromic delights prepared from the fruit of this orchard by asking Lyubov Andreyevna whether she ate frogs in Paris, and she allows herself the comic retort: 'I ate crocodiles'. Shortly afterwards her hypochondria receives similar treatment, when Yasha reminds her that it is time to take her pills:

> PISHCHIK. Don't take medicines, my dear . . . they don't do you any good . . . or harm either. Let me have them. [*Takes the box from her, pours the pills into the palm of his hand, blows on them, puts them all into his mouth and takes a drink of* kvass.] There!

As a result, he later falls asleep whilst still speaking, snores, but suddenly wakes up and asks Lyubov Andreyevna to lend him money for his own mortgate repayments.[16]

The tragic overtones of Lyubov Andreyevna's life — the misfortunes which weigh on her like a stone — find a comic projection in the ridiculous figure of Yepikhodov, nicknamed 'Two-and-twenty misfortunes'. He, like a truly tragic figure, is a stoic in the face of adversity: 'Every day something or other unpleasant happens to me. But I don't complain; I'm accustomed to it, I even laugh at it.' Lyubov Andreyevna's unhappy, destructive love affair has its gross parallel at the level of the servants in the triangular relationship between Yepikhodov, Dunyasha and Yasha, and tragedy even seems threatened at the beginning of Act II, when Yepikhodov reveals that he always carries a gun in case he feels like shooting himself. Nevertheless, despite the subsequent behaviour of Dunyasha, he spends the rest of the act quietly strumming his guitar.

Two incongruously associated aspects of Lyubov Andreyevna's character: on the one hand her cosmopolitan rootlessness, and on the other her immersion in the past and deafness to a changing world, are embodied in the antithetical figures of Sharlotta and Firs. Chekhov had originally ended Act II with a lyrical conversation between these two characters, but he dropped this idea on the advice of Stanislavsky, transferring some of Sharlotta's speeches to the beginning of the act instead.[17]

There is more than a hint of the fairground in the passport-less wandering of Sharlotta, yet it serves as a comment on her mistress and benefactor, who has lived in Mentone and Paris, and who, once back in Russia, confesses almost immediately that she cannot sit still; her return to Paris in Act IV comes as no surprise. When Lyubov Andreyevna expresses pleasure that Firs is still alive, and receives the incongruous reply 'the day before yesterday', we may laugh at what this tells us about Firs, but at the same time be aware of an echo for his backward-looking mistress. There is more pathos in the presentation of Firs and Sharlotta than there is in the portrayal of the other comic characters. In Firs this stems from his age, but in the case of Sharlotta it is perhaps significant that she of all the characters is the nearest to the professional clown.

The comic characters perform a vital function in the delicate mechanism of the play's overall balance. They act as conductors of ridicule, drawing the comedy away from Lyubov Andreyevna herself, allowing her to remain serious, tragic, poetic, yet at the same time they take up and comment on certain aspects of her personality, which if taken to excess, or if seen in a different perspective, are merely comic. The shadowy presence of such aspects can serve to heighten the pathos of her presentation, but if they are allowed more fully into the light, we may then indeed have something nearer to Chekhov's own intentions. A hair's breadth can separate the devices of pathos and comedy — at the shock of loss Lyubov Andreyevna: [*would have fallen, if she were not standing beside a table and an armchair*]; whereas, in the elation of gain, Lopakhin: [*pushes a small table accidentally and nearly knocks over some candle-sticks*].

The play's dominant theme is social change. We are made aware of this from the very opening in the conversation between Lopakhin, the self-made man, and Dunyasha, the maid with pretensions to gentility. Nearly every character is associated to some degree with social ambiguity. Lyubov Andreyevna herself has lowered her status through marriage — her brother tells us at the end of Act I that she had married someone who was not a nobleman (*vyshla za nedvoryanina*). Her elder daughter, Varya, is adopted and is of peasant or lower class origin (*ona u menya iz prostykh*) as she tells Lopakhin in Act II. In effect, Varya seems more like a housekeeper than a daughter of the house. She is characterised in Chekhov's stage directions by her keys, (i.e. *klyuchi* which suggests the Russian word for housekeeper *klyuchnitsa*) and during her quarrel with Yepikhodov in Act III she seems mortally offended by the reference of this estate clerk to her 'superiors' (*starshiye*).[18] Most telling of all, she always addresses her mother and uncle by the polite form of 'you' (*vy*) whereas the true daughter Anya addresses them in the familiar form *ty*.[19]

Anya herself will turn her back on the estate and the old life, under the influence of Trofimov, who, although his own father was a drug store owner, is comically referred to as a 'shabby gentleman'* (*oblezlyy barin*) [cf. Fen: 'moth-eaten gent']. The real gentry, as exemplified by Lyubov Andreyevna, her brother Gayev and the neighbour Simeonov-Pishchik, are chronically short of money. The Gayev family estate will be sold, and Gayev himself will be offered a job in a bank.

Times are obviously changing. The younger servants, Yasha and Dunyasha, give themselves airs and ape their masters. Dunyasha dances at the ball in Act III as though she were a guest, and indeed the real guests are of low social status. Firs comments: 'We used to have generals, barons, and admirals dancing at our balls, but now we send for the post-office clerk and the station-master, and even they don't come too willingly.' The presence of such figures is in itself significant — they represent the modern world of rapid communiction: the railway (newly built) and the telegraph (Lyubov Andreyevna is constantly being summoned back by telegram to her lover in Paris). Thus Lyubov Andreyevna's ball not only acknowledges social change, it invites the new forces which are disrupting the old way of life.

Lopakhin, the self-made merchant of peasant origin, stands at the centre of this social change. He is the bridge between the old world and the new. The ambiguity of his social position is nicely judged; through his money he is the equal of the masters, yet he is also aware of his relationship to the lower orders. Thus on taking his leave in Act I he kisses the hand of Lyubov Andreyevna, embraces the nobleman Pishchik, but does not forget to shake hands with the servants Yasha and Firs.[20] Lopakhin merely says a polite farewell to Gayev, but this is understandable given Gayev's rather squeemish hostility to this upstart who is destined to replace him as owner of the estate.

The loss of a *dacha* is one of the first things we learn about Lyubov Andreyevna. As Anya tells us: 'She has already sold her *dacha* near Mentone. She has nothing left, nothing.'[21] It is, therefore, ironic that later in the same act Lopakhin should tell her of the transformation being effected in the Russian countryside because of the hunger for *dachas* among the new rising force of the urban middle class: 'Up to now in the countryside there have been only masters and peasants, but now *dacha* owners have appeared as well. Every town, even the smallest, is surrounded by *dachas*.'*[22] Lopakhin rubs salt into the wound by suggesting that the Gayev estate should undergo the same fate.

Social change in Russian literature is often presented as a conflict between generations. Turgenev's *Fathers and Children* is perhaps the best known example, and the novel is typical in that it presents the struggle as one of ideas, which are identified by specific decades of the nineteenth century: it is the struggle of the 'men of the sixties' against the 'men of the forties'. This theme, in essence the theme of the Russian intelligentsia, is also present in *The Cherry Orchard*. Gayev, who is of the generation of the 'fathers' in the play, identifies himself towards the end of Act I as a 'man of the eighties':

> GAYEV. You know, I'm a man of the 'eighties. People don't think much of that period, but all the same I can say that I've suffered quite a lot in the course of my life for my convictions. It's not for nothing that the peasants love me. You have to know the peasants! You have to know from which side . . .

At this point he is shut up by a representative of the 'children', his niece Anya. Gayev is always silenced when he makes such speeches; the others find it embarrassing — it is mere rhetoric. In fact words are the only mark of his claim to belong to the intelligentsia of the 1880s. When he says that no one praises that period, he is right. Alexander II had been assassinated in 1881 and the event had ushered in a period of great repression in Russian political and intellectual life. It was a time when all ideas and actions were suspect, a time of 'petty deeds' (*malyy dela*). Intellectually it was largely a cowed and demoralised generation, so that for Gayev to suggest that he has suffered for his convictions as a 'man of the eighties' must strike a Russian audience as ludicrous. The role and nature of the peasant was a permanent preoccupation of the Russian intelligentsia, and at no time more than during the decade preceding the 1880s. There is no evidence in the play that Gayev has any real interest in the peasants, and (as we shall see) the attitude to serfdom will be the corner stone of the criticism voiced by the younger generation against the 'fathers' in the play. Moreover it is curious that Gayev should seek to identify himself with the 'eighties'. As he is now fifty-one years old, it would seem more natural for him to consider himself a 'man of the seventies'; for in 1881 he could not possibly have been younger than twenty-eight, and the period of the 1880s would therefore have largely coincided with his own thirties. Gayev's self-identification with the 1880s doubly proclaims his intellectual immaturity.

Gayev's earlier, embarrassing, speech to the bookcase reveals the values of the 'man of the eighties'. Although he talks of 'fruitful work' (*plodotvoritel'naya rabota*), it appears to be books which, in his view have summoned the Russian intelligentsia to action throughout the whole century. There is no evidence that Gayev himself has read any books; his one passion is that sign of a mis-spent youth — billiards — and he frames his idea not in terms of books but of the bookcase. Thus books are substituted for action, and a bookcase for the books themselves:

> GAYEV. Your silent summons to fruitful work has not slackened through the course of a century, maintaining [*through tears*] in the generations of our kith and kin courage, a faith in a better future, and fostering in us the ideals of good and of social self-awareness.*[23]

The ambiguities in this passage are striking. It is not only the 'fruitful' work which evokes echoes for the symbol of the cherry orchard itself, but Gayev's use of the word *rod* ('kith and kin') also suggest his 'kind': it opens up his argument to include the whole of the gentry class, yet what the bookcase has taught them is not 'social awareness' but 'social self-awareness' (*obshchestvennoye samosoznaniye*). Typically, Chekhov's own laughter at Gayev is conveyed by his direction: [*through tears*].

Some forty years earlier, in his influential essay *What is Oblomovism?* the critic Nikolay Dobrolyubov had assessed the tradition of gentry culture as it had developed up to that point. He claimed that for the gentry intelligentsia reading got in the way of deeds, that rhetoric replaced action, and that its leaders showed little more than self-regard: he saw the summation of its values in the hero of Goncharov's novel *Oblomov*.[24] Gayev, in paying tribute to a full century of this tradition, seems cast in the role of an updated 'Oblomov' (in the emblematic sense suggested by Dobrolyubov). Little appears to have changed: Gayev is lazy, lives in a childish world of the imagination, he too is nannied by an elderly servant, who dresses him much as Zakhar dresses Oblomov. Gayev prefers rhetoric to books and most certainly to action; his social consciousness is merely self-regarding — the social self-awareness of a class. Nevertheless, Oblomov's friend Shtolts, the representative of a newly rising entrepreneurial class, had been Oblomov's constant support, but in Chekhov's play the activities of that entrepreneurial friend of the family, Lopakhin, are ultimately destructive.

Nobody takes the elevated thoughts of Gayev seriously, yet Trofimov is listened to. He is of the younger generation of the intelligentsia and his social origins are quite different from those of Gayev. In Act II Gayev's proclamation of aesthetic and romantic values, in the speech on nature which he is forced to abandon, follows hard on the heels of Trofimov's speech on the future and on the need for work. It is as though Gayev had been spurred into vying with the younger man; for, significantly, Trofimov's words are an indictment of Gayev himself:

TROFIMOV. The vast majority of the intelligentsia that I know is not searching for anything, does nothing and, as yet, is unfitted for hard work. They call themselves an intelligentsia, but they address servants as 'thou', treat peasants like animals. They do not learn well and they read nothing seriously. They do absolutely nothing; only talk about the sciences, and understand little in art.*25

Gayev, the 'man of the eighties', who claims to love the peasants, is just such an intellectual charlatan. He, too, addresses the servant, Yasha, as 'thou' (*ty*), even though his sister addresses Yasha in the polite form: 'you' (*vy*), and the pet name she reserves for Gayev himself — Lena seems to confirm his laziness (*len'*).26

Chekhov's portrayal of Trofimov is not as explicit as he would have liked. The concept of 'eternal student' has not necessarily the comic implications it assumes in the play, as Chekhov explained to his wife, in confiding the fears he had entertained about the play's success: 'I was chiefly afraid about the lack of movement in the second act, and a certain lack of completeness in the student Trofimov. You see, Trofimov is constantly in exile, he is constantly being expelled from the university, and how can one depict things like that?'27 It would have been impossible for Chekhov to have depicted his student as a revolutionary, nevertheless, when Trofimov refuses Lophakin's money, in Act IV, there can be no doubt as to his meaning:

> I'm strong, I'm proud, I can do without you, I can pass you by. Humanity is advancing towards the highest truth, the greatest happiness that it is possible to achieve on earth, and I am in the van!

There is a naive, idealistic, purity about Trofimov which is reminiscent of the revolutionary heroes depicted by N. G. Chernyshevsky in his novel *What is to be done?* His sexual purity is mocked by Lyubov Andreyevna, but by treating Trofimov's idealism and the involuntary protraction of his university career with humour, Chekhov manages to present him in a way acceptable to the censorship of the time. He did not deceive everybody. As *The Cherry Orchard* was in rehearsal, Gorky is reported to have said to its author: 'Now I am convinced that your next play will be a revolutionary one.'28

Nevertheless Chekhov is polemicising with Gorky in the play. Trofimov's words on being 'strong and proud' pick up the pride advocated by Satin in Gorky's play *The Lower Depths*.29 Gorky's

The Cherry Orchard 133

idealistic view of man's potential derives from his semi-mystical philosophy of 'God-building', and it is significant that in criticising the concept through the mouth of Trofimov, Chekhov seems to be suggesting Gayev as its proponent:

LYUBOV ANDREYEVNA. No, let's continue what we were talking about yesterday.

TROFIMOV.What were we talking about?

GAYEV. About pride. [i.e. about the proud man.*]

TROFIMOV. We talked a lot yesterday, but we didn't agree on anything. The proud man, in the sense you understand him, has something mystical about him. Maybe you're right in a way, but if we try to think it out simply, without being too far-fetched about it, the question arises — why should he be proud? Where's the sense in being proud when you consider that Man, as a species, is not very well constructed physiologically, and, in the vast majority of cases is coarse, stupid, and profoundly unhappy, too? We ought to stop all this self-admiration. We ought to — just work.

GAYEV. You'll die just the same, whatever you do.

TROFIMOV. Who knows? And anyway, what does it mean — to die? It may be that Man is possessed of a hundred senses, and only the five that are known to us perish in death, while the remaining ninety-five live on afterwards.

Trofimov, who begins by attacking the mysticism of Gorky's 'proud man', is easily brought round in argument to propounding his own mystical ideas on mortal man, and although his next speech is his serious attack on the intelligentsia which, as we have already seen, is an implied criticism of Gayev, there is, nevertheless, a measure of unconscious irony at his own expense as a member of the intelligentsia:

TROFIMOV. They all look very grave and go about with grim expressions on their faces, and they only discuss important matters and philosophise. Yet all the time anyone can see that our work-people are abominably fed and have to sleep without proper beds, thirty to forty to a room, with bed-bugs, bad smells, damp and immorality everywhere. It's perfectly obvious that all our nice-sounding talk is intended only to mislead ourselves and others.[30]

Lopakhin, the practical business man, and Trofimov, the idealist intellectual, do not always see eye to eye, but in spite of their jibes there is a certain mutual respect. Lopakhin is impressed by Trofimov's extolling of work, and through him the

argument once more turns to the nature of man: he considers
that the grand scale of Russia itself should produce native-born
giants. Significantly Lyubov Andreyevna sees such supermen as
a threat, whereas Chekhov himself, by suddenly forcing
Yepikhodov upon everyone's attention, appears to endorse
Trofimov's original objection to the mysticism of 'proud man'
— the reality of man as he exists:

> LYUBOV ANDREYEVNA. Whatever do you want giants for? They're all right
> in fairy-tales, otherwise they're just terrifying.
> [YEPIKHODOV *crosses the stage in the background, playing his guitar.*]
> LYUBOV ANDREYEVNA [*pensively*]. There goes Yepikhodov. . . .
> ANYA [*pensively*]. There goes Yepikhodov. . . .
> GAYEV. The sun's gone down, ladies and gentlemen.

Here is Chekhov creating mood, but one, which for all its poetic
wistfulness has hard ironic comment at its core.[31] Yepikhodov is
similarly used at the end of the act. The melancholy guitar of
'Two-and-twenty misfortunes' (i.e. *neschast'ye* = unhappiness) is
heard when Trofimov is talking about 'happiness' (*schast'ye*).

> TROFIMOV. You must believe me, Anya, you must. I'm not thirty yet, I'm
> young, and I'm still a student, but I've suffered so much already. As
> soon as the winter comes, I get half-starved, and ill, and worried, poor as
> a beggar, and there's hardly anywhere I haven't been to, where I
> haven't been driven to by Fate. And yet, always, every moment of the
> day and night my soul has been filled with such marvellous hopes and
> visions. I can see happiness, Anya, I can see it coming. . . .
> ANYA [*pensively*]. The moon's coming up.
> [YEPIKHODOV *can be heard playing his guitar, the same melancholy tune as before.
> The moon rises. Somewhere in the vicinity of the poplars* VARYA *is looking for* ANYA
> *and calling: 'Anya! Where are you?'*]
> TROFIMOV. Yes, the moon is rising. [*A pause.*] There it is — happiness —
> it's coming nearer and nearer, I seem to hear its footsteps. And if we
> don't see it, if we don't know when it comes, what does it matter? Other
> people will see it!

The rising moon seems to take up: 'The sun's gone down, ladies
and gentlemen' in the earlier passage. Gayev's setting sun
seems like a valedictory symbol for an age and a class,[32] but it is
replaced by a moon which Trofimov identifies with the future
happiness of mankind. Such a symbol, taken together with
Yepikhodov's mournful guitar, and the calls of a searching

Varya, suggests the same sort of ambivalence that surrounded the arguments on 'proud men' and giants. Moreover the Trofimov, who here at the end of Act II compares himself to winter and welcomes the moon as happiness, invites comparison with the Trofimov who had concluded Act I with an invocation to Anya: 'My little sun! my Spring!'[33]

If the guitar and person of 'Two-and-twenty misfortunes' seem to add a melancholy, pessimistic note to hopes about the nature of man and the happiness to come through social change, there is yet another 'sad' sound of a string to be heard in Act II, and it provides an even more ominous commentary on the theme. Again the mood is pensive: [*They all sit deep in thought; the silence is only broken by the subdued muttering of* FIRS. *Suddenly a distant sound is heard, coming as if out of the sky, like the sound of a string snapping, slowly and sadly dying away*]. Although the sound appears to come from above, Lopakhin suggests it might have an underground explanation — a pit accident. Even more improbably Gayev and Trofimov think of birds (a heron and an eagle owl).[34] Lyubov Andreyevna shudders, finding the sound 'unpleasant, somehow', but it is left to Firs, whose own mumblings the sound had disturbed, to interpret it as an omen: [*A pause.*] FIRS. 'It was the same before the misfortune: the owl hooted and the samovar kept singing.' When he is asked to what 'misfortune' (*neschast'ye*) he is referring, Firs replies: 'before freedom'. He has in mind the greatest social upheaval of nineteenth-century Russia — the liberation of the serfs in 1861, but he does not see this great reform which gave him the new status of a free man, as bringing happiness — it was 'unhappiness' (i.e. misfortune). Similar omens before the liberation of the serfs are referred to in an earlier story by Chekhov, actually entitled *Happiness* (*Schast'ye*), and many commentators have also pointed to the fact that a strange sound occurs in that story, which is also ascribed to the fall of a pit-tub deep below the ground.[35]

The symbolism of the play, which on one level evokes a poetic penumbra of lyrical mood and pensive reflection, in reality exhibits the same mixed elements as the comedy — it contains an undercurrent which is ominous and disturbing. The

central image of the cherry orchard is seen by different characters in different ways. It represents both happiness and
suffering, and its fate also reflects the theme of social change. In
Act I, the orchard, although off-stage, is an obvious presence;
the windows of the nursery open directly on to it, and its beauty
is a focal point of attention. Act II is set outside on the estate,
but *not* in the cherry orchard. The opening directions indicate
that the orchard begins beyond the poplars on one side of the
set. During Act III, when the estate is being sold, there is little
real evidence of the orchard's existence, and in Act IV the
audience is aware of the cherry orchard through its negation in
the off-stage sounds of the axes which are chopping it down.
Thus with each successive act there is a sense of the cherry
orchard receding further and further towards oblivion.

For Lyubov Andreyevna the cherry orchard symbolises her
childhood and the past. It is the most remarkable phenomenon
in the whole province, a thing of beauty, which also produces
fruit (though not as often as it might, and now unfortunately it
can no longer be put to use). Like Gayev's century-old bookcase
it stands as a symbol for the flowering of nineteenth-century
gentry culture, whose fruits and usefulness are now in the
past.[36] Its existence is threatened by a more democratic age, in
which every little bourgeois wants his *dacha* and his own plot of
land, which, as their spokesman Lopakhin hopes, they will one
day set about to cultivate.

The symbolism of trees is strongly developed in Russian
literature — from Turgenev and Tolstoy to writers of the
twentieth century such as Pasternak and Leonov. It is a
recurrent feature of Chekhov's own writing (Dr Astrov in *Uncle
Vanya*, Masha's oak tree in *The Three Sisters*) yet most relevant of
all, as a symbol for nineteenth-century Russian society, is the
extended allegory of the forest in Dobrolyubov's essay *What is
Oblomovism?* Dobrolyubov depicts the gentry intelligentsia as
attempting to lead the ordinary people through a dangerous
forest. They climb the trees to avoid the dangers and to spy the
way ahead, but the trees are comfortable and they have found
fruit there. They ignore the people below until the latter in
desperation begin to hack down their trees:

'Oh! Oh! Don't do that! Stop!' they howl when they see the people setting to work to cut down the trees on which they are ensconced. 'Don't you realise that we may be killed and that with us will perish those beautiful ideas, those lofty sentiments, those human strivings, that eloquence, that fervour, that love for all that is beautiful and noble that have always inspired us? Stop! Stop! What are you doing?'[37]

The trees of Dobrolyubov's allegory were to be taken as representing the institution of serfdom, which supported the gentry and yielded them fruit, whilst at the same time affording them an elevated position which they could claim was for the benefit of others, but axes remove this social myth as they remove the Gayevs' cherry orchard at the end of Chekhov's play.

For Lyubov Andreyevna the orchard is still alive with happy ghosts. She looks out of the window in Act I and believes she sees her mother in a white dress. It is of course merely a tree. But for Trofimov the orchard is peopled with other ghosts, as he tells Anya towards the end of Act II:

> TROFIMOV. Just think Anya: your grandfather, great grandfather and all your ancestors were serf-owners, they owned living souls, and surely you are aware that from every cherry tree in the orchard, from every leaf, from every trunk, human beings are looking at you. Do you not hear the voices? To own living souls that has caused degeneration in us all, those who lived earlier and those living now, so that your mother, you, your uncle no longer notice that you are living on credit, on somebody else's account, at the expense of those people whom you do not allow beyond the entrance hall. . . . We are at least some two hundred years behind, we still have absolutely nothing, no clearly defined attitude to the past, we only philosophise, complain of depression or drink vodka. It is, after all, so clear, that in order to begin to live in the present, we must first redeem our past, finish with it, but it can be redeemed only by suffering, only by unusual, unbroken labour. You must understand this, Anya.*[38]

This is undoubtedly the most important speech in the play. It begins with a broad vision, an exhortation to look beyond the narrow confines of the cherry orchard: 'The whole of Russia is our orchard. The earth is great and beautiful and there are many, many wonderful places on it.' Here Trofimov seems to be almost on the point of endorsing Lopakhin's earlier idea that the grand scale of nature in Russia should produce giants, but the body of the speech contains one of Chekhov's strongest indictments of Russia's past. It is a speech with many resonances. Thus it is significant that Trofimov projects the particular, legal situation of the orchard's present owners into the general and moral position of a whole class. They are in debt, but not to the bank: they are 'living on credit, on somebody else's account, at the expense of those people whom you do not allow beyond the entrance hall'. Similarly the 'redemption' he proposes is no mere financial transaction — it is nothing less than the redemption of the entire past.

Trofimov's assertion: 'To own living souls that has caused degeneration in us all' is an idea of prime importance. It occurs at a meridian point in the play, but before the significance of its various resonances is pursued both backwards and forwards it is essential to look at its linguistic implications. The verb, which Trofimov uses to indicate 'degeneration' — *pererodit'* is based on the root *rod* (the concept celebrated by Gayev in his speech to the bookcase). The first meaning of *rod* is 'birth', 'breed' but it also means 'kith' as well as 'kind'. The adjective derived from it: *rodnoy*, denotes close blood relationship; so that Gayev is the 'blood brother', *rodnoy brat*, of Lyubov Andreyevna. More loosely, however, the adjective can be used as a term of endearment indicating that someone is regarded as 'close', or 'dear'. By using the verb *pererodit'* Trofimov is asserting that a complete change of 'kind' has come about in the nation as a whole, through the owning of 'living souls'. 'Soul' is the legal term for a serf. It is a term which contains a great irony, in as much as serfdom treated living human souls as though they were inanimate objects — mere chattels. Trofimov's phrase 'living souls' evokes the ambiguities of Gogol's famous novel about the buying and selling of serfs — *Dead Souls*. The soul, of course, is also the 'living spirit' — *anima* — and in its nouns Russian grammar makes a distinction between 'animate' and 'inanimate' (*odushevlennyy* and *neodushevlennyy*). Trofimov's point is that serf-owning has blurred this distinction, so that the human needs of people can be ignored, while objects, such as the cherry orchard, are invested with emotional values more proper to people.

Lopakhin believes that he can forget his peasant past. In Act I he tells Lyubov Andreyevna, that although her brother

regards him as an oaf and a *kulak*, ('a tight-fisted peasant') he
feels that he has an affinity with her:

> LOPAKHIN. My father was your father's serf, and your grandfather's, too,
> but you did so much for me in the past that I forget everything and love
> you as if you were my own sister . . . more than my own sister.

The word Lopakhin uses here is not 'sister' but *rodnoy* (*Lyublyu
vas kak rodnuyu . . . bol'she chem rodnuyu*) — i.e. 'I love you as kith
and kin . . . more than kith and kin'.

Lyubov Andreyevna completely ignores this declaration of
affection and kinship. Instead she proclaims her restlessness
and almost immediately exhibits her affection for an inanimate
object, using the very same kinship-like term of endearment —
rodnoy: 'My dear little bookcase' (*shkafik moy rodnoy*). She kisses
it, then addresses her table.

There is no stage direction to indicate that Lopakhin might
have taken this as a rebuff, but the next time he speaks, the
comic juxtaposition of ideas suggests a certain irony: 'I feel I'd
like to tell you something nice, something jolly. [*Glances at his
watch.*] I'll have to go in a moment, there's no time to talk.' He
then broaches his scheme for the cherry orchard.

Earlier, when the aged family retainer, Firs, had brought her
a cushion, Lyubov Andreyevna had extended the endearment
rodnoy to him and kissed him, calling him 'her dear little old
man'* (*moy starichok*) (Fen: 'dear old friend'). In Act III she
shows concern about his health and asks him where he will go if
the estate is sold. Yet in Act IV, although she takes an
emotional farewell of the house itself, and actually personifies it
as 'old grandad', she shows little concern for Firs, the real 'old
grandad' of the house, who is thoughtlessly left behind along
with the furniture. Indeed there is unconscious irony in her
words: 'When we leave here there won't be a soul in the place.'

This final act opens with Gayev and Lyubov Andreyevna
returning from saying farewell to the peasants. With typical
lack of restraint in matters of money, she has given them her
purse, but she is more thrifty with her attention when it comes
to saying goodbye to her faithful old retainer. Firs is ill, she
knows that she will not see him again, yet at the end of the act

she looks impatiently at her watch and says she can spare him some five minutes. When she is told that he has already gone, she makes absolutely no comment but passes immediately to what she sees as her duties in respect of Varya.

There is a general lack of concern about Firs. In Act III the other servants enjoy themselves as guests at the ball, leaving Firs to do all the work, so that his complaint: 'There's no one in the house but me' (*odin na ves' dom*) seems almost prophetic of the ending. Prophetic too is the apparent nonsense reply which Firs makes in Act II, when Gayev complains of being 'fed up' with him for fussing over him about his clothes: 'There's nothing to be done there . . . they went off in the morning without saying anything.'*[39] Yasha, who ironically addresses Firs as 'grandad' (*dedushka*) expresses his boredom more strongly in Act III: 'How you weary me, Grandad! [*Yawns.*] I wish you'd go away and die soon.' A similar unsympathetic sentiment is expressed by Yepikhodov in Act IV at the very time that Anya is trying to find out whether Firs has already left:

ANYA. Has Firs been taken to hospital?

YASHA. I told them to take him this morning. He's gone, I think.

ANYA [*to* YEPIKHODOV, *who passes through the ballroom*]. Semyon Panteleyevich, will you please find out whether Firs has been taken to hospital?

YASHA [*offended*]. I told Yegor this morning. Need you ask ten times?

YEPIKHODOV. This superannuated Firs — candidly speaking, I mean — he's beyond repair, he ought to go and join his ancestors. As for me, I can only envy him.

Saying farewell to Firs has been left to the unsympathetic, even hostilely disposed, younger generation of servants, and the fact that the letter, which should have accompanied him, is still in the house alerts neither Anya nor Varya to the possibility that he might not even yet have gone. It is Trofimov's point that serf-owning has corrupted everybody — masters and servants alike.

Firs, the human embodiment of the old order is left locked up in the old manorial house which is soon to be destroyed. Yet, although the masters have forgotten him, he, as ever, is solicitous for them:

FIRS [*walks up to the middle door and tries the handle*]. Locked. They've gone. . . . [*Sits down on a sofa.*] They forgot about me. Never mind. . . . I'll sit here for a bit. I don't suppose Leonid Andreyevich put on his fur coat, I expect he's gone in his light one. . . . [*Sighs, preoccupied.*] I didn't see to it. . . . These youngsters!

The finer feelings of Leonid Andreyevich (Gayev) himself seem reserved for such things as a bookcase ('an inanimate object, true, but still a bookcase') the house itself or even such abstract concepts as Nature, apostrophised as a person. The confusion of animate and inanimate is reflected even in his speech mannerisms. At moments of embarrassment he frequently asks: 'whom?' (*kogo?*) instead of 'what?' (*chto?*); and the billiard terminology which is constantly on his lips treats the billiard balls as grammatical animates rather than inanimate entities (e.g. *'kladu chistogo, zheltogo v seredinu,* etc.).[40]

The values of *rod* (breed) receive comic treatment at the beginning of Act III in the figure of Simeonov-Pishchik. It involves the confusion of the human with the animal:

PISHCHIK. Actually I'm as strong as a horse. My dear father — he liked his little joke, God bless him — he used to say that the ancient family of Simeonov-Pishchik was descended from the very same horse that Caligula sat in the Senate.

Such absurdity involving names has many parallels in Russian literature. They all go back to Gogol. Thus Maksimov in Dostoyevsky's novel *The Brothers Karamazov* claims to be the identical Maksimov mentioned by Gogol in *Dead Souls*.[41] There is something Gogolian about Pishchik too. At his first appearance in Act I he is described as wearing *sharovary* — those loose, baggy Cossack breeches which seem to link him with the comic heroes of Gogol's Ukrainian tales (one of whom, Ivan Ivanovich Pererepenko, is mortally offended when a 'gander' is added to his noble name).[42] In Act IV Pishchik's desire to have his existence established for others is an obvious literary 'quotation' from the comic character Bobchinsky in Gogol's play *The Government Inspector:*

PISHCHIK. *And when you hear that my end has come, just think of — a horse, and say: 'There used to be a fellow like that once . . . Simeonov-Pishchik his name was — God be with him!'*

The name Pishchik means 'swazzle' (the device used in puppetry to distort the human voice), as such, not only does it hint at the theme of 'animate/inanimate', but also suggests the methods of Gogol's comic characterisation, which had its roots in the Ukrainian puppet theatre (*vertep*). The linking of robust health to an identification with an animal recalls Gogol's 'bear', Sobakevich, in *Dead Souls,* and the absurdity of the supposed origin of Pishchik's *rod* suggests that Chekhov is reworking that famous confusion of animate with inanimate in Gogol's story *The Overcoat,* where the name of the hero is supposedly derived from an actual shoe. One cannot escape the impression that Chekhov is playing one of his elaborate literary jokes: Pishchik does not suggest that his *rod* came from a Roman emperor, but rather from his horse, yet, like Gogol's hero, Bashmachkin, the emperor in question, Caligula, also has a name derived from a shoe (*caliga*), and his forename Gaius (in Russian *Gay*) has provided the root for the name of the play's other champion of *rod* — Gayev.[43]

Trofimov's speech on the cherry orchard contains a statement which is of crucial importance for understanding the ambiguity at the heart of the symbol of the cherry orchard itself: 'we have no clearly defined attitude to the past'* (Fen: 'no clear attitude to our past'). The past for Lyubov Andreyevna has happy as well as painful memories; they exist side by side. She talks of the heavy stone of the past round her neck and shoulders, but immediately afterwards 'laughs happily' when she thinks she sees the ghost of her mother in the orchard.

The sale of the cherry orchard, with both its happiness and its pain, seems unthinkable:

> LYUBOV ANDREYEVNA. I was born here, you know, my father and mother lived here, and my grandfather, too, and I love this house — I can't conceive life without the cherry orchard, and if it really has to be sold then sell me with it. . . . [*Embraces* TROFIMOV, *kisses him on the forehead.* You know, my son was drowned here. . . . [*Weeps.*] Have pity on me, my dear, dear friend.

Yet the estate is sold and it is Firs who is left behind not Lyubov Andreyevna. Nor, after all, is its sale the irreparable loss, which her words might suggest. When Gayev returns in Act III bearing the bad news, Chekhov's directions hint at comedy in their suggestion of 'on the one hand, and yet on the other': [*Enter Gayev; he carries some parcels (i.e. purchases) in his right hand and wipes away his tears with his left*]. He makes no reply to his sister's anxious questions but, still crying, hands Firs 'anchovies' and 'Kerch herrings', and complains of not having eaten and of how much he has suffered. But his expression suddenly changes and he stops crying when he hears the sounds of Yasha playing billiards. In Act IV Gayev even seems to have caught some of Anya's optimism at the prospect of a new life:

> GAYEV [*brightly*]. So it is indeed, everything's all right now. Before the cherry orchard was sold everybody was worried and upset, but as soon as it was all settled finally and once for all, everybody calmed down, and felt quite cheerful, in fact. . . . I'm an employee of a bank now, a financier. . . . I pot the red . . . and you, Lyuba, you're looking better, too, when all's said and done. There's no doubt about it.
> LYUBOV ANDREYEVNA. Yes, my nerves are better, it's true.
> [*Someone helps her on with her hat and coat.*]
> I'm sleeping better, too.

It is true that the brother and sister are allowed their emotional leave-taking of the house, but then they both go off to their different lives: Lyubov Andreyevna to her lover in Paris, and, symbolically, on money sent to redeem the estate to which she has no legal or moral right (in Act III she told us that the money had been sent to buy the estate in the aunt's name as she didn't trust them); money will also figure in Gayev's new life: he is to become a banker. Yet the improbability of such a career is suggested through oblique commentary. When Gayev first mentions the offer of this job in Act II his infantility is immediately stressed: Firs fusses over him with a coat. Moreover in the final act, as we have seen, Gayev refers to himself ironically as a financier, and adds a scrap of his perpetual play-talk: 'I pot the red'. In the leave-taking of these middle-aged children, one senses a pathos verging on the comic. It is aptly parodied in the clowning of Sharlotta:

> GAYEV. Sharlotta! She's singing.
> SHARLOTTA [*picks up a bundle that looks like a baby in swaddling clothes*]. Bye-bye, little baby. [*A sound like a baby crying is heard.*] Be quiet, my sweet, be a good little boy. [*The 'crying' continues.*] My heart goes out to you, baby! [*Throws the bundle down.*]⁴⁴

Hope seems to lie with the younger generation, represented by Anya (under the influence of Trofimov). For them the whole of Russia is their orchard, and an 'ill-defined attitude to the past' is no longer possible. Anya rejects all the nostalgic ties of the estate, when she tells Trofimov at the end of Act II: 'The house we live in hasn't really been ours for a long time. I'll leave it, I give you my word.' But the ties of the past are ambiguous; its associations are also painful. Anya's mother had left the estate, in order never to see again the river where her little son had drowned. Anya ends Act II with a gesture of defiance, not only escaping from Varya, but more importantly exorcising spectres of the past: 'Let us go to the river. It's nice [i.e. 'good'*] there.'

In the final act Anya and Trofimov make their farewells with the minimum of emotion: ANYA. 'Good-bye, old house! Good-bye, old life!' TROFIMOV. 'Greetings to the new life!' [*Goes out with* ANYA]. Gayev and Lyubov Andreyevna are left for their last tearful scene together, but their emotional farewell to their past is punctuated by happy calls from off-stage (together with the enigmatic 'Ah-oo'):[45] ANYA'S VOICE [*gaily*]. 'Mamma!' TROFIMOV'S VOICE [*gaily and excitedly*]. 'Ah-oo!' These calls are repeated a second time, before the older couple finally depart.

In *The Cherry Orchard* Chekhov brings his theatre of action without overt drama to its perfection. No one is killed, and, unlike the other three plays, no shots are fired either on or off-stage, even though Act II opens with Sharlotta carrying a sporting gun and Yepikhodov revealing that he has a revolver, about which he makes dark hints.[46] As in the other plays drama inheres in the ready-made situation around which each act is built. For the most part, we have seen these situations before: arrival, departure, frustrated or misplaced festivities.

The first act opens not unlike *Uncle Vanya* — with a servant and a friend of the family in conversation as they await the appearance of the family itself. But in *The Cherry Orchard* Lopakhin is waiting for a genuine homecoming, and the natural excitement which this event generates is sufficient to sustain the impetus of a whole act. There are discordant notes beneath the surface but what omens there are all seem to augur well. Thus, as in *The Seagull*, the dogs have been barking all night, but Dunyasha interprets this as a sign that they know that the masters are coming. When she herself breaks a saucer (because of Yasha's advances), the usually strict housekeeper Varya says that it is a good sign; even the 'ghost' which Lyubov Andreyevna sees in the garden brings a moment of happiness, and the act ends on a peaceful, pastoral note, with a shepherd off-stage playing a reed pipe.

At first sight the set for Act II appears to be carrying on the pastoral theme, but there are disturbing features in this natural setting: a derelict shrine; large, old gravestones; and a well (which on land once used for burial can hardly indicate springs of purity).[47] There is decay at the heart of this pastoral, and indeed it is almost immediately after Gayev's apostrophising of Nature that the ominous sound of the breaking string is heard. This, in turn, is followed by a portent of dispossession. A shabby stranger passes through the estate, much as the wandering musicians had walked through the Prozorov's garden in *The Three Sisters*. Although it is Varya who appears to be most affected (just as it is Anya who cries after the sound of the breaking string), nevertheless this figure of a 'gentleman' who has seen better days has most relevance for Gayev.[48] It is he who gives him directions and is rewarded by a poetic declamation, which seems a comic echo of his own earlier declamation to Nature.[49] The stranger's scraps of recitation are both about suffering. In the first he almost appears to be addressing Gayev himself: 'Oh, my brother, my suffering brother', whereas the second is about the universal suffering of the peasants.[50] The stranger is drunk and he wants to go to the station. Gayev's first words in Act II had been to comment on the convenience of the railway for going to the town to eat at a restaurant and he had been reproved by his sister for drinking too much and for making speeches. The shabby stranger can be seen as a premonition of the possible future awaiting Gayev himself.

Despite the would-be pastoral setting for Act II, the town itself is mentioned in the opening stage directions: [*Further away is seen a line of telegraph poles, and beyond them, on the horizon, the vague outlines of a large town, visible only in very good, clear weather*].

The suggestive detail of these directions reveals Chekhov the short-story writer rather than the practical dramatist. It is difficult to carry out these instructions to the letter. The town is more a presence which can be vaguely sensed, and amid these natural surroundings such a presence is a threat; for it is from the town that the new owners of little *dachas* will come, transported by the same railway which Gayev now finds so convenient for his trips of self-indulgence.[51] The telegraph poles are another mark of the modern world. They, too, are a threat: they carry telegrams summoning Lyubov Andreyevna back to Paris.

Act II is, therefore, full of omens. There are the guns displayed at its opening; there is Lyubov Andreyevna's sense of impending disaster: 'I keep expecting something dreadful to happen . . . as if the house were going to fall down on us.' Yet in terms of real action nothing dramatic happens, and the act ends with the undoing of omens on the part of the younger generation. Anya rejects the ancestral home and Trofimov tells her that if she has any keys she should throw them into the well — a symbolic act against the spiritual values of a poisoned past. Anya approves of his suggestion and they both happily flee to the river where her brother was drowned.

Like Acts II of both *Uncle Vanya* and *The Three Sisters*, the third act of *The Cherry Orchard* is centred on would-be festivity. The opening stage directions call for light, music and movement, but they also convey a sense of misplaced celebration through the way in which Varya is to be portrayed: [*Varya cries quietly, and wipes away her tears as she dances*]. Here is an ambiguity of mood which will be picked up later in the arrival of Gayev with his tears and his purchases of *hors d'oeuvre*.

Festive entertainment is the dominant motif of the act, but it is all somehow wrong. Lyubov Andreyevna comments: 'The band came at the wrong time, and the party started at the wrong time' (literally 'We, too, have inopportunely contrived a ball'*). The festive mood is all an illusion: the music comes from the local Jewish orchestra (four fiddles, a flute and a double bass); guests of no consequence have been drummed up merely for the numbers; billiards are being played — but only by the servants (Yepikhodov breaks a cue and Yasha appears to have usurped the role of Gayev at the billiard table). The entertainments of Sharlotta, conjuring tricks and ventriloquy, emphasise illusion,[52] and the recitation, which the station master begins, proclaims celebration, but suggests the price of sin: 'Seething people, gaiety, laughter. /The ring of lutes and thunder of cymbals./ All around greenery and flowers'. These are the opening lines which Chekhov's stage directions seem to require, but unlike his use of quotations elsewhere, Chekhov only gives the title (literally 'The Sinful Woman' — *Greshnitsa*):[53]

> [*The* STATION-MASTER *stands in the middle of the ballroom and begins to recite* 'The Sinner' *by Aleksey Tolstoy. The others listen, but he has hardly had time to recite more than a few lines when the sound of a waltz reaches them from the hall, and the recitation breaks off.*]

A poem with this title, recited immediately after Lyubov Andreyevna's teasing defence of love to Trofimov, seems like another instance of Chekhovian indirect commentary, and it picks up a motif present in the two preceding acts. Thus much to the embarrassment of his nieces, her own brother had condemned Lyubov Andreyevna (towards the end of Act I):

> GAYEV. She's a good, kind, lovable person, and I'm very fond of her, but whatever extenuating circumstances you may think of, you must admit that she's a bit easy-going morally. You can sense it in every movement.[54]

Lyubov Andreyevna herself refers to her 'sins' in a long speech in Act II, and asks God to forgive her: 'Oh, Lord, Lord, be merciful, forgive me my sins! Don't punish me any more!' She castigates herself for many 'sins', but she begins with her financial shortcomings: 'Oh, my sins! Look at the way I've always squandered money, continually. It was sheer madness.' The end of this speech is interrupted by the distant sounds of the Jewish orchestra, the very same (as Chekhov stresses in his opening stage directions), which is now playing in Act III; so that, through its title, the opening lines of *The Sinful Woman* appear to link celebration with the specific 'sin' of profligacy: the hiring of the Jewish orchestra.

Lyubov Andreyevna's festivities are entirely misplaced; the 'music' is not really for her, but for Lopakhin who enters towards the end of the act and announces that he has bought the estate:

> Hi! you musicians, come on now, play something, I want some music! Now then, all of you, just you wait and see Yermolay Lopakhin take an axe to the cherry orchard, just you see the trees come crashing down! We're going to build a whole lot of new villas, and our children and great-grandchildren are going to see a new living world growing up here. . . . Come on there, let's have some music!

The Cherry Orchard follows both *Uncle Vanya* and *The Three Sisters* in basing its final act on departure and, as in the earlier plays, this final act is the undoing of the implications of Act I. The opening words of the stage directions take us straight back to the starting point: [*The same setting as for Act I*]. Yet the set is not the same: there are no curtains at the windows, no pictures, and what furniture there is has been piled into one corner as though waiting to be sold.

The parallels between this final act and Act I are striking: in both Lopakhin talks of leaving by train for Kharkov and keeps looking at his watch; in both Yasha is told that his mother is waiting to see him, but is obviously reluctant to see her; in both the characters comment on the cold; and both arrival in Act I and departure in Act IV leave the stage empty for a short time, but the locking of doors in Act IV contradicts the opening of windows in Act I. The play had opened with Lopakhin unintentionally left behind in the house, while the others had gone to the station. Then unrequited love had been lightly adumbrated as a comic theme in the relationship between Dunyasha and Yepikhodov, who hands her a bouquet of flowers (which he has just dropped), but says that the gardener has sent them to be placed in the drawing room. He mentions that the cherry trees are in blossom in spite of three degrees of frost. Towards the end of Act IV there is the non-proposal of Lopakhin to Varya in which three degrees of frost seem to assume a certain symbolic significance for their relationship.[55] But the person left behind at the end is not Lopakhin — it is Firs. Lopakhin and Firs are in this and other respects antithetical characters: both are peasants but one represents the old life, the other the new possibilities. The parallelism with Firs also points to the true nature of Lopakhin's inhibitions concerning the marriage which has been arranged for him.

Lopakhin broaches the subject of his marriage at the very opening of the play, but it is a symbolic utterance, a saying which he attributes to Lyubov Andreyevna. He describes how his drunken father had once beaten him as a boy and had burst his nose, but that Lyubov Andreyevna had taken him inside and washed him, saying: 'Don't cry, little peasant, It'll be better before you're old enough to get married' [literally 'it will heal before your wedding'*]. But for Lopakhin the wounds of the past life have never really healed — in spite of everything he feels he is still 'a little peasant', and Lyubov Andreyevna, although she may not intend it, is herself helping to keep these wounds open.

We have seen how in the opening act, she makes no comment on his confession of affection and his feeling that she is *rodnaya*, and when in Act II Lyubov Andreyevna criticises him for his way of life and his opinions, Lopakhin once more returns to the subject of his drunken peasant father and his terrible upbringing. At this Lyubov Andreyevna bluntly suggests that he should marry her adopted daughter Varya, stressing that she is of the right social origins: — 'She comes from the common folk, and she's a hard-working girl: she can work the whole day without stopping.'

Shortly after this Firs enters and Lopakhin, in repeating the words just uttered by Lyubov Andreyevna to the deaf old man, gets an unexpected reply: LOPAKHIN. 'They say, you've aged a lot.' FIRS. 'I've been alive a long time. They were going to marry me off before your Dad was born.' [*Laughs.*] Once more the question of marriage is obliquely linked to Lopakhin's origins — his father, but Firs is talking about enforced peasant marriage before the emancipation.[56] Lopakhin teases him about the 'good old days': 'Oh, yes, it was a good life all right! At least, people got flogged!' Firs again mishears, but his reply only serves to confirm Lopakhin's point about the status of the peasant in the old days (while further suggesting the ambiguity of Lopakhin's present social position):

FIRS. [*not having heard him*]. Rather! The peasants belonged to the gentry, and the gentry belonged to the peasants; but now everything's separate, and you can't understand anything.[57]

Later, after giving money to the vagrant, Lyubov Andreyevna asks Lopakhin for a further loan. Then, virtually in the next breath, she tells Varya that she has arranged her marriage, and congratulates her. Varya is in tears at her lack of tact; it is as though she is being given away for money. Lopakhin, too, seems embarrassed, at least he counters by showing off his 'culture' in a cruel jibe: 'Okhmeliya, get thee to a nunnery.'* The quotation, though inaccurate, is apt.[58] But the suggestion that Varya might be better suited to a religious life is one made not only by Lyubov Andreyevna but also by Varya herself.[59]

In Act III Lyubov Andreyevna explains to Varya that no one is forcing her to marry Lopakhin, but the phrase she uses: 'No one's trying to force you'* (*nikto ne nevolit*) semantically evokes the spectre of serfdom (i.e. *nevolya*). Here, as elsewhere, there is an 'ill-defined attitude to the past', a submerged suggestion of the old ways: the marrying of serfs according to their masters' wishes.[60] Indeed in Act IV Lyubov Andreyevna says that she is leaving with two cares on her mind, and both of them seem almost feudal. The first is care of the ailing Firs (and we see how well she copes with that); the second is to make arrangements for Varya. She prevails on Lopakhin to propose before she leaves, and he admits to feeling that once Lyubov Andreyevna has left he will not be able to do so. The fact that Yasha has already drunk up the champagne does not augur well for a celebration. When Lopakhin is confronted with Varya, he is unable to bring himself to propose.

A certain lack of seriousness in Lopakhin's relationship with Varya is suggested in Act I when he suddenly peers round the door at Varya and Anya and makes a mooing sound, to which Varya responds with a tearful threat of violence.[61] Later in the same act she 'crossly' tells him that it is time he left. Lopakhin's jibe about Ophelia in Act II hits very near the mark, and her obvious distress ('He scared me, my heart is beating so') may not be entirely due to the encounter with the shabby stranger.[62]

When in Act III she aims a blow at Lopakhin, mistaking him for Yepikhodov, the directions indicate that, at first, she apologises [*angrily and sarcastically*] and when Lopakhin announces that he has bought the estate, Varya demonstratively throws her keys on the floor and walks out. It is clear that throughout the play there is constant tension between the couple. The adopted daughter's displays of anger stem from insecurity: in each case there lies behind them a linking of Lopakhin to the fate of the household. The self-made man Lopakhin, for his part, will not necessarily do what is expected of him, particularly if there is pressure from a lady for whom he entertains such ambiguous feelings, as he does for Lyubov Andreyevna.[63]

Lopakhin is one of the most interesting characters in the play. He has been given certain autobiographical features; for like the author he is the son of a petty shopkeeper, whose grandfather was a serf; like him he had an unpropitious childhood, but has made his own way in the world. Lopakhin's success, of course, has been in business but he also has certain pretensions to culture. At the opening of the play he has a book which he was trying to read before he fell asleep. In Act II he mentions a play which he has seen (though it might only be a vaudeville). He also 'quotes' from *Hamlet*. At the same time he is aware of his own lack of education and of his terrible handwriting. Trofimov comments that he has fingers like an artist, and that he has a subtle and gentle soul. Nor is Lopakhin blind to beauty; he speaks enthusiastically of the poppy crop which he sowed in the spring. Here was beauty which he created, but beauty, which unlike the cherry orchard, could also be made to yield a profit. Besides the man of practical affairs there is also something of the idealist in Lopakhin, and Trofimov is perhaps right in suggesting that he goes too far in believing that the *dacha* owners will one day engage in productive farming.

Gayev calls him a boor, and there are certainly aspects of his behaviour which might suggest this. In Act III he displays insensitivity when he boasts to its owners of having bought their estate, and a lack of tact in Act IV, when he allows his workmen to start felling the orchard before the family has left.[64] Yet, as we have seen, Lyubov Andreyevna is not always tactful in her dealings with Lopakhin, and her brother at times is down-right rude.

Lopakhin's delight in purchasing the estate is understand-able. He, too, has his ghosts, and his speech in Act III picks up many of the points made by Trofimov about the evils of serfdom:

> LOPAKHIN. Don't laugh at me! If only my father and grandfather could rise from their graves and see everything that's happened . . . how their Yermolay, their much-beaten, half-literate Yermolay, the lad that used to run about with bare feet in the winter . . . how he's bought this estate, the most beautiful place on God's earth! Yes, I've bought the very estate where my father and grandfather were serfs, where they weren't even admitted to the kitchen!

The old order has certainly changed. Lopakhin, the new owner of the cherry orchard will have none of the old manorial life, but the axes which ring out its destruction in the final act have a particularly ominous sound for a Russian audience — the axe was the traditional weapon of peasant rebellion: 'Your play can be called a terrifying, bloody drama, which God preserve, if it should ever break out. How awful and terrifying it is when the muffled strokes of axes ring out off-stage.'[65] The curtain falls on three different but equally potent symbols of change: Firs left behind, forgotten in the deserted house; the ring of axes outside; and once more the strange sound of the breaking string.

Chekhov called *The Cherry Orchard* a comedy but it is not a comedy with a happy ending. Two years before his death, Chekhov told a young student:

> You say that you have wept over my plays. Yes, and not only you alone. But I did not want to write them for this purpose, it is Alekseyev who has made such crybabies out of them. I wanted something different. I only wished to tell people honestly: 'look at yourselves, see how badly and boringly you live!' The principal thing is that people should understand this, and when they do, they will surely create for themselves another and a better life. I will not see it, but I know it will be entirely different, not like what we have now. And as long as it does not exist, I'll continue to tell people: See how badly and boringly you live! Is it that which they weep over?[66]

Here is Chekhov himself speaking with the voice of Trofimov; here too is Lopakhin telling Lyubov Andreyevna: 'Oh, if only we could be done with all this, if only we could alter this distorted unhappy life somehow!' At the same time it is also Lyubov Andreyevna reproaching Lopakhin: 'I'm sure it wasn't at all amusing. Instead of going to see plays, you should take a good look at yourself. Just think what a drab kind of life you lead, what a lot of nonsense you talk!'[67] The play's sympathies are far from one-sided, and it is given to Lyubov Andreyevna to utter the words which Chekhov himself could well have taken as an epigraph for his 'comedy'.

CONCLUSION

THE CHEKHOVIAN PLAY is a logical and coherent development of a tendency dominant in the Russian theatre (and, indeed, in the novel) to concentrate interest less on plot than on portraiture, psychology and ideas. Chekhov's art is unmistakably Russian: the apparent directness of his naturalism is conditioned by the reflexes of a culture whose traditional symbol, the icon, unites simplicity of form with 'meaning beyond', and whose literature, under the straight rod of censorship, has adopted oblique subtlety as its second nature.

Like all Russian writers Chekhov is steeped in the literature of his own country. He uses literary allusion along with sounds, symbols and a whole range of non-verbal devices to add unexpected dimension to the flat prose of everyday life. His plays are clear, unassuming prisms which concentrate light on the banal and the commonplace, yet tinge them with multi-coloured edges. But such an art requires a sophisticated audience, with wide literary sympathies; for Chekhov quotes not only from Russian literature, but also from that of Western Europe. One of the first and most evocative of such allusions, the *Hamlet* motif in *The Seagull*, launches a theme of central importance for Chekhov's theatre; for, in different ways, each of his major plays is concerned with usurpation.

In *The Seagull*, itself, usurpation is that of the realm of art, but Treplev's frustrated struggle to replace Trigorin, yields to a deeper level of the theme: the usurpation by art of life itself. In *Uncle Vanya* the disputed realm is science (*nauka* — in the broader sense in which it is used in Russian). The wealth of the estate and the energies of its custodians have been diverted to support the false man of science, the bogus authority,

Serebryakov, whose social origins and implied concern for issues such as female emancipation seem to have promised more, in terms of intellectual leadership, than the barren aestheticism which is the reality of his time-serving academic career. Those who have long laboured to support him have now grown disillusioned with his peevish self-centredness, and the true 'man of science' in the play is the hard working Dr Astrov with his profound concern at man's usurpation as a profligate steward in the estate of nature.

In these first two plays the theme is presented more in terms of generations: the young against the middle-aged; the middle-aged against the elderly. The last two plays explore usurpation as a social phenomenon. In *The Three Sisters* the parvenu philistinism of Natasha and Protopopov ousts the cultured values of a privileged military caste, represented by the Prozorov family. At the same time the play communicates a sense of unease at these values, which are those of a family living in the past, and only capable of seeing the future as a return to lost roots; a family for whom the reticence of 'good manners' prevents meaningful action — above all when the 'honour' of the military ethic leads to pointless tragedy. In *The Cherry Orchard* the social clash is even more explicit, and now the parvenu usurper Lopakhin receives something nearer to positive endorsement. Indeed, the question of social and intellectual leadership adumbrated in *Uncle Vanya* is here thrown into new prominence, and with it the theme of the generations assumes more specific social and political colouration.

The literary ghost haunting Chekhov's portrayal of his feckless, inadequate characters is Goncharov's hero Oblomov. Not surprisingly, Chekhov objected to such comparisons and his energetic denial of a preoccupation with 'Oblomovism' is not unlike the reaction of Dostoyevsky when charged with a contrary obsession (that he was too interested in 'morbid manifestations of the will'). With equal justice Chekhov might also claim that the real point was not 'interest' but 'exposure'. Nevertheless, the Oblomov of Goncharov's novel is at once both a negative and a sympathetic character, and a similar ambiguity inheres in all Chekhov's 'Oblomovs'. Indeed, who are the real usurpers, be it of art, science or social hegemony? Are the usurpers those in power, or those who seek to replace them? This question, although clearly posed, is never unambiguously answered.

For the present enacted on stage the past casts a long shadow, the future a bright but fitful light. But if it is part of Chekhov's point that his characters have 'no clearly defined attitude to the past', their anticipation of the future is no less ambiguous. Are they serious in their hopes and their strivings, or is it just 'philosophising' or a mere comforting delusion — the dream's usurpation of renounced reality?

Usurpation, which is Chekhov's central theme, is also in a sense his method. The primacy of action in the plays is challenged and replaced by what could well be considered less legitimate theatrical matter — a range of symbolic and allusive devices more conducive to reflection than to pure drama. Thus mood encroaches on the functioning of plot, conversation stands in for action, and direct statement is replaced by indirect commentary. Indeed, *The Cherry Orchard* takes substitution a stage further by embodying the faults of Lyubov Andreyevna in the characters who surround her.

The two stages which confront the audience at the opening of *The Seagull*, and the two concepts of theatre which they represent, are posed by Treplev as being incompatible. Yet to the audience itself one can be seen to embrace the other. Here is a metaphor for the ambivalence of Chekhov's own dramatic art, in which the symbolism of the inner stage derives from the conventional naturalism of the outer, each relying on the other, so that 'usurpation' by each of the province of the other is virtually complete. As in the image of the double stage, the poles of other contradictions are also contained one within the other in a state of mutual usurpation: negative characters bathe in positive sympathy; laughter emerges *'through tears'*; and the banality of ordinary everyday existence is transcended by eternal truth.

The structure of each play is tight. Lines that appear tangential, even incongruous, are in fact inward-referring and congruent. On the other hand, allusion charges the plays with meaning that is not fully stated. Thus there is a personal element submerged in the plays. Trigorin and Treplev seem to reflect an artistic debate going on within Chekhov himself, and his commonsense doctors (Dorn and Astrov) hint at another aspect of self-identification. Nevertheless, in the recurrent motif of the love of an older man for a young woman (Trigorin/ Nina; Serebryakov/Yelena; Voynitsky/Yelena; Vershinin/Masha) literature seems to have prefigured life. The theme is absent from his last play, written after his marriage to Olga Knipper. Not only did Chekhov portray friends and acquaintances in his plays, but it is also clear that at times he used them as the vehicle for private jokes.

Whatever may have been the private springs which fed Chekhov's art — however ordinary and unelevated in appearance the nature of his dramatic material; despite even the undoubted 'Russianness' of his characters and themes — it is nevertheless beyond dispute that his theatrical genius transcends that which is merely personal, commonplace, topical or even narrowly national. His plays reach out to a world-wide audience, to whom they speak of problems, relationships and values which are eternal, and thus his appeal is universal.

NOTES

REFERENCES to Chekhov's works are to the Academy of Sciences edition: A. P. Chekhov, *Polnoye sobraniye sochineniy i pisem v tridtsati tomakh*, Moscow, 1974 onwards. For convenience this edition will be recorded as: *PSS*, followed by a volume number in Roman and a page reference in Arabic numerals, but as the volumes devoted to letters are numbered independently, reference to these volumes will have the indication '(Letters)' before the Roman numeral.

INTRODUCTION

1. M. Valency, *The Breaking String: The Plays of Anton Chekhov*, New York, 1966, p. 17 (cf. also *ibid*. p. 222).

2. Cf. Francis Fergusson, '*The Cherry Orchard*: A Theatre-Poem of the Suffering of Change', in *Chekhov, A Collection of Critical Essays,* ed. R. L. Jackson, Englewood Cliffs, New Jersey, 1967, p. 152.

3. Harvey Pitcher, *The Chekhov Play*, London, 1973, p. 78.

4. *Ibid*. pp. 4, 214.

5. Nils Ake Nilsson denies any significance other than compositional to such remarks. See his 'Intonation and Rhythm in Chekhov's Plays' in Jackson, pp. 172–3. Valency, however, considers that 'it is seldom that the associative links are entirely lacking', but adds: 'It is entirely probable that the seemingly disjunctive nature of Chekhov's dialogue reflects his own habit of mind.' See Valency, p. 237. Pitcher considers such speech habits a trait common to Russians. See Pitcher, p. 28.

6. 'During the pauses it is as though inaudible words are carried across the stage on light wings', Yu. Aykhenval'd (quoted in *PSS*, XIII, p. 510).

7. K. S. Stanislavsky, *Moya zhizn' v iskusstve*, Moscow, 1962, p. 328.

8. Cf. Chekhov's long letter to Suvorin on *Ivanov* (30 Dec. 1888) *PSS* (Letters), III, pp. 108–16.

9. Valency, p. 45.

10. Styan, however, sees Voynitsky's surprising of the 'amorous' scene between Astrov and Yelena as 'a grotesque stage trick'. See J. L. Styan, *Chekhov in Performance. A Commentary on the Major Plays,* Cambridge, London, New York, Melbourne, 1971, p. 126.

11. Harvey Pitcher denies 'lack of communication' as a theme in Chekhov's

plays. See Pitcher, p. 25.

12. Cf. I. S. Turgenev, *Polnoye sobraniye sochineniy i pisem v dvadtsati vos'mi tomakh* (*Sochineniya*) III, Moscow, 1962, pp. 75–6.

13. *Ya vas lyublyu (k chemu lukavit'?)*
     No ya drugomu otdana,
     Ya budu vek yemu verna.
     Cf. Turgenev, *Poln. sob. soch.* (*Soch.*), III, p. 58. Pushkin's 'Novel in Verse' is itself full of literary allusions. For Russians literary echoes not only permeate literature, they also permeate life. See Peace, *Russian Literature and the Fictionalisation of Life*, Hull, 1976.

14. In Ostrovsky's play *The Forest* an actor manages to pass an outspoken judgement on local society by reciting a speech from Schiller's *Die Räuber*, and cannot be brought to account because, as he says, it has been passed by the censor. See A. N. Ostrovsky, *Polnoye sobraniye sochineniy v dvenadtsati tomakh*, Moscow, 1974, III, p. 337.

15. Styan, p. 339.

16. For the influence of Gogol on Chekhov see Peace, *The Enigma of Gogol, An Examination of the Writings of N. V. Gogol and their Place in the Russian Literary Tradition*, Cambridge, 1981, pp. 52, 89, 150, 191, 204, 247, 299, 321 n. 31, 330 n. 38, 337 n. 16.

17. See *Russkaya literatura XVIII veka*, compiled by G. P. Makogonenko, Leningrad, 1970, p. 290. Rayfield compares *Platonov* with *The Brigadier*. See D. Rayfield, *Chekhov: The Evolution of his Art*, London, 1975, p. 98 (but cf. Platonov's own rejection of the 'raisonneur' figures of Fonvizin, *PSS*, XI, p. 38).

18. Makogonenko, pp. 495–6. The following part of this exchange seems particularly pointed semantically:
     KRIVOSUDOV. But I fobbed him off. He would have gone on with a whole lot of improbable things about the case, but I shut him up.
     NAUMYCH [*to FEKLA*]. A pound of mustard.
     KRIVOSUDOV. I got him off my hands.
     NAUMYCH. How much, sir, my master to you is indebted [*to* FEKLA] a skirt length of silk.*

19. A. S. Dolinin (quoted in *PSS*, XII, p. 368; cf. also *ibid.* p. 316).

20. Rayfield, p. 94.

21. J. Tulloch, *Chekhov: A Structuralist Study*, London and Basingstoke, 1980, pp. 7, 90.

22. *PSS*, XII, p. 56.

23. Cf. Rayfield, p. 101. Chekhov spoke to V. G. Korolenko of writing a drama to be called *Ivan Ivanovich Ivanov* — 'you understand. There are thousands of Ivanovs, an ordinary man, absolutely not a hero . . .', *PSS*, XII, p. 412. Chekhov also commented: 'The word Russian often crops up when I describe Ivanov.' See *The Oxford Chekhov*, trans. and edit. Ronald Hingley, London, New York, Toronto, 1967, II, p. 295.

24. *PSS*, XII, pp. 29–30.

25. *Ibid.* p. 37.

26. His uncle Shabel'sky says that he himself played at being Chatsky as a young man, *PSS*, XII, p. 33. Rayfield notes the influence of *Woe from Wit* on both *Platonov* and *Ivanov*. See Rayfield, p. 98.

27. *PSS*, XII, p. 38.

28. *Ibid.* p. 72.

29. *Ibid.* p. 57.

30. *Ibid.* p. 59.

31. *Ibid.* p. 250 (cf. Hingley on Chekhov's 'endearing distrust of clichés and literary stereotypes', *The Oxford Chekhov*, II, p. 6).

32. *PSS*, XII, p. 71.

33. Cf. *ibid.* pp. 50, 54–6.

34. *PSS* (Letters), III, p. 111 (a somewhat similar view on the Russian as a sieve was expressed to Gorky. See Jackson, p. 202).

35. N. A. Dobrolyubov, *Sobraniye sochineniy*, Moscow 1935, I, pp. 183–4 (cf. also the use of Dobrolyubov's term 'A Realm of Darkness' — *temnoye tsarstvo* — in *Ivanov*, *PSS*, XII, p. 34).

36. *PSS*, XII, p. 33.

37. *PSS* (Letters), III, p. 132.

38. *Ibid.* p. 421.

39. *Ibid.* pp. 201–2, 203.

40. *PSS*, XII, p. 165.

41. *PSS* (Letters), VIII, pp. 319, 596 and *PSS*, XIII, pp. 419, 459.

42. *PSS* (Letters), XI, p. 142.

43. Valency, p. 246.

44. *PSS* (Letters), II, pp. 332, 512.

45. Ye. M. Saltykov-Shchedrin, *Sobraniye sochineniy v dvadtsati tomakh*, Moscow, 1976, XVI(1), p. 197.

46. I. A. Goncharov, *Sobraniye sochineniy v shesti tomakh*. Moscow, 1972, IV, p. 510.

47. Cf. Stanislavsky, *Moya Zhizn'*, p. 275 and Vs. Meyerhold, 'Naturalistic Theater and Theater of Mood', Jackson, pp. 62–8.

48. Stanislavsky, *Moya Zhizn'*, p. 329.

49. Vl. Prokof'ev, *V sporakh o Stanislavskom*, Moscow, 1976, p. 86.

50. Valency, p. 298.

51. 'Written after a vow not to work for the theatre again, it is an act of vengeance', Rayfield, p. 202.

THE SEAGULL

1. I have amended Fen's 'at half-past nine' (cf. *PSS*, XIII, p. 7: '*rovno v polovine devyatogo*').

2. This is a literal rendering of the Polevoy translation of *Hamlet* used in the text (*PSS*, XIII, p. 12). The original is:

    QUEEN. O Hamlet, speak no more:

Thou turns't mine eyes into my very soul;
And there I see such black and grained spots
As will not leave their tinct.
HAMLET. Nay but to live
In the rank sweat of an enseamed bed
Stewed in corruption, honeying and making love
Over the nasty sty (Act. III, sc. iv).

This is quoted correctly by Hingley p. 74, but Fen gives Treplev's reply as: 'And let me wring thy heart, for so I shall,/ If it be made of penetrable stuff' (Fen. p. 128).

Polevoy's translation of *Hamlet* was not the only one available to Chekhov, but it was the only one which softened Hamlet's reply to his mother. See Thomas G. Winner, 'Chekhov's *Seagull* and Shakespeare's *Hamlet*: A Study of Dramatic Device', *American Slavic and East European Review*, 1956, XV, pp. 106–7.

3. There is also a premonition of Treplev's suicide; for the '*Hamlet* question' meant 'to be or not to be' in Russia. See James H. Billington, *The Icon and the Axe: An Interpretive History of Russian Culture*, New York, 1966, p. 354.

4. *PSS*, XIII, p. 36. 'but all the same, he does feel in a way that he doesn't belong here, that he's a cadger, living on charity. It's not to be wondered at — he's got pride' (Fen. p. 155).

5. Rudin distinguishes between 'self-respect' (*samolyubiye*) and 'self-love' (*sebyalyubiye*). The latter, he says, is suicide. Turgenev, *Poln. sob. soch (Soch.)*, VI, p. 267.

6. *PSS*, XIII, p. 9. 'in my passport I'm described as a member of the lower middle class, born in Kiev. Well, my father was a member of the petty bourgeoisie, as you know — although he was a well-known actor too — and his native town was Kiev' (Fen, p. 124).

7. Hingley translates the word as 'provincial shopkeeper', and thus provides Treplev with an identification which is more pointedly autobiographical. See *The Oxford Chekhov*, II, p. 236 (and note on p. 355).

8. *PSS*, XIII, p. 40. 'You're incapable of writing even a couple of miserable scenes! You're just a little upstart from Kiev! A cadger!' (Fen, p. 159).

9. I.e. '*syuzhet dlya nebol'shogo rasskaza*' (PSS, XIII, p. 31). The full irony of this phrase is lost in 'a subject (plot) for a short story' (Fen, p. 151; Hingley, p. 91).

10. Treplev says: 'You remember, in Pushkin's play *The River Nymph* the miller says he's a raven. So in the same way she kept calling herself "the seagull" in her letters.' c.f Pushkin, *Polnoye sobraniye sochineniy v desyati tomakh* (4th edit.), Leningrad, 1977–9, V, pp. 379–80. *The River Nymph* is, of course, Fen's translation of *Rusalka*, see n. 36 p. 167 below. Dargomyshky turned Pushkin's poem into an opera.

11. Guy de Maupassant, *Sur l'Eau*, (ed. E. Flammarion) Paris, 1925, p. 42.

12. *Ibid.* pp. 43–4. Maupassant is aware of his own 'rat-like' activities as a

writer (*ibid.* pp. 113, 115–16). There are many echoes in *Sur l'Eau* for Chekhov's play, e.g.: 'Comment se fait-il que le public du monde n'ait pas encore crié: "Au rideau" n'ait pas demande l'acte suivant avec d'autres êtres que l'homme, d'autres formes, d'autres fêtes, d'autres plantes, d'autres astres, d'autres inventions, d'autres aventures? (*ibid.* p. 59). Maupassant speculates on the moon, and the moon and poetry (*ibid.* pp. 99–107). A passage on the individual swamped in the crowd recalls the words of Dorn in Act IV about his experiences in Genoa (*ibid.* pp. 153–4) and there is an account of the effects of tuberculosis, which Chekhov must have read with interest (*ibid.* pp. 48–52).

13. Fen omits the stage direction. See also n. 9 above.

14. See E. J. Simmons, *Chekhov, A Biography*, London, 1963, pp. 287–9, 318, 321, 324–7, 330, 331, 352–4.

15. *Ibid.* pp. 252, 279, 331–3.

16. R. Hingley, *A New Life of Anton Chekhov*, London, Toronto, Melbourne, 1976, p. 198.

17. Simmons, pp. 340, 373–5.

18. Hingley, *New Life*, p. 196. Arkadina may have been based on the actress L. B. Yavorskaya, to whom Chekhov had promised a play entitled: *Dreams (Grezy)* (cf. the role of dreams in Treplev's play). See *PSS*, XIII, p. 360. Arkadina may also have been based on another actress, L. I. Ozerova, who in a letter to Chekhov of 27 February 1897 calls the play 'our *Seagull*' (*ibid.*). The name Ozerova recalls *ozero* — 'lake': a dominant symbol for art in the play. For a discussion of the symbolism of water in the play see Winner, pp. 105–6.

19. *PSS*, XIII, p. 29. 'As for the years when I was starting — my younger better years — in those days my writing used to be one continuous torment' (Fen, p. 148).

20. See Hingley, *New Life*, pp. 227–8.

21. *PSS* (Letters), I, p. 242.

22. See Simmons, p. 125.

23. 'These were the days of the seemingly incompatible twins Naturalism and Symbolism', P. Henry, Introduction to A. P. Chekhov, *The Seagull*, Letchworth, 1965, p. 11.

24. Guy de Maupassant, *La Vie Errante* (ed. E. Flammarion), Paris, 1925, p. 11.

25. *Ibid.*

26. See T. G. Masaryk, *The Spirit of Russia: Studies in History, Literature and Philosophy* (trans. Eden and Cedar Paul), London, 1968, II, p. 247.

27. *PSS*, XIII, p. 383.

28. Fen omits this last sentence, cf. *PSS*, XIII, p. 10.

29. *PSS*, XIII, p. 8. Fen renders this as 'squeezed out' (p. 123), Hingley has 'drag out' (p. 70). The fishing imagery is also found in *Hamlet*, cf. Polonius: 'Your bait of falsehood takes this carp of truth' (*Hamlet*, Act II, sc.i). In the next scene Hamlet calls him a 'fishmonger'. Other echoes of

Shakespeare's play may be seen in Trigorin's cloud shaped like a grand piano, (cf. the variously shaped cloud with which Hamlet 'falsely baits' Polonius (*ibid.* Act III, sc.ii). Pitcher also sees an amusing echo of Hamlet's 'inky cloak' in the play's opening lines on Masha's black dress (Pitcher, p. 46); cf. *Hamlet*, Act I, sc.ii.

30. *Vysokhlo, uteklo* (*PSS*, XIII, p. 27). Fen translates this as though the action were still in progress: 'drying up, draining away' (p. 145), Hingley has 'dried up', 'soaked into the ground' (p. 87).

   Although Treplev quotes Hamlet's: 'Words, words, words' on this occasion, another of his jibes from the same scene might also seem appropriate: 'Let her not walk i' the sun: conception is a blessing; but not as your daughter may conceive' *Hamlet*, Act II, sc.ii (cf. also Winner pp. 103–11).

31. As in the story *A Case History (Sluchay iz praktiki)* where the red eyes of the devil are also equated with materialism.

32. 'I don't want any, Mamma, I'm not hungry' (i.e. 'replete') (*ne khochu, mama, ya syt*). The adjective *sytyy* — 'satisfied', 'replete' relates to a secondary theme '*Sytyy chelovek*' ('satisfied man') which occurs in the arguments of Sorin with Dorn (Act II) and more ominously in this final act where it is related to the theme of death. The figure of Sorin, as will be seen, has relevance for the position of Treplev himself.

33. W. Gareth Jones, '*The Seagull's* Second Symbolist Play-within-the-Play', *Slavonic and East European Review*, LIII, No. 130, January 1975, pp. 7–22.

34. *PSS*, XIII, p. 54. Fen smooths this out: 'We've still got something of yours down here' (p. 176 — cf. 'We still have that thing of yours, Boris', Hingley, p. 115).

35. *PSS*, XIII, p. 59. 'It won't be very nice' (Fen, p. 182) should perhaps be stronger; i.e. *nekhorosho* = 'bad'. Hingley has: 'It'll be a pity' (p. 115).

36. Treplev's name suggests 'towsling', 'knocking about' (i.e. from verb *trepat'*). It seems significant that he himself uses this verb at the beginning of Act I to describe his mother's reputation — *imya yeye postoyanno treplyut v gazetakh* ('they constantly knock her name about in the papers', or as Fen and Hingley translate it: 'bandied about' (Fen, p. 123; Hingley, p. 70).

37. There is a suggestion of 'bear' in his name (*medved'* = 'bear').

38. *PSS*, XIII, p. 6. The translations smoothe out the linguistic peculiarity of '*indifferentizm*' a comically pretentious word, serving to characterise Medvedenko (e.g. 'indifference', Fen, p. 120; 'I just don't mean a thing to you', Hingley, p. 115). Fen translates six versts as 'six miles', Hingley is more accurate with 'four miles'.

39. *PSS*, XIII, p. 5. 'It isn't money that matters' (Fen, p. 119); 'Money doesn't matter' (Hingley, p. 67).

40. *PSS*, XIII, p. 12. I have preserved the original word order to convey Chekhov's irony. Arkadina's 'triumphs' are immediately placed a quarter of a century ago (for an audience in the late 1890s) and at a

provincial fair. Fen has: 'I remember I saw her play marvellously at the Poltava fair in '73'. A sheer delight. Marvellous acting' (Fen, pp. 127–8). A fair was held every year at Poltava in the Ukraine in July on the feast of Elijah the Prophet. Theatricals were just one of the many entertainments provided. See A. N. Ostrovsky, *Poln. sob. soch.*, III, pp. 272, 542.

41. E.g. V. Yermilov, who points out that the positive endorsement of Nina as an actress goes back to the first production and the interpretation of the role by Komissarzhevskaya (V. Yermilov, *Dramaturgiya Chekhova*, Moscow, 1954, p. 93). Aninka and Lyubinka in Saltykov's novel are considered as little better than prostitutes and are driven to attempt suicide by swallowing a brew made from phosphorous matches. See M. Ye. Saltykov-Shchedrin, *Sobraniye sochineniy v dvadtsati tomakh*, Moscow, 1972, XIII, pp. 233–47.

42. *PSS*, XIII, p. 17. Cf. 'You could hear a pin drop' (Fen, p. 134); 'You could have heard a pin drop' (Hingley, p. 244).

43. In Act II Dorn twice sings: 'Tell her, my flowers': at the beginning, after Masha's statement about the tragedy of her life; and on a second occasion when Masha's unhappiness appears to be linked with Nina's attraction to the town life of an actress. Shortly after this Nina presents Dorn with actual flowers, which Polina promptly destroys.

In Act IV Nina will look back at her life and describe her former feelings as 'flowers': 'How nice it all used to be, Kostya! Do you remember? How tranquil, warm, and joyous, and pure our life was, what feelings we had — like tender, exquisite flowers. . . . Do you remember?' Trigorin tells Nina in Act II: 'I feel as though I'm devouring my own life, that for the sake of the honey I give to all and sundry I'm despoiling my best flowers of their pollen, that I'm plucking the flowers themselves and trampling on their roots. Am I out of my mind?'

44. The name Sorin may be derived from *sorit'* — to squander (i.e. of money), *sornyak* is 'weed'.

45. In taking up with her his nephew's need for money, he is in a sense arguing his own case.

46. His denigration of Dorn's 'philosophy' also looks forward to a similar negative treatment of 'philosophy' in *The Three Sisters*.

UNCLE VANYA

1. For discussion of the writing of *Uncle Vanya* see *PSS*, XIII, pp. 387–92, and *The Oxford Chekhov*, II, p. 300. The play was printed in 1897 and various provincial theatres performed it before the Moscow Arts Theatre.

2. Notice of S. V. Flyerov-Vasil'ev (quoted in *PSS*, XII, p. 391).

3. Cf. the feelings of Chekhov himself at the height of the cholera epidemic of 1892: 'Not to belong to oneself, to think only of diarrhoea, and

shudder at night when the dogs bark and there's a knock at the gate (have they not come for me?).' Letter to A. S. Suvorin, 16 August 1892, *PSS* (Letters), V, p. 104.

4. (Telegin) *Yedu li ya po polyu, Mariya Timofeyevna, gulyayu li v tenistom sadu. Smotryu li na etot stol, ya ispytyvayu neiz asnimoye blazhenstvo.* Cf. Pushkin's poem of 1829: *Brozhu li ya vdol' ulits shumnykh/ Vkhozhu l' vo mnogolyudnyy khram/ Sizhu l' mezh yunoshey bezumnykh/ Ya predayus' moim mechtam* (Pushkin, *Poln, sob. soch.*, III, p. 130).

5. At the beginning of Act III — 'I've grown quite lazy, I can't help it! '(*oblenilas' ne mogu*). Cf. the root *len'* which is also found in Yelena's name, so that *oblenilas'* also suggests 'I have got like Lenya' (i.e. Yelena), *PSS*, XIII, p. 91.

6. *PSS*, XIII, p. 69. SONYA. 'That's splendid. It's so rare for you to stay the night with us. I don't suppose you've had dinner?' ASTROV. 'No, I haven't.' SONYA. 'Then you'll dine with us. We have dinner soon after six nowadays.' [*Drinks her tea.*] 'The tea's cold!' (Fen, p. 193). 'dinner' — *obed* — is the midday meal. In the aristocratic circles of St Petersburg, in Pushkin's time, it was often served at six o'clock, since they did not get up until midday.

7. They are the Christian name and patronymic of Oblomov.

8. Cf. Christopher Marlowe, *The Tragical History of Doctor Faustus*, Act V, sc.i.

9. *The Wood Demon*, Act IV, sc. ix. *PSS*, XII, p. 195. (Lacedaemonii is another name for Spartans).

10. Valency links this theme to Chekhov's own illness. See Valency, p. 198.

11. The same call: *tsyp, tsyp, tsyp* is used as open mockery of Tuzenbach by Solyony in *The Three Sisters*, Act III.

12. *PSS*, XIII, p. 70. Fen translates a 'writing *perpetuum mobile*' as 'a non-stop writer'; and *galka* (jackdaw), *PSS*, XIII, p. 67, as 'magpie' (Fen, p. 190).

13. The pause is omitted from Fen, p. 195 (cf. *PSS*, XIII, p. 71). The bird call actually used by Marina is *tsyp, tsyp, tsyp,* and although this is the same call used to mock Tuzenbach in Act I of *The Three Sisters* (*PSS*, XIII, pp. 129, 134) nevertheless in the later play Fen translates it as 'cluck, cluck' (pp. 260, 267).

14. *PSS*, XIII, p. 106. Cf. 'You old gander! Ga-ga-ga!' (Fen p. 235).

15. Ilya Serman, *Konstantin Batyushkov*, New York, 1974, p. 78. Magarshak, however, identifies the reference with F. Batyushkov, the Russian editor of *Cosmopolis*. See Magarshak, *The Real Chekhov*, p. 94. The identification is doubtful.

16. Marina tells us that Sonya's mother would not sleep at nights because she was worried about her husband's gout. Her daughter, however, needs her sleep to cope with work on the estate, and refuses to indulge her father's whims: 'And I haven't the time, I must get up early tomorrow — I've got to see to the haymaking' (*PSS*, XIII, p. 77). The thunderstorms must surely delay this, and later Sonya tells her uncle:

'All the hay has been cut, it rains every day, everything is rotting' (*ibid.* p. 82).

17. Quoted in *PSS*, XII, p. 397. Cf. also: 'One wants to call to the helm of power real workers and labourers, flourishing in obscurity and place them in high positions instead of the untalented but distinguished Serebryakovs', Stanislavsky, *Moya zhizn'*, p. 284.

18. *PSS*, XII, p. 392.

19. *Ibid.* p. 389.

20. *Ibid.* p. 412.

21. In *The Wood Demon*, Khrushchev (Astrov's forerunner) was outspoken in his criticism of Serebryakov, and his denunciation of his authority is an indictment of Russia itself: 'Therefore according to the opinion of the distinguished scholar and professor, I am mad. I bow before your excellency's authority and will immediately drive home, and shave my head. No, it is the land which still holds you which is mad' (*PSS*, XII, p. 178).

One of the actors, and a director of the Moscow Arts Theatre, A.A. Sanin regretted that the social element of the play had suffered in their production. See *PSS*, XII, p. 410.

22. The words spoken to the wicked stepmother by her mirror in Pushkin's tale about the Dead Princess and the Seven Knights (*Skazka o mertvoy tsarevne i semi bogatyryakh*). Later Astrov confesses that he is affected by beauty: 'What still does affect me is beauty. I can't remain indifferent to that' and he admits that the beauty of Yelena could turn his head.

23. Magarshak thinks that Act I is set in June, and Act II at the beginning of July. See Magarshak, *The Real Chekhov*, pp. 80–1.

24. Hingley, *New Life*, pp. 232–3. Further 'rat-like' features may be seen in the fact that Suvorin suspected that he himself had provided material for the portrayal of Professor Serebryakov in *The Wood Demon* (see Rayfield, pp. 105, 249 n. 4). Suvorin's wife saw *Uncle Vanya* as reflecting the relationships within her own family. After a performance by the Moscow Arts Theatre in St Petersburg, she wrote of the play to Chekhov (April 1903): 'I know it by heart and I constantly laugh. It produces reflection and melancholy in other people, but laughter in me, because I can hear and see very many of the people who are near to me' *PSS*, XIII, p. 392.

25. *'Brüderschaft'* is a mutual toast drunk by two acquaintances to mark a new intimacy, which, in particular, allows them to address one another as *ty* ('thou') as opposed to the more formal *vy* ('you').

26. He quotes the opening speech of Gogol's play *The Government Inspector*, which deals with the havoc created in the provinces by the advent of a bogus authority.

27. Selling the estate itself appears to replace the selling of a forest which was proposed in *The Wood Demon*. However, in *Uncle Vanya* Serebryakov mentions the possibility of selling a forest but rejects it. (Cf. *PSS*, XII, p. 177 and XIII, p. 99).

28. *PSS*, XIII, p. 104. SONYA [*softly*]. 'Nanny, dear, Nanny' (Fen, p. 233).

29.   *PSS*, XIII, p. 105. 'On the wall a map of Africa, obviously serving no useful purpose here' (Fen, p. 234).

30.   Quoted in *PSS*, XIII, p. 409. The map of Africa was connected in Chekhov's mind with Astrov's attitude to Yelena. In a letter to Olga Knipper he wrote that Astrov, realising that everything was over, should talk to Yelena in Act IV in the same tone as he talked about the heat in Africa. See 'Letter to Olga Knipper', 30 September 1899. *PSS* (Letters), VIII, p. 272. In 1893 Chekhov had written to Lika Mizinova: 'Money, Money. If I had money, I would go off to South Africa, about which I am now reading very interesting letters. One must have an aim in life, and when one travels one has an aim' (*PSS* (Letters), V. p. 224). Chekhov is probably referring to *Letters from Africa* by G. Sienkiewicz (*ibid*. p. 490). A detail in the irony of Goncharov's presentation of Oblomov is his 'reading' a travel book about Africa (I.A. Goncharov, *Sobraniye sochineniy v shesti tomakh*, Moscow, 1972, IV p. 176).

31.   *PSS*, XII, p. 182 Yelena also calls her lot 'a canary's happiness' (*schast'ye moye kanareyechnoye*), *ibid*. p. 195.

32.   *PSS*, XIII, p. 106. 'You shouldn't take any notice deary. We all live on God, You, and Sonya, and Ivan Petrovich are just the same — none of us sits with folded hands, we are all working — all of us!' (Fen, p. 235). *Prizhivaly* — 'hangers on' were a traditional feature of old fashioned country estates (cf. *Oblomov, Ibid*. pp. 110, 183).

33.   I.e. *Nado delo delat'* (Styan's gloss: 'work' is not entirely accurate. See Styan, pp. 137, 141). In a letter to Chekhov of 28 November 1899 Nemirovich-Danchenko commented on the audience's laughter at Serebryakov's words (*PSS*, XII, pp. 411–12). It must be borne in mind that the word *delo* in radical circles often had a revolutionary connotation.

34.   For a discussion of divergent critical views on this ending see Styan, pp. 140–1.

35.   In *The Wood Demon* one of the female characters, Yulya, is actually called 'uncle' (*dyadya*) by Fedor Ivanovich, to which she objects: 'I am not an uncle' (*ya ne dyadya*) (*PSS*, XII, p. 201). In this earlier play the forerunner of Telegin bears a surname derived from *dyadya* — Dyadin.

36.   *PSS*, XIII, p. 93. 'Uncle Vanya says I have mermaid's blood in my veins' (Fen, p. 221). The mythological creature in question is *rusalka* — a drowned maiden whose amorous advances had power to lure men to their deaths.

37.   *PSS*, XIII, p. 107. 'That's an old trick. You're not mad, you're simply a crank. A silly old fool. I used to think that every crank was sick or abnormal. But now I believe it's normal for a man to be a crank. You are perfectly normal' (Fen, p. 236).

38.   He alludes to Paratov, a character in Ostrovsky's play *A Bride without a Dowry (Bespridannitsa)* who characterises himself as 'a man with big moustaches and small abilities' (Ostrovsky, *Poln. sob. soch.*, V, p. 44). It is

interesting that 'cold tea' plays a comic role in this play too (it is really alcohol, *ibid*. p. 18) but tea-drinking is typical of the merchant milieu in which Ostrovsky sets his plays — indeed *chayepitiye* (tea-drinking) is almost synonymous with indolence.

39. Tulloch links Astrov's ideas to Chekhov's own 'environmentalist' approach to medicine. See Tulloch, pp. 5, 91.

40. Chekhov's word is 'pit' not 'well' (cf. *PSS*, XIII, p. 79; Fen, p. 205). Voynitsky's 'light' imagery seems to take up his retort to his mother in Act I that he was a radiant person who illuminated no one: '*O, da ya byl svetloyu lichnost'yu,ot kotoroy nikomu ne bylo svetlo* (*PSS*, XIII, p. 70); 'Oh, yes! I used to be an inspiring personality who never inspired anybody!' (Fen. p. 194).

41. *PSS*, XIII, p. 79. 'You are cultured and intelligent, Ivan Petrovich — surely you ought to realise that the world is being destroyed not by fire and pillage, but by hatred and enmity and all this petty quarrelling' (Fen, p. 205).

THE THREE SISTERS

1. Chekhov had already exploited the tensions beneath the surface of a name-day celebration in a story of 1888, *The Party* (*Imeniny*).

2. E.g. Valency, p. 219.

3. *Na dvore solnechno, veselo* (*PSS*, XIII, p. 119). The translations gloss this as: 'There is cheerful sunshine outside' (Fen, p. 249); 'outside the sun is shining cheerfully' (Hingley, p. 171).

4. Beverly Hahn sees snow 'taking on a steady conscious metaphoric force' in the early story *Misery (Toska)*. See Beverly Hahn, *Chekhov: A Study of the Major Stories and Plays*, Cambridge, London, New York, Melbourne, 1977, p. 60.

5. This is literally: 'A couple of devils' / 'Of course it's nonsense' (*PSS*, XIII, p. 120). Fen adds a stage direction (not in the original): [*To TUZENBACH*].

6. But Chekhov saw it as a sign of inward grief: 'People who have been carrying grief about inside them for a long time and have got used to it only whistle a bit, and are frequently lost in thought' (Letter to Olga Knipper, 2 January 1901, *PSS*, XIII, p. 442).

7. *Ya by lyubila muzha* (*PSS*, XIII, p. 122) — 'I would have been very fond of my husband' (Fen, p. 251).

8. L. N. Tolstoy, *Polnoye sobraniye sochineniy*, Moscow, 1928–58, X, pp. 153–4, 156–7.

9. Towards the end of Act I Irina links the fact that Masha is 'out of humour' to her marriage (*PSS*, XIII, p. 123). In Ostrovsky's play *The Bride without a Dowry* (see above pp. 167–8 n. 38) not only is there also a quotation from *Ruslan and Lyudmila*, but Paratov pointing to his wedding ring tells Larisa: 'There are the golden chains, by which I am shackled

for all my life' (Ostrovsky, *Poln. sob. soch.*, V, pp. 46, 76). *Lukomor'ye* ('bend in the sea') could be an oblique reference to Chekhov's own experience of provincial thraldom. Taganrog is situated on a great bend of the sea — the Sea of Azov. An earlier version of the play had Irina going to Taganrog, and this may have been the original impetus for the theme of 'Moscow' in the play (*PSS*, XIII, p. 426). Certain features of Kulygin derive from one of Chekhov's Taganrog teachers, V. K. Vinogradov (i.e. his becoming clean-shaven after his promotion, *ibid.* p. 424). But the character was most probably modelled on the actor cast to play the part, A. L. Vishnevsky. If this is so it is further evidence of the sort of Chekhovian humour at work in *The Seagull*. Commenting on this, L. A. Sulerzhitsky adds 'That's what it is to make friends with a writer' (*vot-te i druzhi s pisatelem*) (*ibid.* 424).

10. Rayfield likens the quotation to a rosary used by Masha in extreme anguish Rayfield, p. 218.

11. Cf. the title of Lermontov's play: *The Strange Man (Strannyy chelovek)* and the use of 'strange' in *The Hero of Our Time*. See M. Yu Lermontov, *Geroy nashego vremeni* (with an Introduction, Notes and Vocabulary by D. J. Richards), Letchworth, 1974, p. 183 n. 112.

   Solyony's name suggests the verb *nasolit'* — 'to spite, to annoy' (literally 'to over salt'). It seems significant that his first words in the play occur immediately after Tuzenbach's reference to the suicide attempts of Vershinin's wife in which the verb *nasolit'* is used to explain her motives ('apparently just to annoy her husband' — *ochevidno chtoby nasolit' muzhu*, *PSS*, XIII, p. 122. See p. 163 n. 36 above for a comparable semantic echo for the name Treplev.

12. It is not entirely clear for whom these remarks are meant. They could be addressed to Tuzenbach (who has just spoken) as a counter to his dismissive words to Chebutykin. (cf. Magarshak, *The Real Chekhov*, p. 131) or they could be intended for Chebutykin himself, even though his very next words show no reaction (cf. *PSS*, XIII, p. 431, and Styan p. 167).

13. This is not from *The Gipsies*.

14. Later he will again say: 'I have a triple-barrelled name — Baron Tuzenbach-Krone-Alschauer — but actually I'm a Russian. I was baptized in the Greek Orthodox faith, just like yourself. I haven't really got any German characteristics, except maybe the obstinate patient way I keep on pestering you. Look how I bring you home every evening' (*PSS*, XIII, p. 144).

15. The original name here had been Belinsky, but Chekhov changed it to Dobrolyubov, see *PSS*, XIII, p. 431.

16. See Hingley, *New Life*, pp. 14–15 for Chekhov's own experiences in the Taganrog school.

   In 1887 The Minister of Education, I. D. Delyanov, had tried to control access of the lower orders to secondary education through his 'Circular on Cooks' Children' (*Tsirkulyar o kukharkinykh detyakh*). Knowledge of Latin and Greek was used, as in previous decades, as a means of controlling educational opportunity. (After 1871 more than forty per cent of the time on the curriculum was devoted to classical languages.) The circular mentioned particularly the children of coachmen, washer-women and petty traders. Inclusion of the latter category would certainly have prevented Chekhov himself from receiving secondary education, had the act been introduced some twenty years earlier.

17. *PSS*, XIII, pp. 163–4. 'Tara-tara-tara. / Tum-tum' (Fen, p. 302). The origin of this nonsense communication is ascribed to a similar incident between Chekhov and an unnamed actress in the well-known restaurant *Slavyanskiy bazar* in February 1896 (see *PSS*, XIII, p. 413–14). A similar refrain also occurs in the poem which Chekhov would later quote in *The Cherry Orchard* — Nekrasov's 'Reflections at a Front Door' (*Razmyshleniya u paradnogo pod"ezda*) 'Returning, some hum "tram-tram", but other peti-tioners weep' (*Vozvrashchayas', inoy napevayet "tram-tram / Inyye prositeli plachut*), N. A. Nekrasov, *Sobraniye sochineniy v vos'mi tomakh*, Moscow, 1965, I, p. 301.

18. 'Oh, I'm so happy, happy, happy! / And I'm so bored, bored, bored!" (Fen, p. 304); 'I'm happy, happy, happy' (Fen, p. 305).

19. The full echo effect is easily obscured in translation: 'I love you, I love you, I love you . . . I love your eyes. . ./I'm in love, in love . . . I love that man. . .' (Fen, pp. 218, 277); 'I love you, love you, love you. I love your eyes. . ./I'm in love, in love with that man' (Hingley, pp. 194, 218).

20. Styan also considers the play to end in a 'curiously choric manner', see Styan, p. 231.

21. It had originally been intended to parade Tuzenbach's body across the stage. The idea appears to have been Chekhov's (see M. N. Stroeva, '*The Three Sisters* in the Production of the Moscow Arts Theatre' in Jackson, p. 131, and *PSS*, XIII, p. 433). Valency, however, ascribes the idea to Stanislavsky (Valency, p. 210) and Hingley thinks that the facts are not entirely clear (*The Oxford Chekhov*, III, p. 7, 314). A letter to Olga Knipper of 20 January 1901, appears to suggest the idea as Stanislavsky's, see *PSS* (Letters), IX, p. 188.

22. When Stanislavsky added a scratching mouse to Chekhov's play and claimed that it awakened in him a process of 'creative supra-consciousness' (*tvorcheskoye sverkhsoznaniye*) its real origin may have been, rather, subconscious — prompted by literary echoes. In Pushkin's 'Verses composed at night during sleeplessness' the sound of the clock is compared to 'the womanish babbling of one of the Parcae' and to 'the mouse-like scuttling of life'. The poet ends (like Masha) by looking for meaning in all this, see *Pushkin, Poln. sob. soch.* III, p. 186.

Pushkin's images are carried on, perhaps consciously, in Turgenev's *A Nest of Gentlefolk* in another evocation of provincial boredom: 'the little clock ticks in haste on the wall, a mouse, hidden away, scratches and gnaws behind the wallpaper, and three old maids, just like the Parcae, move their needles quickly and silently', I. S. Turgenev, *Poln. sob. soch.* (*Soch.*), VII, p. 162. (See Stanislavsky, *Moya zhizn'*, pp. 290–1 and Stroeva in Jackson, p. 127, where it is clear that darkness and a pendulum were also part of Stanislavsky's interpretation.)

23. Shakespeare, *Julius Caesar*, Act I, sc.ii.

24. See *PSS*, XIII, p. 448, and Pitcher p. 124. The 'inactivity' of the three sisters is comparable to that of Oblomov, but in an inverted sense: he lives in the capital, St Petersburg, a life which he rejects, and dreams of living in the depths of country on his estate at Oblomovka. But although he has every incentive to go there (he cannot stay in his present apartment, and the affairs on his estate need urgent attention) he seems incapable of realising his dream. (cf. Goncharov, p. 79).

25. 'You see, the eight has to go on the two of spades.' There is, perhaps, another literary echo here: Pushkin's *Queen of Spades*, where cards which cannot fail to win in fact lose and decide the fate of the hero.

26. *PSS*, XIII, p. 176. 'So I've just made up my mind — if I'm really not going to be able to live in Moscow, that's that. It's my fate that's all. Nothing can be done about it. It's God's will, everything that happens, and that's the truth' (Fen, p. 315).

27. Literally 'He did not have time to say "Akh!" before the bear fell on him' (*PSS*, XIII, p. 125). *Akhnut'* — 'to say Akh!' — has the secondary meaning of 'to strike a heavy blow'.

   The quotation comes from Krylov's fable about ingratitude: *The Peasant and the Workman*. Solyony's other literary references are to works which both end on the theme of 'fate'. The final section of *The Hero of Our Time* is entitled 'The Fatalist' and *The Gipsies* ends with the line: 'There is no defence from our fates' (*I ot sudeb zashchity net*). See Pushkin, *Poln. sob. soch.*, IV, p. 169.

28. Magarshak speculates on this as 'a conclusive connection to the rather inconclusive argument about happiness', *The Real Chekhov*, p. 148. Fen comments on Berdichev: 'A town in Western Russia well-known for its almost exclusively Jewish population' (Fen, p. 282). She translates '*zhrebiy broshen'*' ('the die is cast') as 'Well, I have thrown in my hand' (p. 282; cf. *PSS*, XIII, p. 147).

29. This number must apparently include Anfisa (as well as Rodé and Fedotik who appear, rather, to be standing, or even moving around).

30. *PSS*, XIII, p. 129. The Fen translation omits Masha's pointed comment. Hingley has 'Which was what father wanted' (p. 180). The irony emerges even more clearly when it is recognised that Irina's words are literally 'and his son has chosen for himself an academic career'.

31. From the beginning, in his rough notes, Chekhov saw Chebutykin as enjoying being at the duel, *PSS*, XIII, p. 426 (cf. also Styan p. 219).

32. *PSS*, XIII, p. 172. The Fen translation alters the word order as a gloss on the reason for Chebutykin's waiting 'radiating a mood of benevolence which does not leave him throughout the act, is sitting in a chair in the

garden. He is wearing his army cap and is holding a walking stick, as if ready to be called away at any moment' (Fen. p. 311).

33. The image seems to derive from *The Gipsies:*

> So sometimes before winter
> At the misty morning time
> When there rises from the fields
> A flock of late cranes
> And with a cry makes off into the distance to the south
> Shot through with mortal lead
> One sadly remains behind
> With a hanging wounded wing.

Pushkin, *Poln. sob. soch.,* IV, p. 168.

Originally Chekhov had written 'crane' (*zhuravl'*) instead of migratory bird', see *PSS*, XIII, p. 439.

34. V. Yermilov sees Tuzenbach's warning that Vershinin will mention his wife and daughters, and the fact that he then does so, as a classical incident of vaudeville, see Yermilov, p. 231.

35. Stanislavsky even toyed with the idea of having Protopopov come on stage, see Stroeva in Jackson p. 130. As Magarshak points out Protopopov is identified with a bear through the name and patronymic wished on him by Masha (Mikhail Protapych) and this in turn echoes Solyony's quotation about the sudden attack of a bear, see *The Real Chekhov*, pp. 133–4.

36. The recipe was communicated to Chekhov himself by his wife in a letter of 12 September 1900, see note in *PSS*, XIII, p. 431.

Chekhov must have been struck by the irony of the young actress giving the older doctor medical advice, and in its refurbishing here for the incompetent doctor Chebutykin, we may suspect another of Chekhov's private jokes. Oblomov's father loved to read out disconnected facts from out-of-date papers (Goncharov, p. 142).

37. *PSS*, XIII, p. 160. 'walking firmly and soberly' (Fen, p. 298).

38. *PSS*, XIII, p. 157 (i.e. *zagorozhennyye shirmamy* — 'fenced in by screens'). 'There are two beds, one on the right, the other on the left, each screened off from the centre of the room' (Fen, p. 294).

39. It should also be noted how 'tiredness' and indifference are linked in the play, particularly at the end of Act II, where Olga and Kulygin repeatedly claim tiredness, when confronted by questions or problems they do not wish to face. Most significant of all is Chebutykin's claim to be tired immediately after whispering the news of Tuzenbach's death in Act IV.

40. Olga's words are not: 'I am not listening' (*ne slushayu*) but literally 'I am not hearing' (*ne slyshu*) *PSS*, XIII, p. 169. Fen omits the direction [*behind the screen*] and translates Olga's speech: 'Nevertheless, I don't want to hear it, You can say any nonsense you like, I'm not listening' (p. 307). Cf. Hingley [*From behind the screen*] 'That's enough of that. I'm not

listening anyway' (Hingley, p. 218).

41. The child-dominated Natasha seems to view Olga less as a sister-in-law than as a future headmistress of her children: 'Our headmistress is tired! You know, when my Sofochka grows up and goes to school, I'll be frightened of you.'

42. When Chekhov was asked whether Irina really knew, he replied: 'Irina does not know that Tuzenbach is going to a duel, but she guesses that something bad happened yesterday, capable of having serious and at the same time bad consequences. But when a woman guesses, she says: "I knew, I knew"', *PSS*, XII, p. 422.

43. See Stanislavsky, *Moya zhizn'*, p. 291.

44. 'Among the other civilians' is Fen's rendering of: *'mezhdu shtatskimi voobshche'* (*PSS*, XIII, p. 142) — literally 'among the civilians in general'. Cf. 'But civilians in general are often so rude, disagreeable and bad mannered' (Hingley, p. 193).

45. 'At the dining-room table it is she who offends against the rules of good behaviour by striking her plate with her fork and exclaiming: "Let's have a glass of vodka! Oh, life is sweet! What the hell!"', Margarshak, *The Real Chekhov*, p. 139.

46. *PSS*, XIII, p. 177. 'When you have to take your happiness in snatches, in little bits, as I do, and then lose it, as I have lost it, you gradually get hardened and bad-tempered. [*Points at her breast.*] Something's boiling over inside me, here' (Fen, p. 316). Both Fen and Hingley treat Masha more leniently by seeing the confession: *'malo po-malu grubeyesh'* (literally 'you gradually grow coarse, ill mannered') as merely a question of 'hardness' (cf. Hingley p. 226 'you gradually get hardened').

47. *PSS*, XIII, p. 144. 'It hasn't got what I always longed for and dreamed about. It's the sort of work you do without inspiration, without even thinking' (Fen, p. 278). Cf. Hingley, p. 195: 'It's sheer drudgery with nothing romantic or intellectual about it.'

48. *PSS*, XIII, p. 120. 'Honestly, I've been feeling as if my strength and youth were running out of me drop by drop, day after day. Day after day, all these four years that I've been working at the school . . . I just have one longing and it seems to grow stronger and stronger. . .'/ IRINA. 'If only we could go back to Moscow! Sell the house finish with our life here, and go back to Moscow' (Fen, p. 250). Like Fen, Hingley also translates *'mechta'* 'dream', 'day-dream' as 'longing' (cf. Hingley p. 172).

49. *PSS*, XIII, p. 129. 'There's nothing our good Baron loves as much as a nice bit of philosophising' (Fen, p. 260). Cf. Hingley p. 180: 'The baron wouldn't mind starving so long as you let him say his little piece.'

50. *PSS*, XIII, p. 184 'If only we could educate the industrious people and make the educated people industrious' (Fen, p. 325).

51. 'You ask what is life? That is just the same as asking what is a carrot. A carrot is a carrot and nothing more is known about it.' Letter to Olga Knipper of 20 April 1904 (quoted in Valency, p. 301, who also quotes

sentiments analagous to Tuzenbach's speech, written by Gorky, *ibid.* p. 69). Chekhov was obviously at times plagued by the 'philosophising' of his own father: 'Dad is philosophising as before and poses such questions as: "Why does the snow lie here?" or "Why are there trees there and not here?"' Letter to Al. P Chekhov, 21 March 1892, *PSS* (Letters), V, p. 29.

52. I have restored the adjective '*pereletnyye*' — 'migrating'. See *PSS*, XIII, p. 178, and n. 33. p. 172 above. Cf. Gromov in *Ward No. 6*: 'Go and preach that philosophy in Greece, where it is warm and smells of orange blossom, but here it is not suited to the climate', *PSS*, VIII, p. 100.

53. See n. 52 above and cf. *PSS*, XIII, p. 175.

54. For 'stylistic' reasons translators seek to vary the repeated phrase: *vse ravno* (*PSS*, XIII, p. 188) — 'What does it matter? Nothing matters' (Fen, p. 330); 'None of it matters, Nothing matters' (Hingley, p. 237).

55. The stage directions describe it as '*tort*' (cake) but Ferapont himself calls it a pie (*pirog*). Olga seems to suggest that this humble bearer of the 'pie' will be the first to taste it: 'Nanny, give him some pie. Go on Ferapont, they will give you some pie there' (*PSS*, XIII, p. 125). Both Fen and Hingley translate *tort* and *pirog* equally as 'cake' (cf. Fen, p. 255 and Hingley, p. 176). It is, however 'pie' which is served for lunch, and apple pie is offered for supper (*PSS*, XIII, pp. 134, 136).

56. Styan, p. 169.

57. *PSS*, XIII, pp. 137, 148. Neither Fen nor Hingley preserves this complete identity of expression: 'What a sweet little thing'/'They're awfully nice' (Fen, pp. 270, 283); 'Oh, how lovely!'/'Oh, aren't they lovely!' (Hingley, pp. 188, 198).

58. Cf. Ostrovsky's play: *Ne vse kotu maslenitsa* (*A Cat Can't Always Live In Clover*) which takes its title from the final line: *Ne vse kotu maslenitsa, byvayet i velikiy post* ('It's not always Shrove-tide for the tom cat, there is also Lent').

59. *PSS*, XIII, p. 139. 'The faint sound of an accordion is heard coming from the street' (Fen, p. 272); 'From the street comes the faint sound of an accordion' (Hingley, p. 190).

60. 'The audience, of course, expects Natasha's arrival at any moment, like Malvolio's, to put a stop to the celebration', Styan, p. 192.

61. *PSS*, XIII, p. 140. Fen translates '*prostokvasha*' (yoghourt) as 'sour milk' (Fen, p. 273); Hingley (p. 191) has 'yogurt'.

62. In the Moscow Arts Theatre rehearsals, Chekhov was not pleased by the large amount of noise called for by Stanislavsky. He undertook to organise the sound effects himself. See Stanislavsky, *Moya zhizn*', p. 292.

63. Letter to Stanislavsky, 2 January 1901, *PSS* (Letters), IX, p. 171 (cf. Styan, p. 208). There may be another allusion to Shakespeare's play in the way Solyony constantly sprinkles his hands. See Rayfield, p. 218.

64. *PSS*, XIII, p. 164. 'I hardly need to make my moral yet more clear: that might be teasing geese, I fear!' (Fen, p. 303).

65. *PSS*, XIII, p. 163–4. 'MASHA (*sings*). 'Tara-tara-tara . . .'/VERSHININ. 'Tum-tum . . .'/MASHA. 'Tara-tara . . .'/ VERSHININ. 'Tum-tum, tum-tum. . .' [*Laughs.*] (*Enter* FEDOTIK.)/FEDOTIK (*dancing about*). 'Burnt, burnt! Everything I've got burnt!' (Fen, p. 302). (*Pogoret'* — to burn up entirely' can also mean: 'to lose all one's possessions in a fire'.)

66. *PSS*, XIII, p. 175. Fen translates '*gop, gop*' as 'Heigh-ho' and '*au*' as 'ahoo' but reduces them to one ('Heigh-ho') in this passage: 'From the back of the stage comes a shout "Heigh-ho" (Fen, p. 314). Cf. Hingley, p. 224 'Hallo-there! Halloo-oo!'

67. Cf. Ostrovsky's *The Forest*: PETR. 'But it's already all up, brother . . .' (*Da ved' uzh au brat*), Ostrovsky, *Poln. sob. soch.* III, p. 307.

68. The rest of the verse (which Chebutykin does not sing) goes on 'And I bitterly weep / That I have little significance' (*I gor'ko plachu ya / Chto malo znachu ya*). see *PSS*, XIII, p. 466. Fen's 'I am sitting on a tomb-di-ay' is suggestive, but *tumba* is really a bollard.

69. *PSS*, XIII, p. 180. This last sentence is not in either the Fen or the Hingley translation. They are obviously following a variant found in the censors' copies, see *PSS*, XIII, p. 306. TUZENBACH. 'Say something!' / IRINA. 'What? What am I to say? What?' (Fen, p. 321); TUZENBACH. 'Say something.' / IRINA. 'Why, what am I to say?' (Hingley, p. 230).

THE CHERRY ORCHARD

1. See letters to Olga Knipper, 7 March 1901, and 22 April 1901 (quoted *PSS*, XIII, p. 479).

2. I.e. 'where all pandemonium might be let loose' (*gde by chert khodil koromyslom*). As the literal meaning of *koromyslo* is a 'yoke' (used for carrying pails etc.) the phrase suggests the devil as a yoke. (Cf. the comic role of the devil in Gogol's *Evenings in a Village near Dikanka*.)

3. See *PSS*, XIII, p. 492.

4. *Ibid.*, p. 497.

5. *Polnoye sobraniye sochineniy i pisem A. P. Chekhova*, Moscow, 1944–51, XX, p. 265.

6. *PSS*, XIII, pp. 497–8.

7. F. M. Dostoyevsky, *Sobraniye sochineniy v desyati tomakh*, Moscow, 1958, X, p. 212.

8. Letter to A. S. Suvorin, Beginning of May, 1889, *PSS* (Letters), III, p. 202.

9. Styan, however, sees it differently: 'A frog in his throat surprises us with an unexpected sign of the warmth of his emotions. Even a fool can be affected by an irrevocable departure' (Styan, p. 333).

10. *PSS*, XIII, p. 197. The translators put these qualities in the past: 'She used to be a good soul. An easy-going simple kind of person' (Fen, p. 333). 'She was always such a nice woman, unaffected and easy to get on with' (Hingley, p. 241).

11. *PSS*, XIII, p. 210. 'If only this burden could be taken from me, if only I could forget the past' (Fen, p. 348). Hingley also has 'burden' (p. 253).

12. *PSS*, XIII, p. 129. 'I love him, of course I love him. I do, I do . . . It's a millstone round my neck, and I'm going to the bottom with it — but I love him and I can't live without him' (Fen, p. 376). Hingley also has 'millstone' (p. 276).

13. F. M. Dostoyevsky, *Pis'ma*, ed. and comment. A. S. Dolinin, Moscow and Leningrad, 1928, II, p. 71.

14. Styan comments on the use Chekhov makes of these telegrams throughout the play to chart Lyubov Andreyevna's changing attitude to her lover. See Styan, p. 265.

15. *PSS* XIII, p. 210. Fen noticeably tones this down: 'Oh, my childhood, my innocent childhood! I used to sleep in this nursery; I used to look on to the orchard from here, and I woke up happy every morning. In those days the orchard was just as it is now, nothing has changed. [*Laughs happily.*] All, all white! Oh, my orchard! After the dark, stormy autumn and the cold winter, you are young and joyous again; the angels have not forsaken you!' (Fen, p. 347–8). Hingley also glosses '*chistota*' (purity) as 'innocent childhood', but also has 'angels in heaven' (p. 253).

16. 'Lyubov's addiction to pills and her incessant coffee-drinking suggest obliquely something disturbed and guilty about her worldliness', Hahn, p. 14. In Act II we learn that she has already attempted to poison herself.

17. Stanislavsky, *Moya zhizn'*, p. 553. For the original variant see *PSS*, XIII, pp. 329–30.

18. *PSS*, XIII, p. 238. The translations treat this 'seniority' as one of age: 'Those who are older than me' (Fen, p. 381); 'older and wiser heads than yours' (Hingley, p. 280).

19. Chekhov seems not to have taken Varya very seriously either: she is a 'nun', a 'silly girl', letters to Olga Knipper, 1 November 1903, and to Nemirovich-Danchenko, 2 November 1903. *PSS* (Letters), XI, p. 293. Quoted in *The Oxford Chekhov*, III, p. 329.

20. Nevertheless the servants do not treat him as one of them: 'Dunyasha and Yepikhodov stand in the presence of Lopakhin. They don't sit down. After all Lopakhin is very much at ease, behaves like a squire and calls the servants "thou", while they call him "you"' (letter to Stanislavsky, 10 November 1903) — quoted in *The Oxford Chekhov*, III, p. 329 — *PSS* (Letters), XI, p. 303.

21. *PSS*, XIII, p. 201. '*dacha*' is glossed as 'villa' by Fen (p. 338) and Hingley (p. 245).

22. At the time of writing the play Chekhov was himself building a *dacha*, see *PSS*, XIII, p. 490.

23. *PSS*, XIII, pp. 206–8. The translations smoothe out the peculiarities of this speech: 'For a hundred years you have never failed to fill us with an urge to useful work; several generations of our family have had their

courage sustained and their faith in a better future fortified by your silent call; you have fostered in us the ideal of public good and social consciousness' (Fen, p. 345). Fen loses the stage direction: [*through tears*]. Cf. Hingley: 'In the course of the century your silent summons to creative work has never faltered, upholding [*through tears*] in several generations of our line confidence and faith in a better future and fostering in us the ideals of virtue and social consciousness' (Hingley, p. 251).

24. N. A. Dobrolyubov, 'What is Oblomovshchina', *Selected Philosophical Essays*, (trans. J. Fineberg) Moscow, 1956, pp. 174–217.

25. *PSS*, XIII, p. 223. 'Nearly all the members of the intelligentsia that I know care for nothing, do nothing, and are still incapable of work. They call themselves "intelligentsia", but they still talk contemptuously to their servants, they treat the peasants as if they were animals, they study without achieving anything, they don't read anything serious, they just do nothing. As for science, they only talk about it, and they don't understand much about art either' (Fen, p. 364).

26. In Act IV Lopakhin predicts that Gayev will not stay at the bank: *leniv ochen'* ('he is very lazy'), *PSS*, XIII, p. 246.

27. Letter to Olga Knipper, 19 October 1903 (quoted in *PSS*, p. 495), *PSS* (Letters), XI, p. 279.

28. See *PSS*, XIII, p. 514.

29. See *ibid.* p. 518. Gorky's play was produced by the Moscow Arts Theatre in December 1902. The words referred to are: 'Man! That is marvellous! It sounds . . . Proud! Man!' Satin calls for the elevation of man, not for his humbling through pity. See M. Gorky, *Polnoye sobraniye sochineniy*, Moscow, 1970, VII, p. 177.

30. Tulloch sees merely rhetoric in these words, and disputes the veracity of the social conditions which Trofimov describes. Tulloch, pp. 9–10, 200.

31. Lopakhin's words on the size of Russia and native-born giants seem a conscious echo of a famous passage in Gogol's *Dead Souls*: 'Should there not be a prodigious knight here where there is room for him to spread himself and pace up and down? — *Zdes' li ne byt' bogatyryu, kogda yest' mesto, gde razvernut'sya i proytis' yemu?* See N. V. Gogol', *Sobraniye khudozhestvennykh proizvedeniy v pyati tomakh,* Moscow, 1960, V. p. 316.

Bogatyr' is a knight of epic, giant-like stature, and Yepikhodov's name in this context is comically appropriate. Its first element *yepi* suggests a debased pronunciation of 'epic' (*epicheskiy*), whereas the second element *khod* appears to derive from the verb 'to go' (*khodit'*) — he is therefore a comic 'epic-mover' (he is first introduced to us through his squeaky boots).

'"The spirit of the epic", Bowra concludes, "is its attempt to find significance in the achievements of man and to show him in his essential nobility"' (Tulloch, p. 101). It is in this sense that Yepikhodov appears on the stage at this moment as Chekhov's answer to Gorky's 'proud man'.

32. Cf. the motif of the setting sun in *Oblomov* (I. A. Goncharov, *sobraniye sochineniy v shesti tomakh*, Moscow, 1972, IV, pp. 190, 256, 493–4): 'In Chekhov's mind sunsets were, as his letters show, always associated with coughing up blood, and inspire horror', Rayfield, p. 108. After the sound of the breaking string Lyubov Andreyevna suggests that they should leave, as it is already becoming evening (*uzhe vechereyet*), *PSS*, XIII, p. 226. She consoles Anya, whom she notices weeping, but at the end of Act III it is Anya's turn to console her mother — with an image of evening: 'your heart will be filled with happiness, like the sun in the evening; and then you'll smile again' (*PSS*, XIII, p. 241).

33. *PSS*, XIII, p. 214. '*Solnyshko moye! Vesna moya!*' Fen translates this as: 'My one bright star! My spring flower!' (p. 353). The comparison to winter at the end of Act II is ambiguous: *kak zima, tak ya goloden, bolen vstrevozhen, beden kak nishchiy* (*PSS*, XIII, p. 228). The translations treat the first *kak* as a shorthand for *kak tol'ko* (i.e. not 'as', 'like' but 'as soon as'): 'As soon as winter comes, I get half-starved and ill and worried, poor as a beggar' (Fen, p. 368); 'In winter time I'm always half-starved, ill, worried, desperately poor' (Hingley, p. 270).

34. 'The superstition that the owl (eagle-owl) brings misfortune is widespread among various peoples', commentary of N. I. Prokof'yev to Afanasiy Nikitin, *Khozhdeniye za tri morya*, Moscow, 1980, p. 188.

35. Harvey Pitcher gives a list of 'breaking strings' in Chekhov's works. See Pitcher, p. 218 n. 36.

36. Stanislavsky comments on two possible stressings of the adjective for 'cherry' (*vishnevyy*) in the play's title. Chekhov said that it should be pronounced *vishnyovyy sad* not *vishnevyy sad*. 'This time I understood the subtlety: *vishnevyy sad* is a business-like commercial orchard which brings a profit. Such an orchard is necessary even now. But a *vishnyovyy sad* brings no profit. It preserves within itself and its blossoming whiteness the poetry of a bygone gentry life. Such an orchard grows and blossoms for a whim, for the eyes of pampered aesthetes. It is a pity to destroy it, but it is necessary since the process of the country's economic growth demands it' (Stanislavsky, *Moya zhizn'*, p. 328).

37. Dobrolyubov, *Selected Philosophical Essays*, p. 204. In *The Wood Demon* Khrushchev's criticism of Professor Serebryakov seems to carry on this imagery: 'There are no real heroes, no real talents, there are no people who might lead us out of this dark forest' (*PSS*, XII p. 194).

38. *PSS*, XIII, pp. 227–8. Cf. Fen p. 368 'Just think, Anya; your grandfather your great grandfather and all your forefathers were serf owners — they owned living souls. Don't you see human beings gazing at you from every cherry tree in your orchard, from every leaf and every tree-trunk, don't you hear voices? . . . They owned living souls — and it has perverted you all, those who came before you, and you who are living now, so that your mother, your uncle and even you yourself no longer realise that you're living in debt at other people's expense, at the expense of

people you don't admit further than the kitchen. We are at least two hundred years behind the times; we still have no real background, no clear attitude to our past, we just philosophise and complain of depression, or drink vodka. Yet it's perfectly clear that to begin to live in the present, we must first atone for our past and be finished with it, and we can only atone for it by suffering, by extraordinary, unceasing exertion. You must understand this, Anya.'

39. *PSS*, XIII, p. 221. 'Tut, tut! You went off this morning and never told me you were going' (Fen, p. 361).

40. But cf. Lebedev in the first version of *Ivanov:* 'Whom will you drink?' (*kogo budesh' pit'*) instead of: 'what will you drink?' (*PSS*, XI, p. 286).

41. Dostoyevsky, *Sob. soch.*, IX, p. 525.

42. For the connotation of the word 'gander' in Gogol's story see Peace, *Enigma of Gogol*, pp. 78–9, 337 n. 16.

43. A notice of the play in *New Time* (*Novoye vremya*) spoke disparagingly of 'more animation in the inanimate objects than in the characters' (*PSS*, XIII, p. 511).

44. Styan, however, sees this as Sharlotta's mockery of Lyubov Andreyevna and Varya. Styan, pp. 247, 325.

45. See p. 112, above and p. 175 n. 66.

46. 'I can't help thinking that there is something new in my play, however boring it might be. There is not a single shot in the whole of the play', letter to Olga Knipper, 25 September 1903, *PSS* (Letters), XI, p. 256, quoted Magarshak, p. 190).

47. Beverly Hahn sees the play as 'a pastoral mode of comedy' (Hahn, p. 20). 'There is no cemetery — there had once been one, but two or three gravestones leaning in disorder are all that remain', letter to Stanislavsky, 23 November 1903, *PSS* (Letters), XI, p. 312 (see Styan, p. 274).

The Brockhaus-Efron entry on cemeteries begins with a frightening description of putrefaction and the possible dangers to health, but rather unexpectedly asserts that: 'frequently cemetery wells are even noted for their remarkable, good, pure and tasty [*sic*] water'. F. A. Brokgauz and I. A. Efron (eds.). *Entsiklopedicheskiy slovar'*, St Petersburg, 1895, XV, pp. 278–83. However in another 'literary' context Parson Brontë's churchyard was a health hazard for the inhabitants of Haworth, see Mrs Gaskell, *The Life of Charlotte Brontë* (with an introduction and notes by Clement K. Shorter), London, 1900, p. 127; and Isabel C. Clarke, *Haworth Parsonage: A Picture of the Brontë Family*, London, 1925, p. 148.

48. Typically, Gayev attributes the shaking of his hands to the fact that he has not recently played billiards.

49. For Gayev's speech the stage directions literally read: [*Quietly, as though declaiming*]; those for the stranger are simply: [*He declaims*], *PSS*, XIII, pp. 224, 226.

50. The first is a garbled version of S. Ya. Nadson's poem of 1880: 'My

friend my brother, my weary, suffering brother / Whoever you are do not lose heart' (*Drug moy, brat moy, ustalyy stradayushchiy brat / Kto b ty ni byl, ne paday dushoy*). The poem deals with the return of 'love' to earth. Love (*Lyubov'*) is the name of Gayev's sister, and in this context the end of the first stanza is particularly striking: 'Believe! The time will come — and Baal will perish / And love will return to the land' (*Ver'! Nastanet pora — i pogibnet Vaal / I vernetsya na zemlyu lyubov'*), see S. Ya. Nadson, *Polnoye sobraniye stikhotvoreniy*, Moscow and Leningrad, 1962, p. 110.

The second fragment comes from a well-known poem by N. A. Nekrasov about the suffering of the common people of Russia, *Reflections at a Front Door* (*Razmyshleniya u paradnogo pod"ezda*). See p. 170 n. 17 above. The quotation, almost from the end of the poem, identifies their sufferings as a song ('This moan is called a song with us' — *etot ston u nas pesney zovetsva*). Contrasting the death of the unfeeling aristocrat to the life of the peasant, Nekrasov writes: 'The advancing days of an untroubled Arcadian idyll will set: under the captivating skies of Sicily, in fragrant sylvan shade, watching the purple sun sink into an azure sea, making patches of gold — lulled by the gentle sound of the Mediterranean wave — like a child you will fall asleep, surrounded by the care of a dear and loved family' (N. A. Nekrasov, *Sob. soch.*, I, pp. 302–3).

51. Stanislavsky had actually wanted to bring a train on to the set. Letter to Stanislavsky, 23 November 1903, *PSS* (Letters), XI, p. 312. (see Styan p. 275).

52. 'She picks up a rug from a chair and offers to *auction* it, no less' (Styan, p. 301). The general point is good, although in fact Sharlotta only offers to *sell* the rug, not *auction* it (*ya zhelayu prodavat'*. Sharlotta's Russian is slightly stilted; she constantly uses *zhelat'* instead of *khotet'* (a fact which emerges from Chekhov's emendations, see *PSS*, XIII, p. 477). She also uses the 'polite' verb for 'to eat' (*kushat'*) for her dog. Nevertheless, Chekhov did not wish to have her 'foreignness' caricatured: 'Sharlotta doesn't speak Russian with an accent; only occasionally does she mispronounce the ending of a word and make mistakes in the masculine and feminine endings of adjectives', letter to Nemirovich-Danchenko, 2 November 1903, *PSS* (Letters), XI, p. 294.

The confusion of gender may be a similar grammatical indicator of character for the rather masculine Sharlotta, as is Gayev's confusion of animate and inanimate.

53. Although in *The Three Sisters* Chekhov merely indicates the title of a song ('The Maiden's Prayer'). For an interpretation of the relevance of *The Sinful Woman* to Act III see Rayfield, p. 224.

54. 'Easy going morally' is stronger in the original (i.e. *porochna* — 'depraved' 'wanton', *PSS*, XIII, p. 212). (Cf. 'loose woman' — Hingley, p. 255.)

55. Reinforced by Varya's banal and pathetic: 'And our thermometer's broken.'

56. It is not clear to whom Firs is addressing these remarks, but ostensibly

his conversation is with Lopakhin. If, however, Firs means the father of Lyubov Andreyevna, he could well be talking about the marriages of minors that were often contracted in peasant families. Cf. Tatyana's nurse in Pushkin's *Eugene Onegin*: 'My Vanya was younger than me, my dear, and I was thirteen', (Ch. III, stanza xviii) Pushkin, *Poln. sob. soch.* V, p. 55.

57. 'Separate' is Fen's translation of Firs' strange hybrid word — *vrazdrob'*, *PSS*, XIII, p. 222 which Hingley renders as 'at sixes and sevens' (p. 264).

58. *PSS*, XIII, p. 226. 'Go to a nunnery, Ohmeliya!' (Fen. p. 367); 'Amelia, get thee to a nunnery' (Hingley, p. 268). The uneducated corruption of Ophelia to Okhmeliya suggests that the name derives from drunkenness (cf. *okhmelet'* — 'to get drunk'). Drink (and coercion) seem to be strangely associated with marriage in this play. In Act I we learn that when Lopakhin's nose has been burst by his drunken father, Lyubov Andreyevna had commented: 'It will heal before your marriage.' Lyubov Andreyevna's own unhappy marriage had ended when her husband died from drinking champagne, and when in Act IV Lopakhin is sent in to make his proposal his first thought is to drink champagne.

59. Cf. Lyubov Andreyevna's first remarks in the play about her adopted daughter: 'And Varya is just the same as ever, looking like a nun.'

60. When Aksyushka in Ostrovsky's play *The Forest* is asked whether she owns herself or is the property of others (*Ch'ya ty? Svoya ty ili chuzhaya?*) she replies that no one is forcing her to marry (using the verb: *nevolit'*), see: Ostrovsky, *Poln. sob. soch.* III, p. 269. Aksyushka is a distant relative of the mistress of the house, Gurmyzhskaya, who feels entitled to dispose of her ward in marriage as she sees fit (*ibid.* pp. 264–5) and the same differentiation of address (thou/you) exists between them as between Lyubov Andreyevna and Varya.

61. *PSS*, XIII, p. 201. Fen glosses this sound as 'bleating' (p. 338); Hingley, more accurately has 'mooing' (p. 245). As this sound interrupts Anya and Varya's discussion of the future of the estate, it may be seen as an instance of 'indirect commentary' on Lopakhin's part.

62. *PSS*, XIII, p. 227. The translations, however, make it quite unambiguous: 'That man scared me. My heart keeps thumping' (Fen, p. 367); 'that man scared me. I still feel quite shaken' (Hingley, p. 268).

63. Valency even sees Lyubov Andreyevna as the secret love of Lopakhin's life, Valency p. 273.

64. It is not clear what Lopakhin's bottle of champagne is meant to celebrate. Is it his final possession of the estate, or the departure of a woman whose own husband had died from an excess of it?

65. From a letter which Chekhov received from a student in Kazan (Viktor Baranovsky) quoted in *PSS*, XIII, p. 502–3. Commenting on the symbolic role of the axe in Russian culture James H. Billington writes: 'The sound of an axe off-stage at the end of Chekhov's last play *The Cherry*

Orchard announced the coming end of Imperial Russia', Billington, p. 28.

66. See Simmons, p. 581. The student's name was Tikhonov. Alekseyev was the real name of Stanislavsky.

67. Cf. *PSS*, XIII, p. 220. As Hingley makes clear, this is a general statement not aimed solely at Lopakhin: 'I don't suppose it was a bit funny. You people shouldn't go and see plays, you should try watching your own performance instead. What drab lives you all lead and what a lot of rubbish you talk!' (Hingley, p. 263).

Index

Chekhov